The Comic Strip
Collection

Lucky

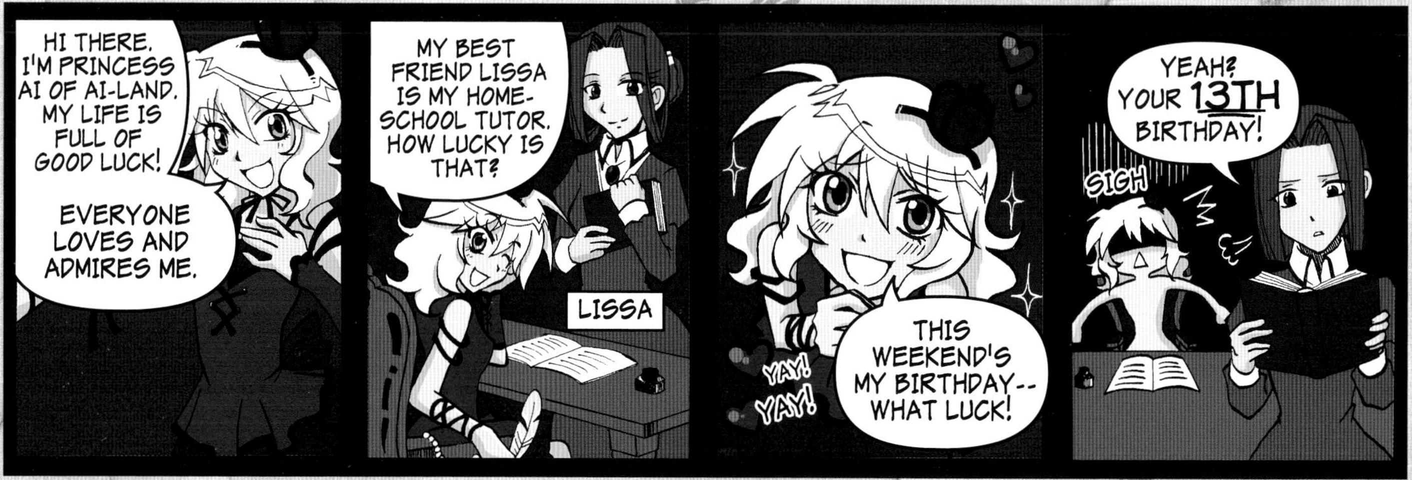
HI THERE. I'M PRINCESS AI OF AI-LAND. MY LIFE IS FULL OF GOOD LUCK!
EVERYONE LOVES AND ADMIRES ME.
MY BEST FRIEND LISSA IS MY HOME-SCHOOL TUTOR. HOW LUCKY IS THAT?
LISSA
THIS WEEKEND'S MY BIRTHDAY-- WHAT LUCK!
YAY! YAY!
YEAH? YOUR 13TH BIRTHDAY!
SIGH

Teen

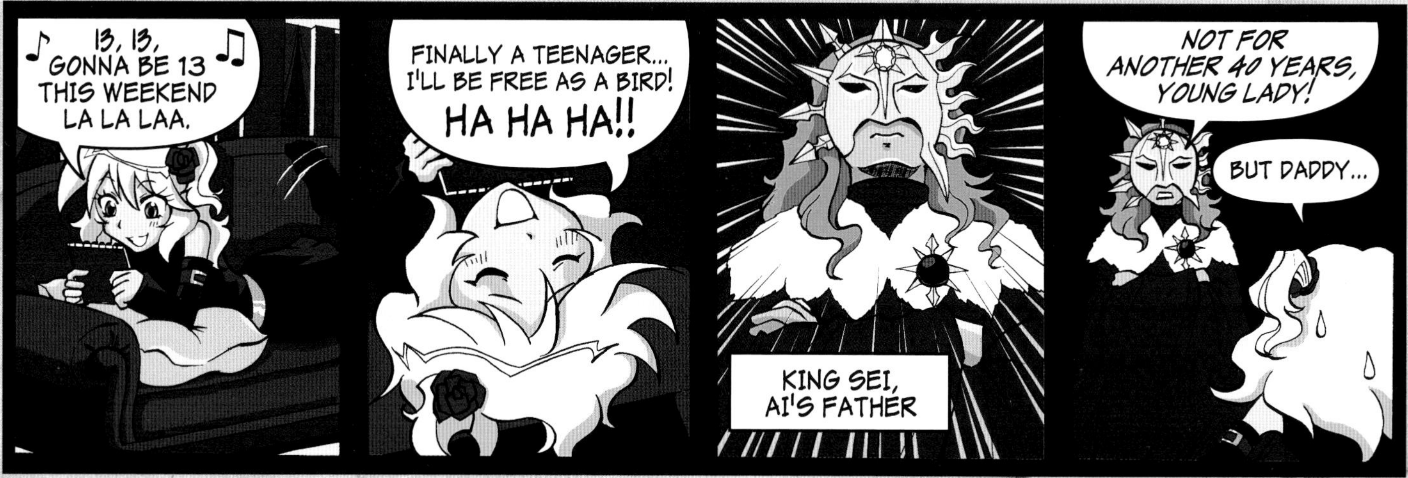
♪ 13, 13, GONNA BE 13 THIS WEEKEND LA LA LAA. ♫
FINALLY A TEENAGER... I'LL BE FREE AS A BIRD! HA HA HA!!
KING SEI, AI'S FATHER
NOT FOR ANOTHER 40 YEARS, YOUNG LADY!
BUT DADDY...

Birthday Present

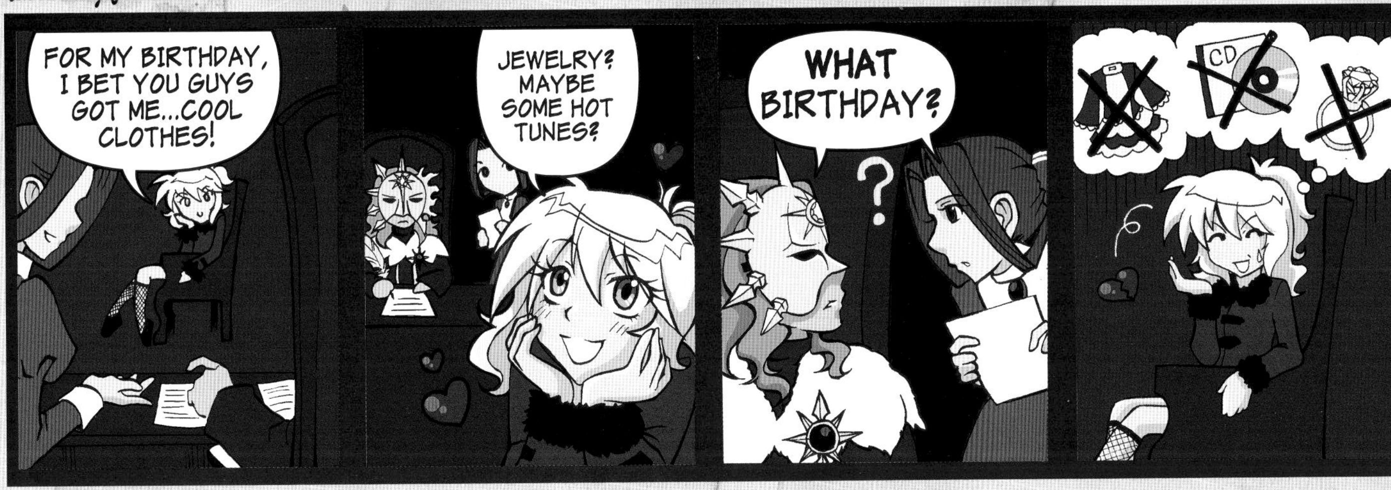
FOR MY BIRTHDAY, I BET YOU GUYS GOT ME...COOL CLOTHES!
JEWELRY? MAYBE SOME HOT TUNES?
WHAT BIRTHDAY?
CD

Invite List

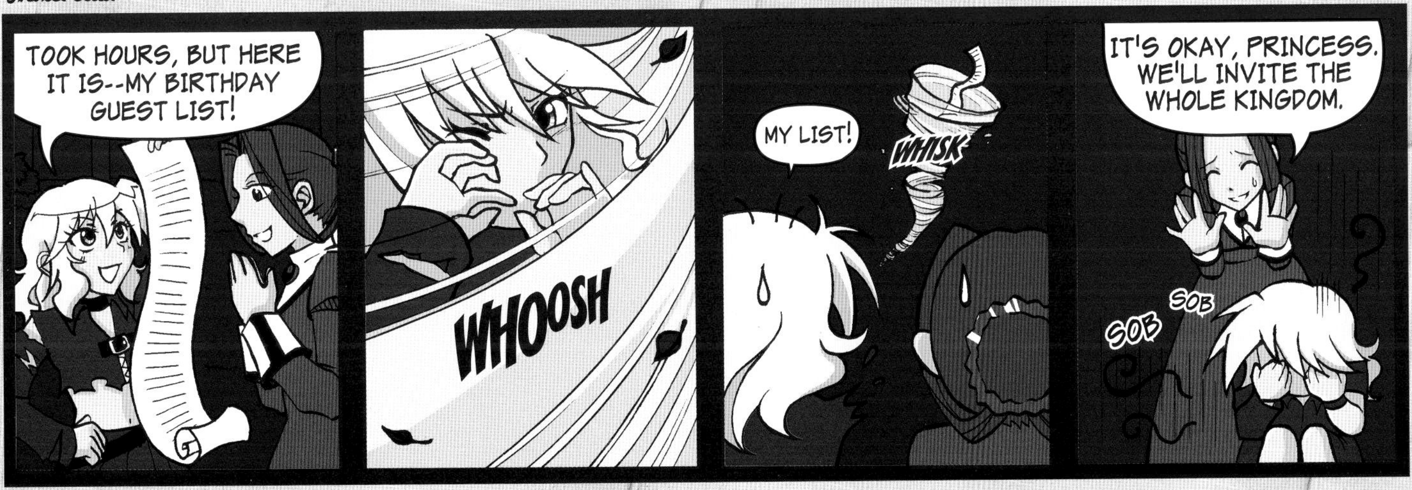
TOOK HOURS, BUT HERE IT IS--MY BIRTHDAY GUEST LIST!
WHOOSH
MY LIST!
WHISK
IT'S OKAY, PRINCESS. WE'LL INVITE THE WHOLE KINGDOM.
SOB
SOB

Birthday Cake

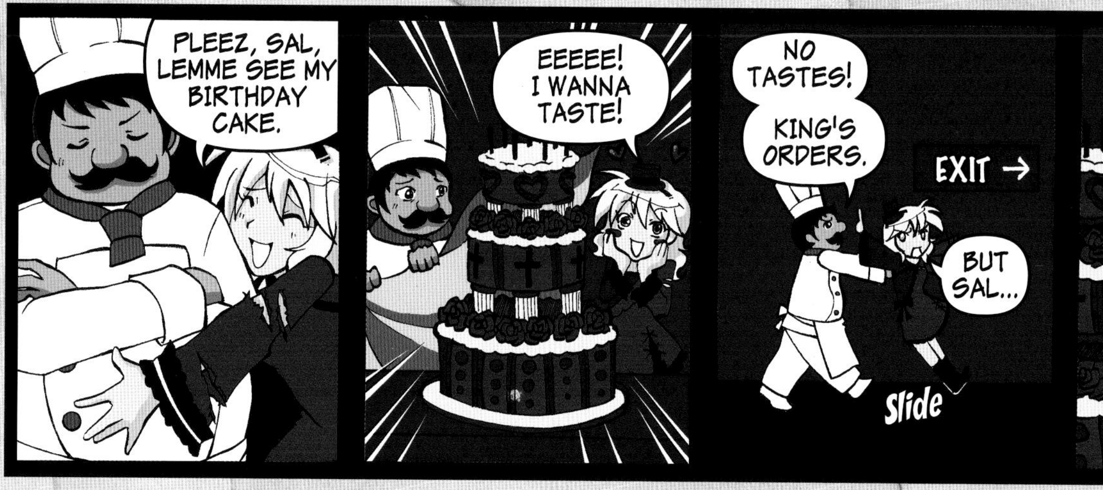
PLEEZ, SAL, LEMME SEE MY BIRTHDAY CAKE.
EEEEE! I WANNA TASTE!
NO TASTES!
KING'S ORDERS.
EXIT →
BUT SAL...
Slide
EXIT
HEY!
DELICIOSO!

Birthday Fashion

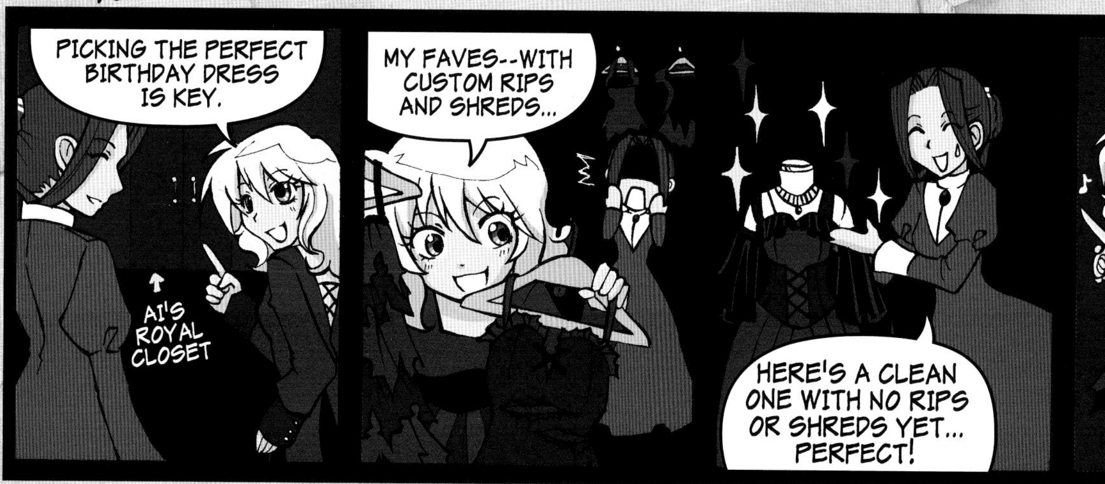
PICKING THE PERFECT BIRTHDAY DRESS IS KEY.
AI'S ROYAL CLOSET
MY FAVES--WITH CUSTOM RIPS AND SHREDS...
HERE'S A CLEAN ONE WITH NO RIPS OR SHREDS YET... PERFECT!
NOW IT'S PERFECT!
SNIP
SNIP
SNIP

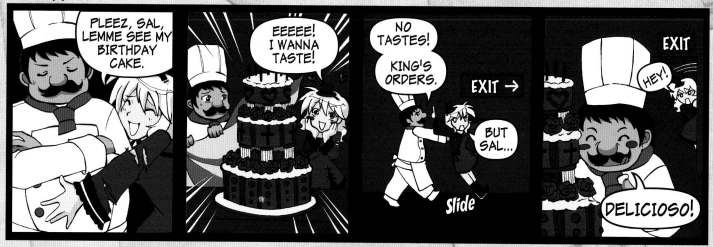

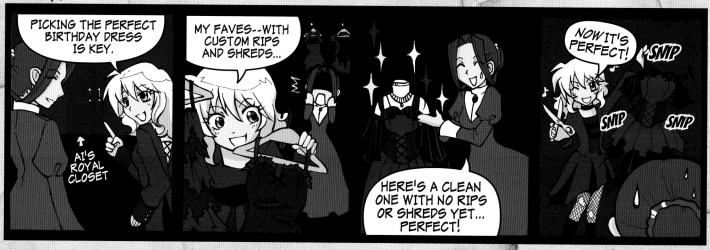

dear dAiry

I'm so psyched to finally be the big ONE-THREE. You know what that means, right? Yes indeed--I'm finally a teen! I've only been waiting for 12 long, arduous years... But now, the entire Kingdom of Ai-Land is gathered to celebrate this humongous event--my birthday! Ah, life as a Princess certainly has its rewards. ☺ But it's not all cake, which is why I need to enjoy the fun times while I can.

love always

Ai

Dougen Slash Patrol

DSP

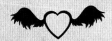

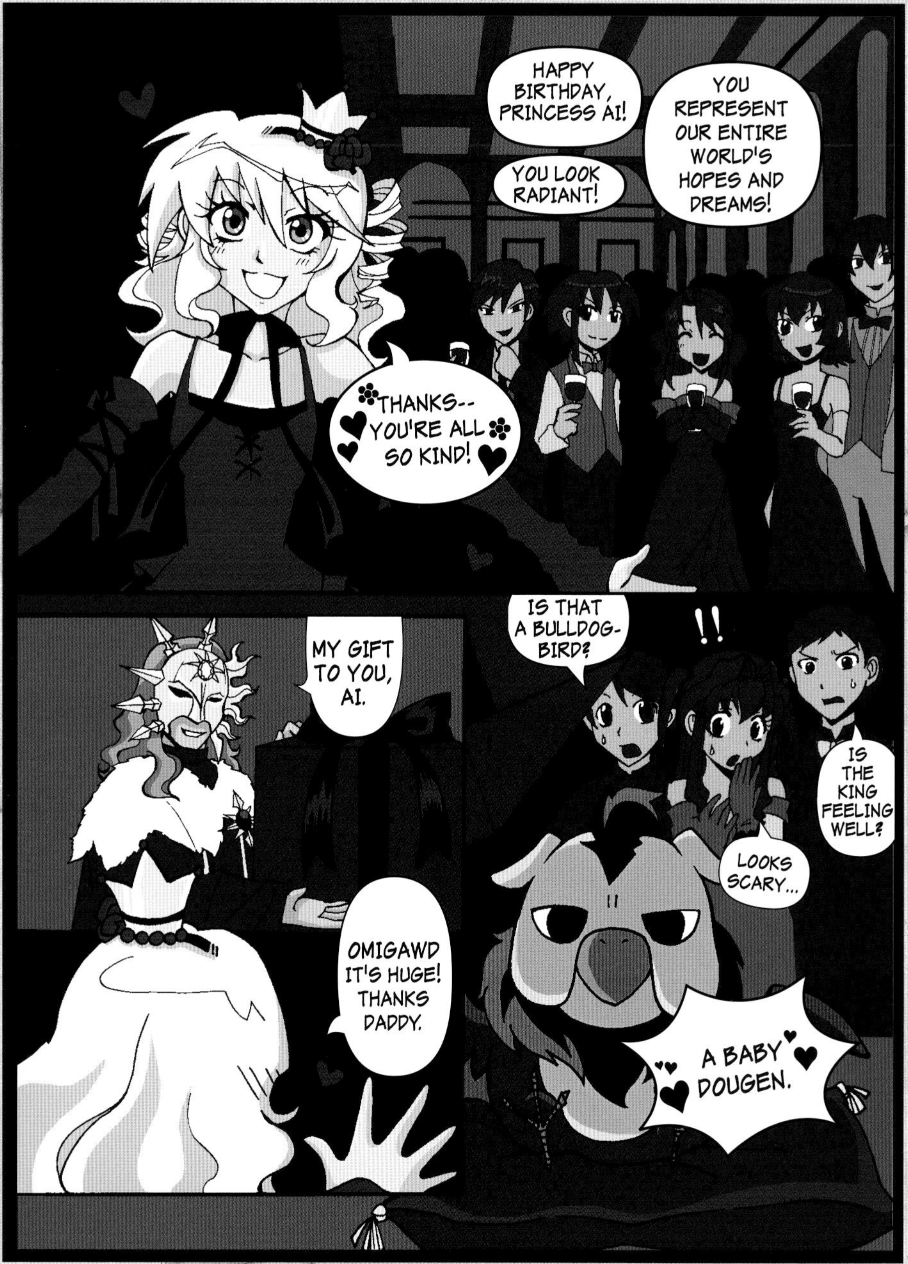
HAPPY BIRTHDAY, PRINCESS AI!
YOU LOOK RADIANT!
YOU REPRESENT OUR ENTIRE WORLD'S HOPES AND DREAMS!
THANKS-- YOU'RE ALL SO KIND!
MY GIFT TO YOU, AI.
OMIGAWD IT'S HUGE! THANKS DADDY.
IS THAT A BULLDOG-BIRD?
!!
IS THE KING FEELING WELL?
LOOKS SCARY...
A BABY DOUGEN.

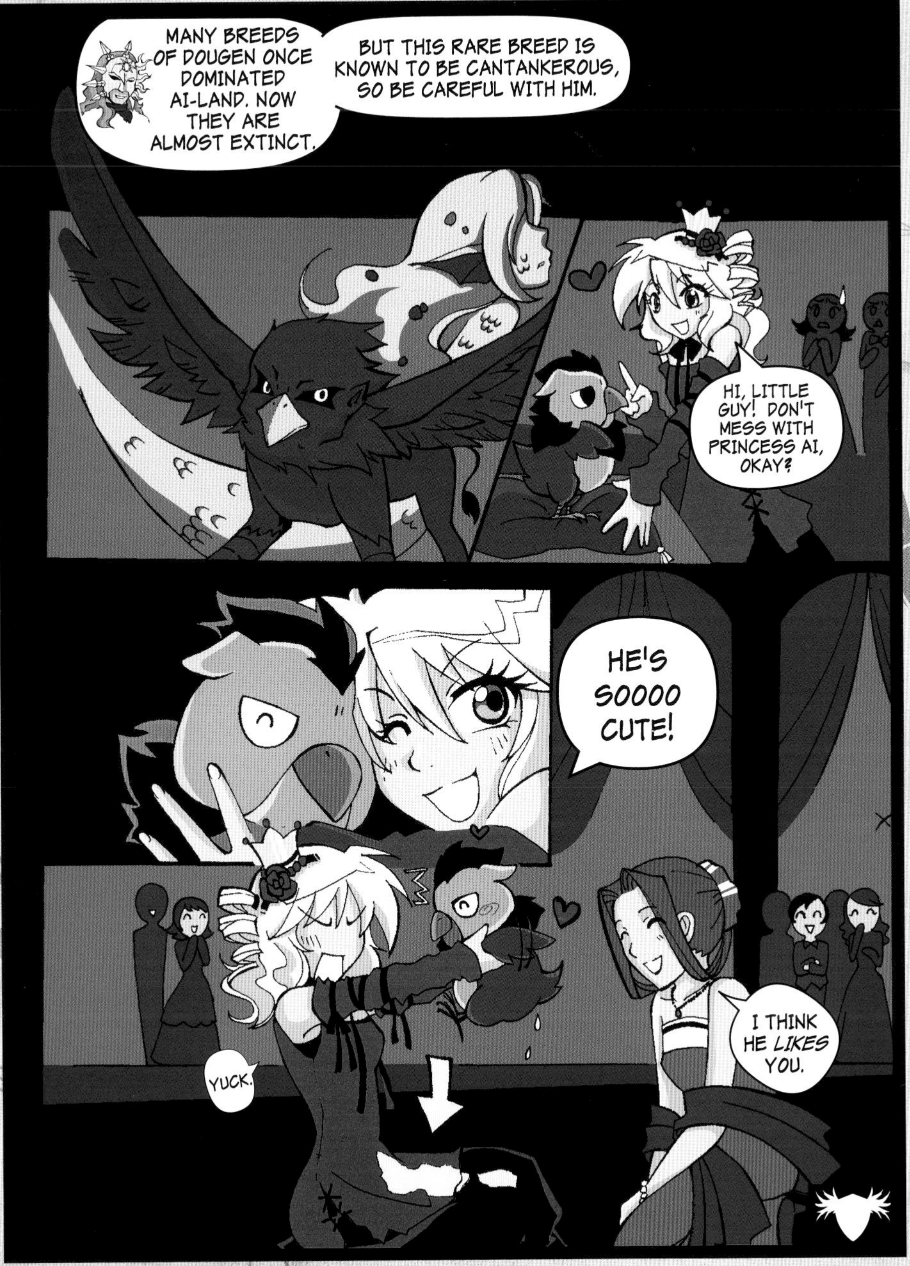
MANY BREEDS OF DOUGEN ONCE DOMINATED AI-LAND. NOW THEY ARE ALMOST EXTINCT.
BUT THIS RARE BREED IS KNOWN TO BE CANTANKEROUS, SO BE CAREFUL WITH HIM.
HI, LITTLE GUY! DON'T MESS WITH PRINCESS AI, OKAY?
HE'S SOOOO CUTE!
YUCK.
I THINK HE *LIKES* YOU.

Pet Food

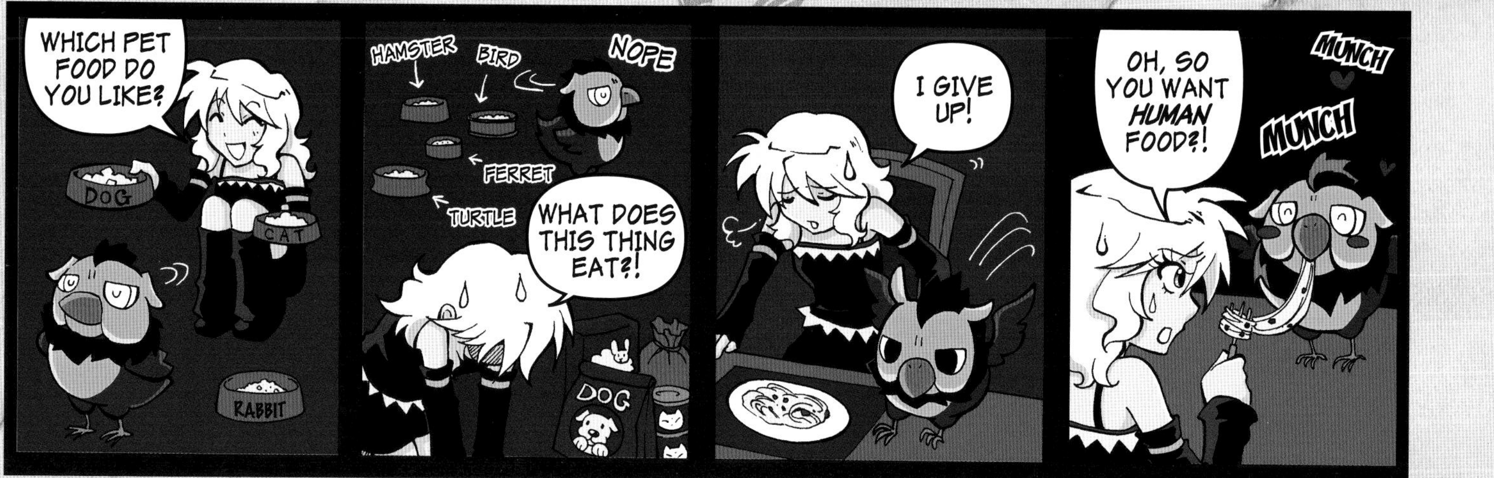
WHICH PET FOOD DO YOU LIKE?
DOG
CAT
RABBIT
HAMSTER
BIRD
NOPE
FERRET
TURTLE
WHAT DOES THIS THING EAT?!
DOG
I GIVE UP!
OH, SO YOU WANT *HUMAN* FOOD?!
MUNCH
MUNCH

Nocturnal

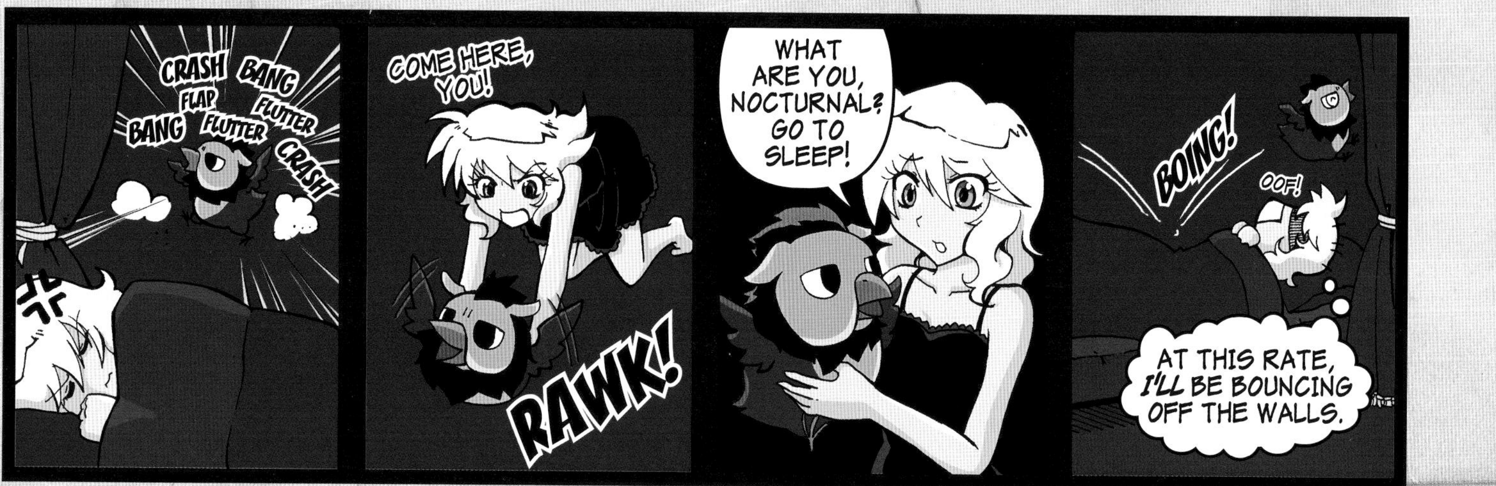
CRASH
BANG
FLAP
FLUTTER
BANG
FLUTTER
CRASH
COME HERE, YOU!
RAWK!
WHAT ARE YOU, NOCTURNAL? GO TO SLEEP!
BOING!
OOF!
AT THIS RATE, *I'LL* BE BOUNCING OFF THE WALLS.

Pet Shots

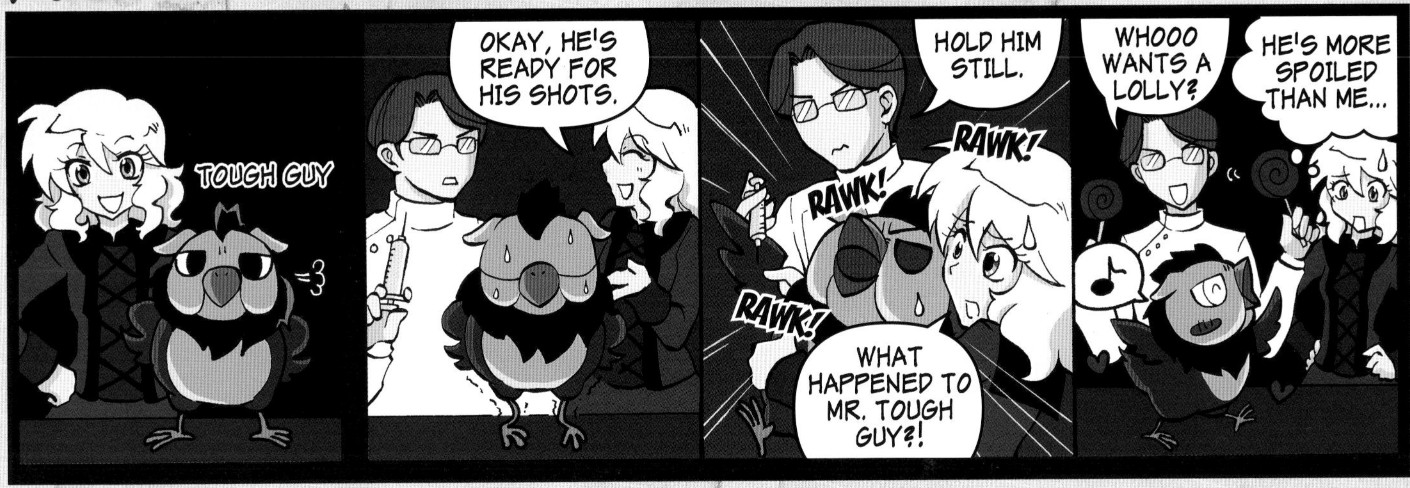
TOUGH GUY
OKAY, HE'S READY FOR HIS SHOTS.
HOLD HIM STILL.
RAWK!
RAWK!
RAWK!
WHAT HAPPENED TO MR. TOUGH GUY?!
WHOOO WANTS A LOLLY?
HE'S MORE SPOILED THAN ME...

Pet Clothes

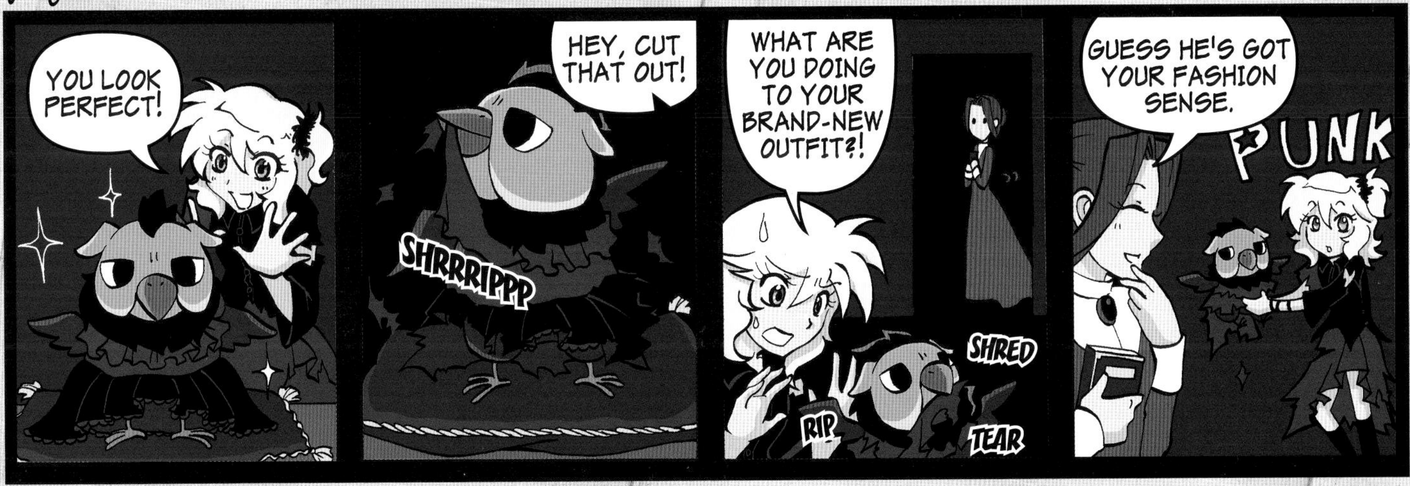
YOU LOOK PERFECT!
HEY, CUT THAT OUT!
SHRRRIPPP
WHAT ARE YOU DOING TO YOUR BRAND-NEW OUTFIT?!
SHRED
RIP
TEAR
GUESS HE'S GOT YOUR FASHION SENSE.
PUNK

Walk

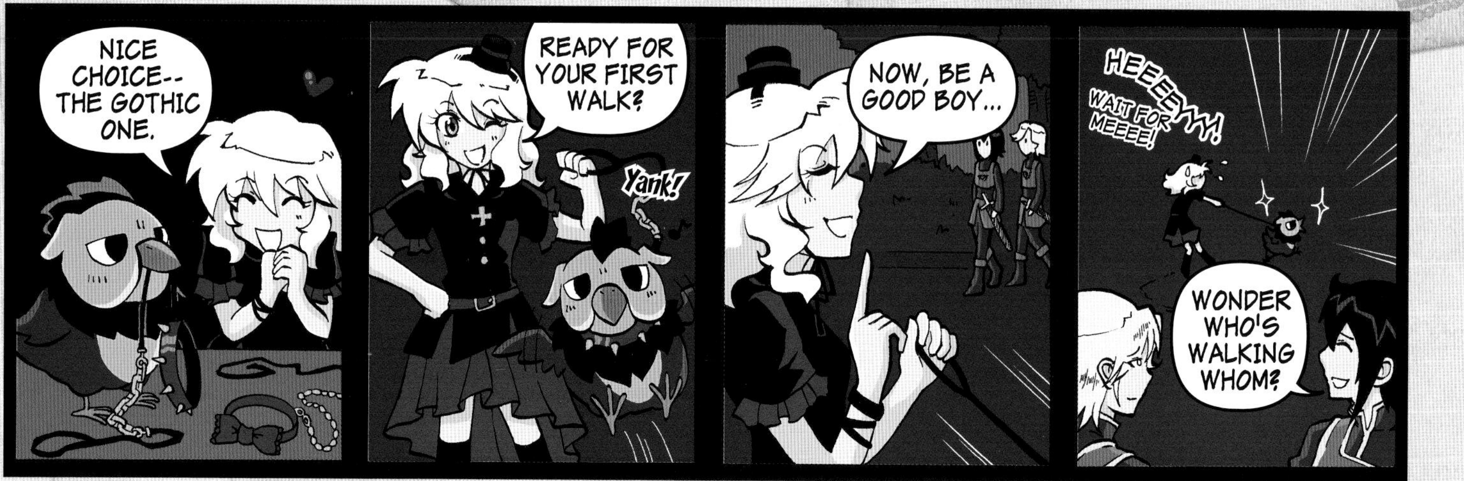
NICE CHOICE-- THE GOTHIC ONE.
READY FOR YOUR FIRST WALK?
Yank!
NOW, BE A GOOD BOY...
HEEEEYYY!
WAIT FOR MEEEE!
WONDER WHO'S WALKING WHOM?

Bath

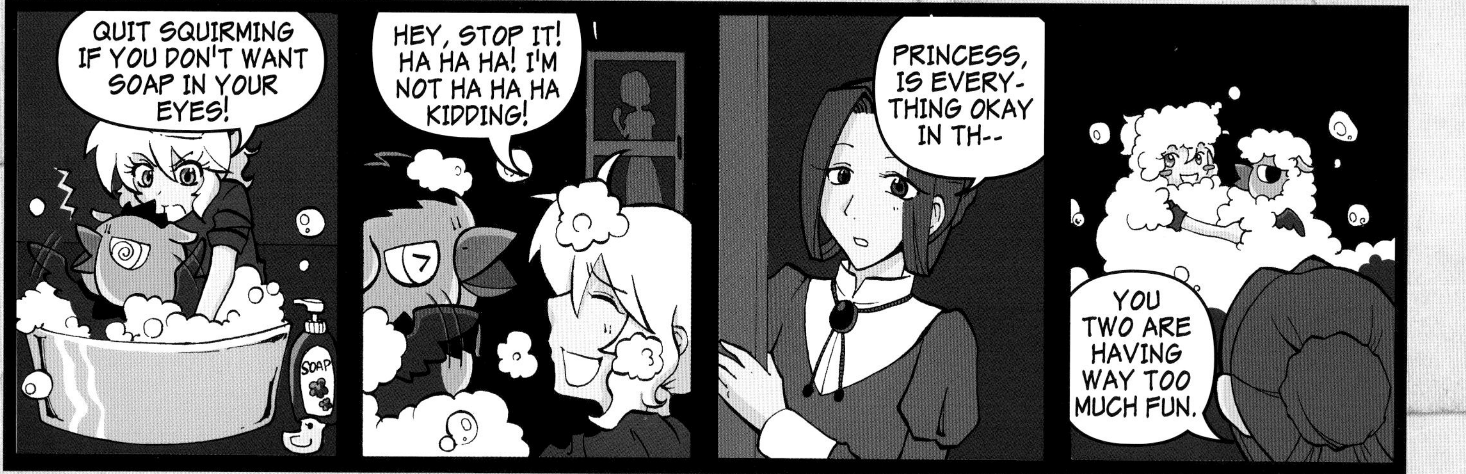
QUIT SQUIRMING IF YOU DON'T WANT SOAP IN YOUR EYES!
SOAP
HEY, STOP IT! HA HA HA! I'M NOT HA HA HA KIDDING!
PRINCESS, IS EVERY-THING OKAY IN TH--
YOU TWO ARE HAVING WAY TOO MUCH FUN.

dear d**Ai**ry

Life here in the Ai-Land castle is good, especially now that I've got my fun-loving, rascal baby-Dougen pet to entertain Lissa and me. I hear that Dougen are a special breed of living beings here on Ai-Land, but they are almost entirely extinct. That's why I'm so glad Daddy gave me one for my 13th birthday! I guess it helps that he's the King. Now if I can only find a way to train this little guy...

love always

Ai

11

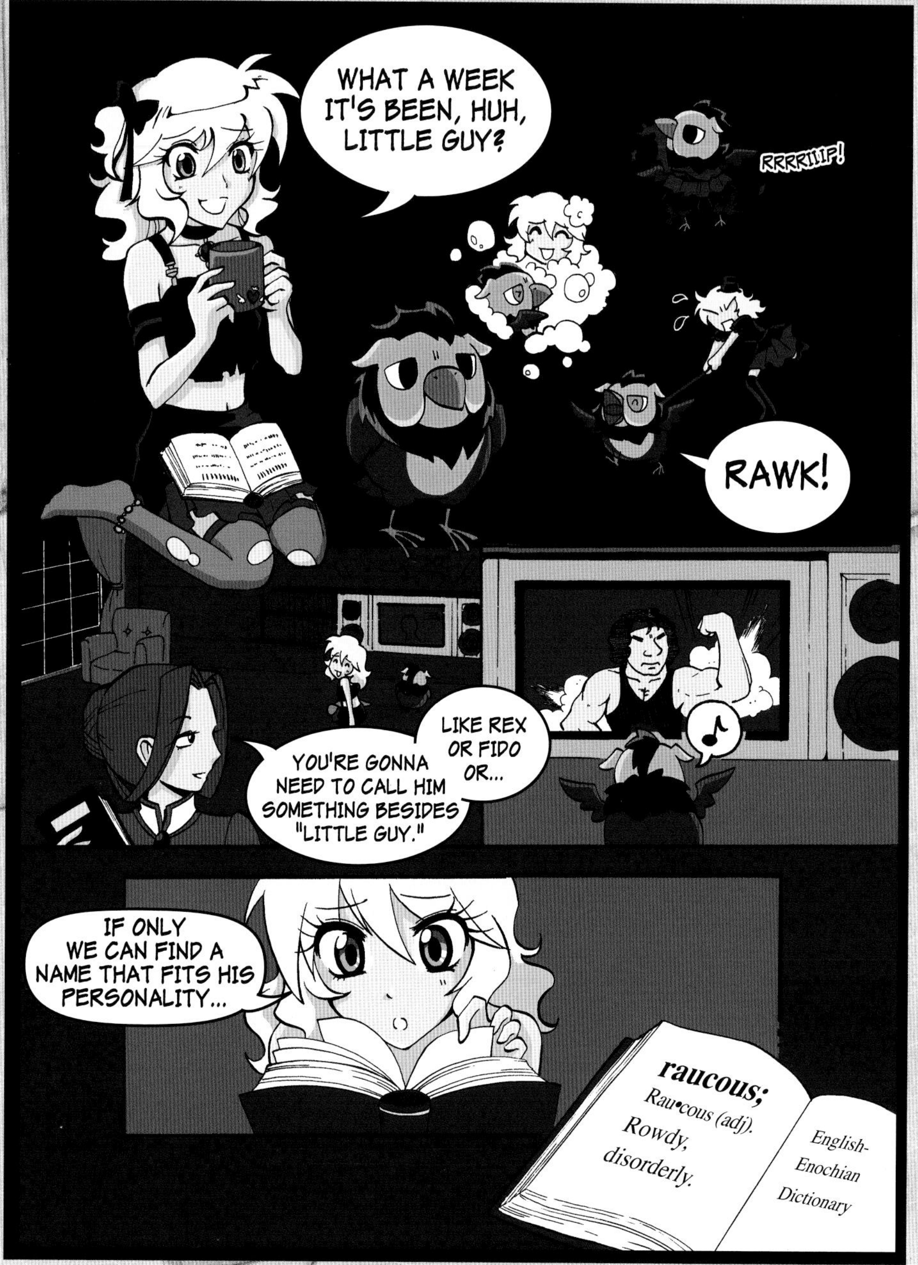
WHAT A WEEK IT'S BEEN, HUH, LITTLE GUY?
RRRRIIIP!
RAWK!
YOU'RE GONNA NEED TO CALL HIM SOMETHING BESIDES "LITTLE GUY."
LIKE REX OR FIDO OR...
IF ONLY WE CAN FIND A NAME THAT FITS HIS PERSONALITY...
raucous;
Rau•cous (adj). Rowdy, disorderly.
English-Enochian Dictionary

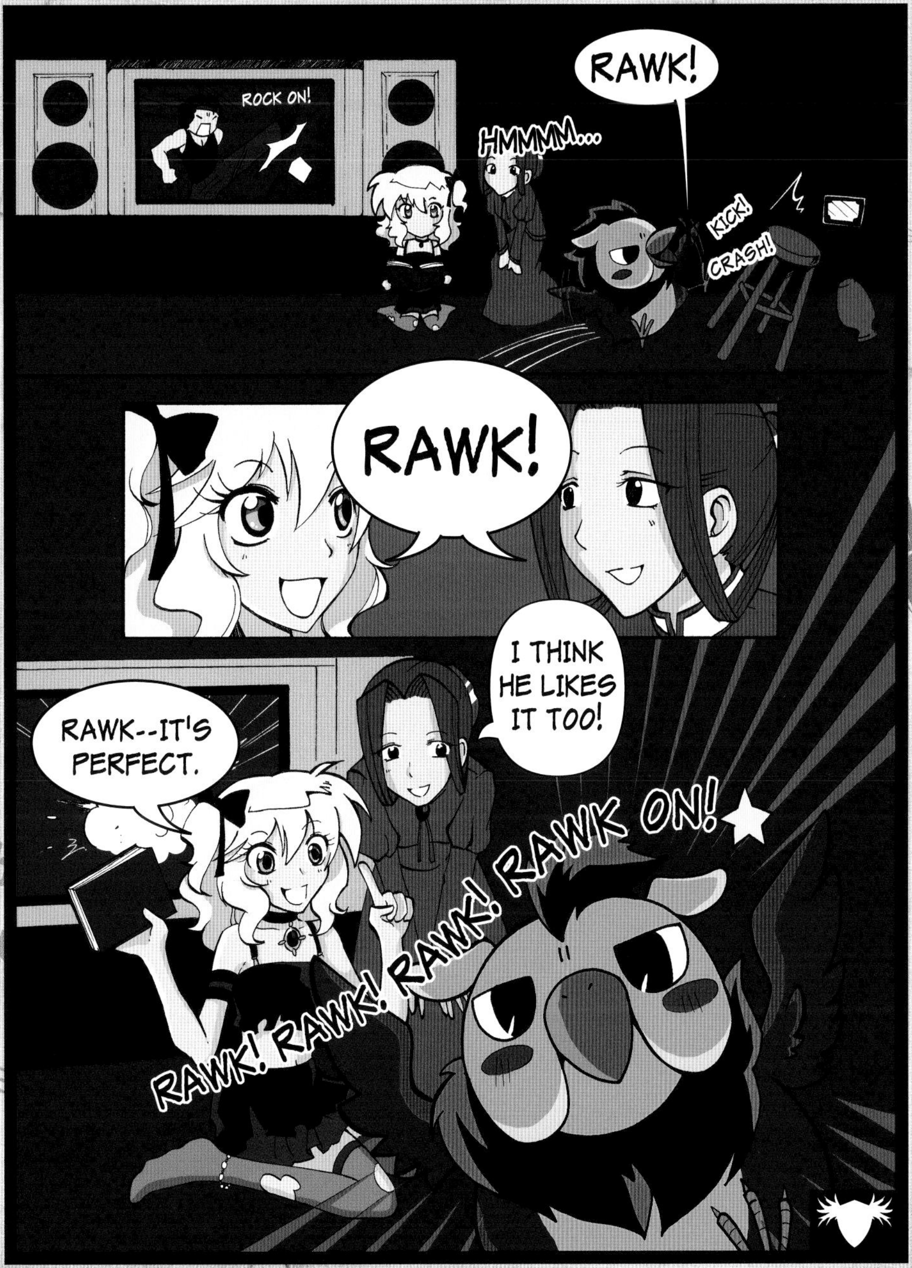
ROCK ON!
HMMMM...
RAWK!
KICK!
CRASH!
RAWK!
RAWK--IT'S PERFECT.
I THINK HE LIKES IT TOO!
RAWK! RAWK! RAWK! RAWK ON!

Other Side

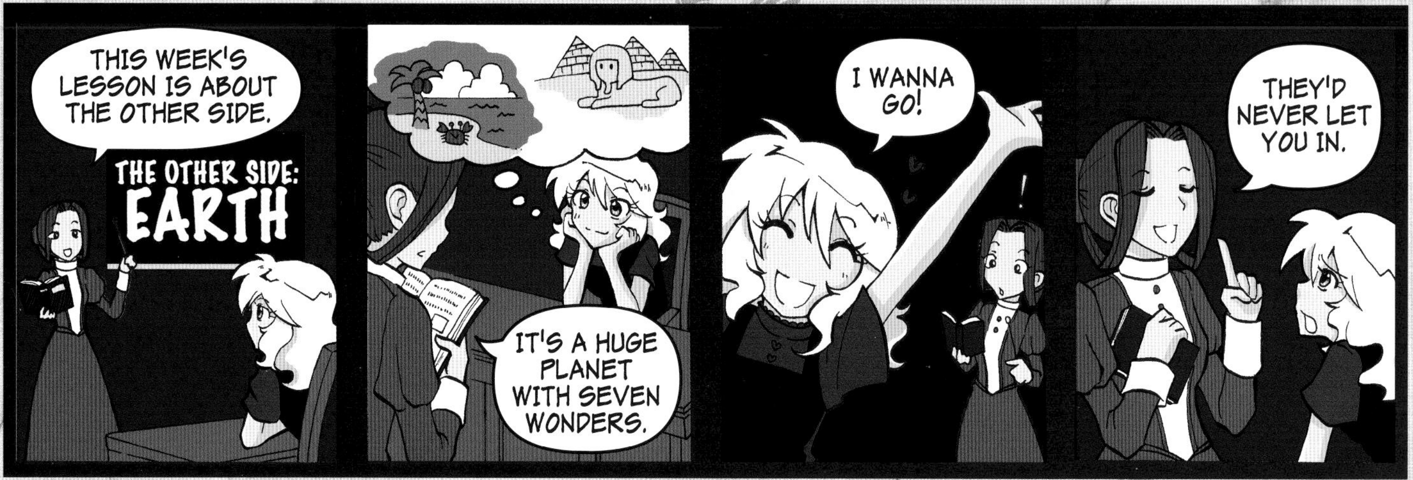
THIS WEEK'S LESSON IS ABOUT THE OTHER SIDE.
THE OTHER SIDE: EARTH
IT'S A HUGE PLANET WITH SEVEN WONDERS.
I WANNA GO!
THEY'D NEVER LET YOU IN.

Nations

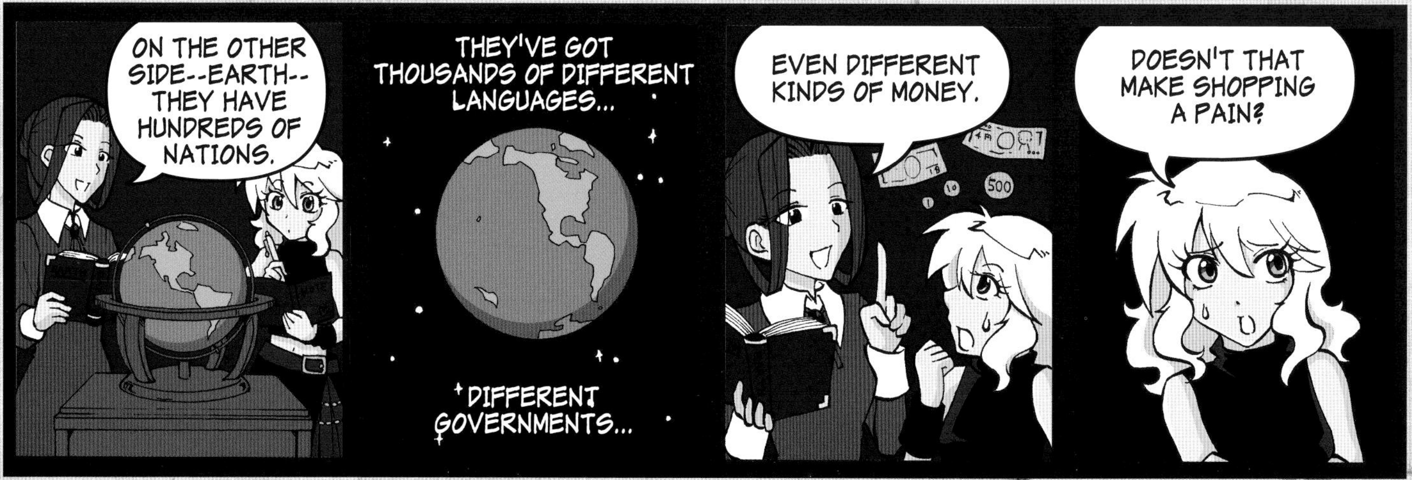
ON THE OTHER SIDE--EARTH--THEY HAVE HUNDREDS OF NATIONS.
THEY'VE GOT THOUSANDS OF DIFFERENT LANGUAGES...
DIFFERENT GOVERNMENTS...
EVEN DIFFERENT KINDS OF MONEY.
500
DOESN'T THAT MAKE SHOPPING A PAIN?

Religion

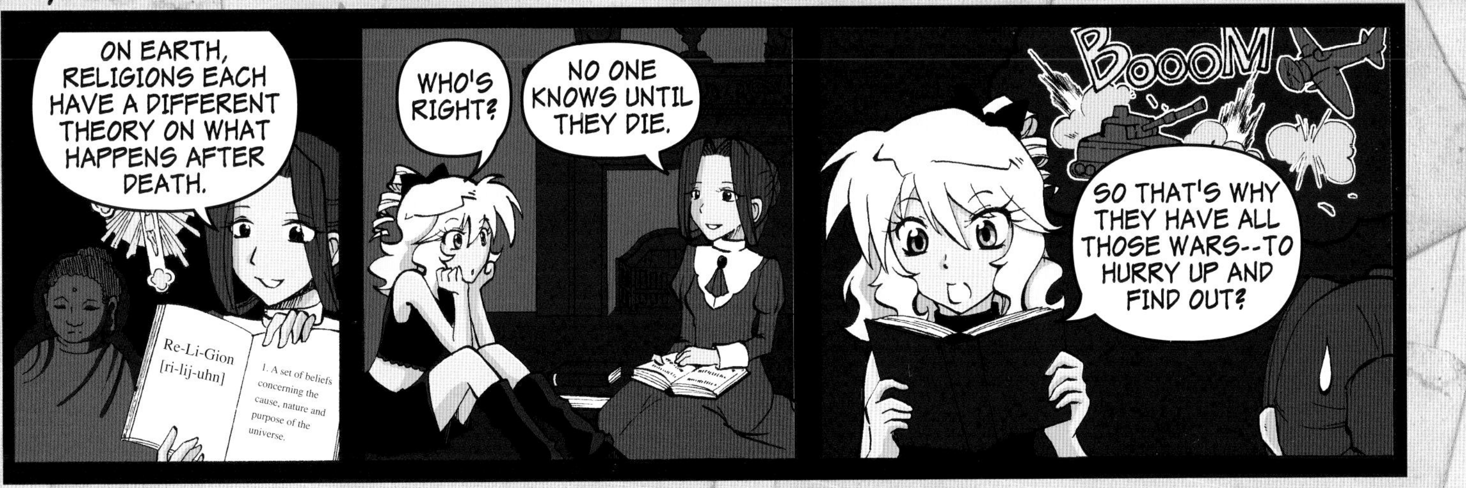
ON EARTH, RELIGIONS EACH HAVE A DIFFERENT THEORY ON WHAT HAPPENS AFTER DEATH.
Re-Li-Gion [ri-lij-uhn]
1. A set of beliefs concerning the cause, nature and purpose of the universe.
WHO'S RIGHT?
NO ONE KNOWS UNTIL THEY DIE.
BOOOM
SO THAT'S WHY THEY HAVE ALL THOSE WARS--TO HURRY UP AND FIND OUT?

Ai-Land vs. the Other Side

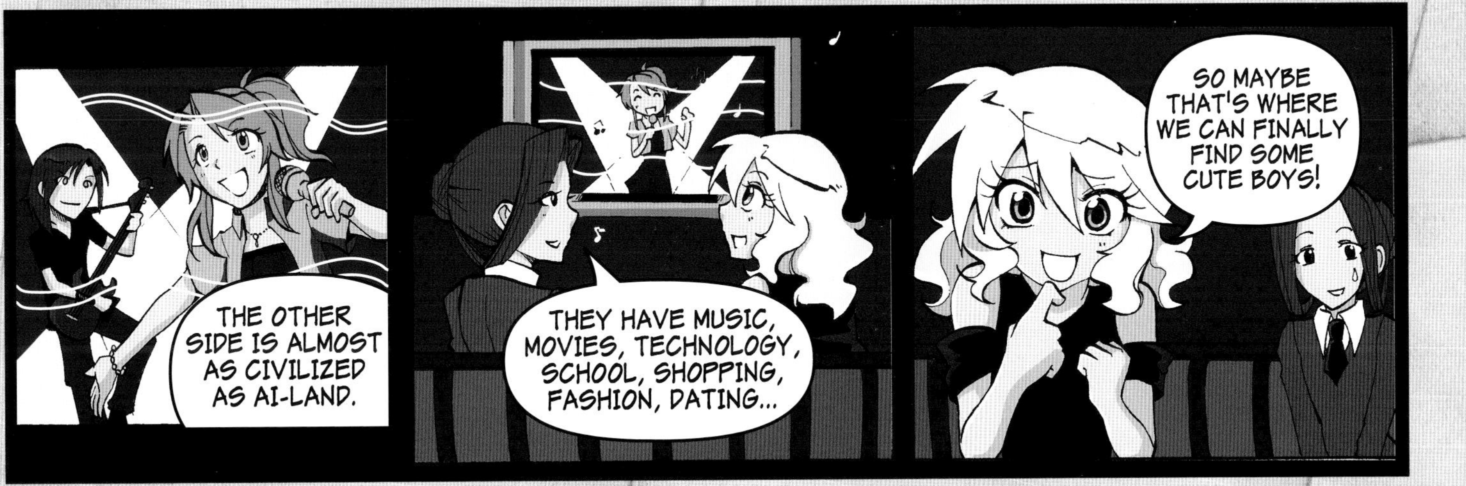
THE OTHER SIDE IS ALMOST AS CIVILIZED AS AI-LAND.
THEY HAVE MUSIC, MOVIES, TECHNOLOGY, SCHOOL, SHOPPING, FASHION, DATING...
SO MAYBE THAT'S WHERE WE CAN FINALLY FIND SOME CUTE BOYS!

Transportation

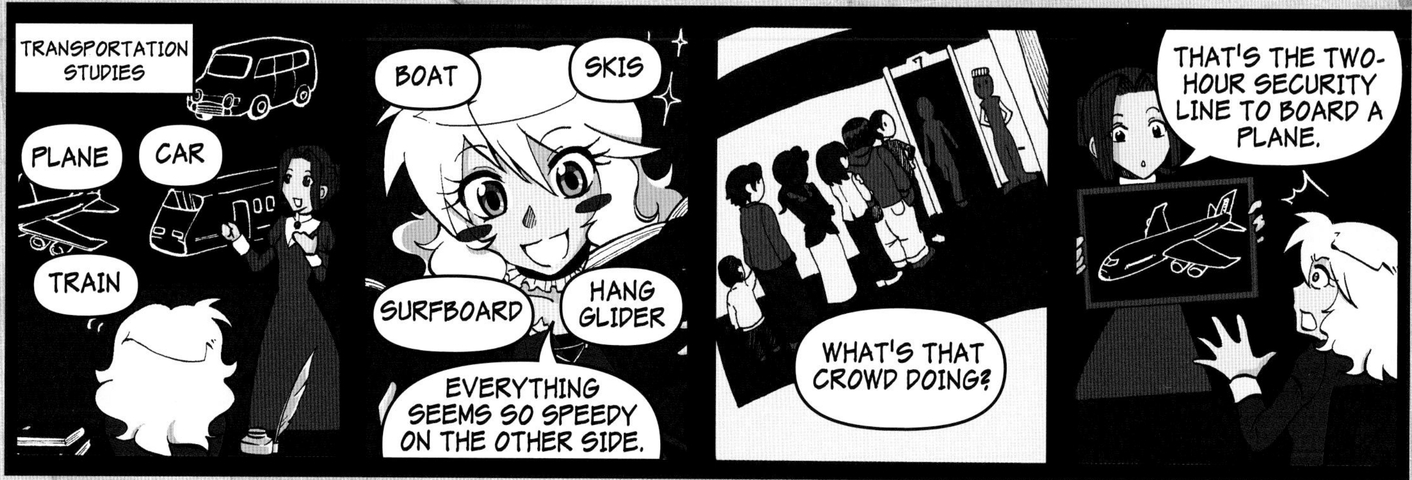
TRANSPORTATION STUDIES
PLANE
CAR
TRAIN
BOAT
SKIS
SURFBOARD
HANG GLIDER
EVERYTHING SEEMS SO SPEEDY ON THE OTHER SIDE.
WHAT'S THAT CROWD DOING?
THAT'S THE TWO-HOUR SECURITY LINE TO BOARD A PLANE.

Bad for You

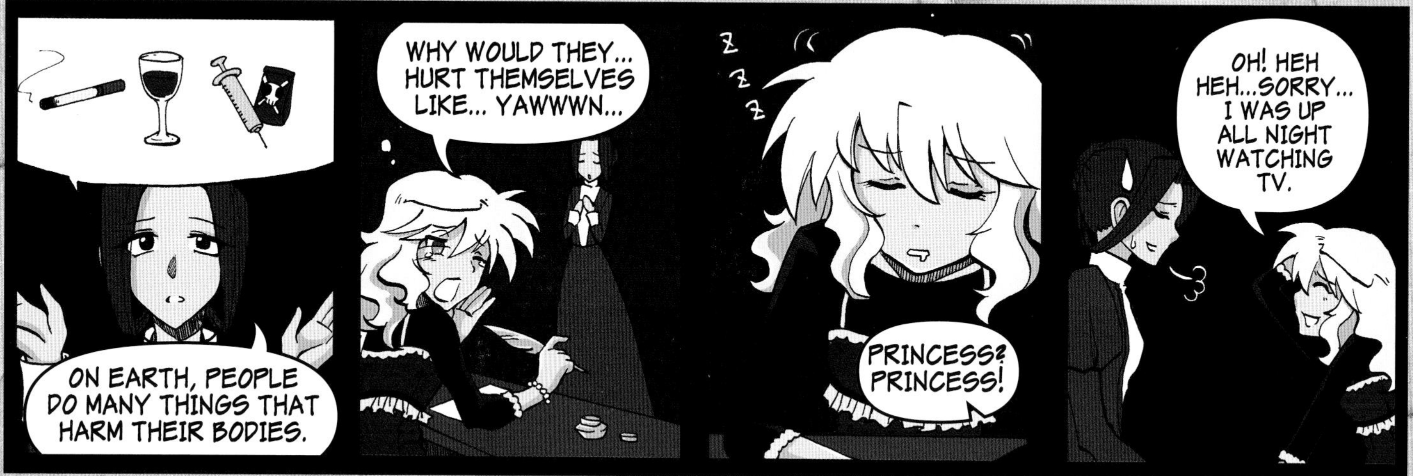
ON EARTH, PEOPLE DO MANY THINGS THAT HARM THEIR BODIES.
WHY WOULD THEY... HURT THEMSELVES LIKE... YAWWWN...
Z
Z
Z
PRINCESS? PRINCESS!
OH! HEH HEH...SORRY... I WAS UP ALL NIGHT WATCHING TV.

dear diry

It's been such an amazing week learning all about the Other Side, a place they call planet "Earth." Life can get so boring stuck in this castle, and Ai-Land is such a small world compared to this "Earth" place. Now it's become my ultimate goal to somehow travel there one day. Too bad there's no easy way to get there from Ai-Land. In the meantime, I'll just dream of all the hot-looking boys there... Uh-oh, gotta go study for the big test!!

love always

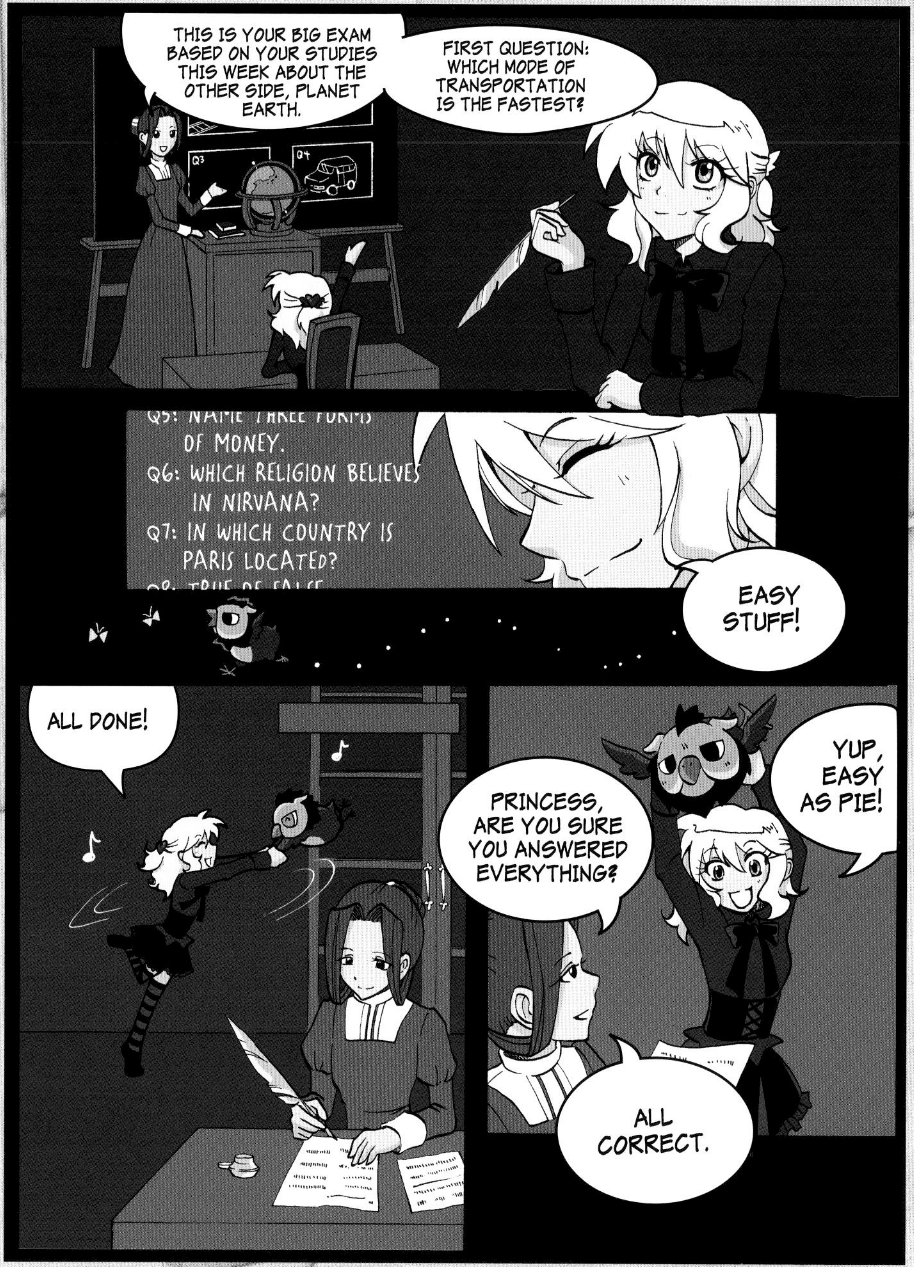
THIS IS YOUR BIG EXAM BASED ON YOUR STUDIES THIS WEEK ABOUT THE OTHER SIDE, PLANET EARTH.
FIRST QUESTION: WHICH MODE OF TRANSPORTATION IS THE FASTEST?
Q3
Q4
Q5: NAME THREE FORMS OF MONEY.
Q6: WHICH RELIGION BELIEVES IN NIRVANA?
Q7: IN WHICH COUNTRY IS PARIS LOCATED?
EASY STUFF!
ALL DONE!
PRINCESS, ARE YOU SURE YOU ANSWERED EVERYTHING?
YUP, EASY AS PIE!
ALL CORRECT.

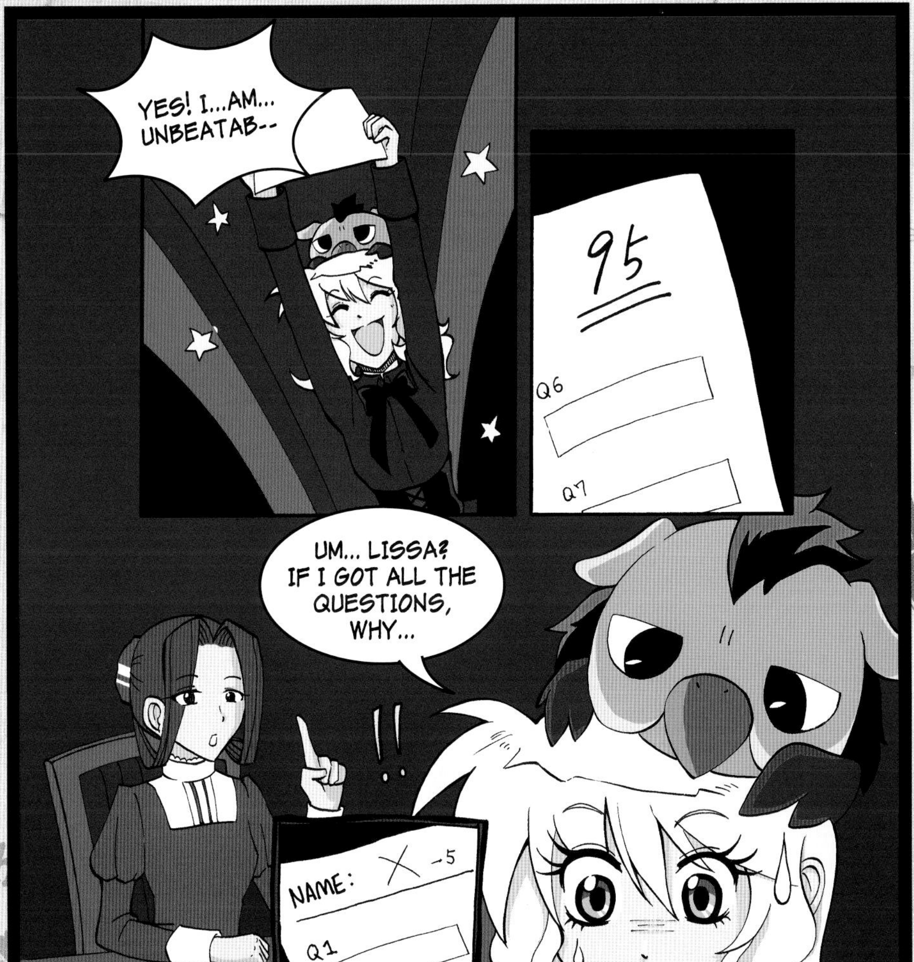
YES! I...AM... UNBEATAB--
95
Q6
Q7
UM... LISSA? IF I GOT ALL THE QUESTIONS, WHY...
!!
NAME: X -5
Q1
YOU FORGOT YOUR NAME.

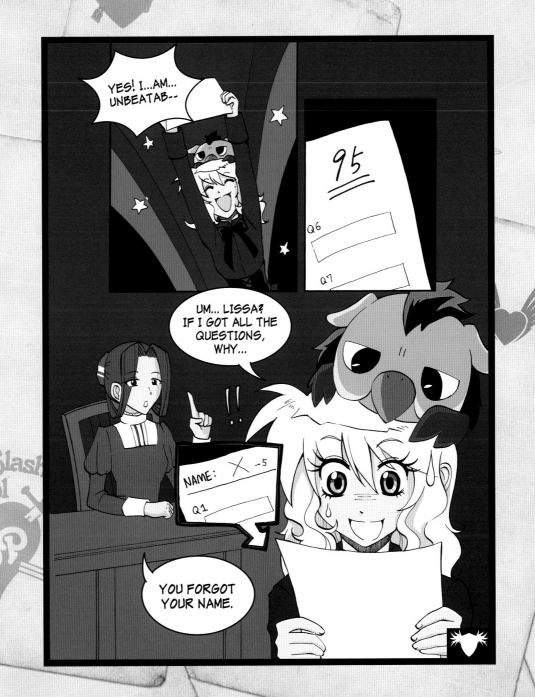

Wings

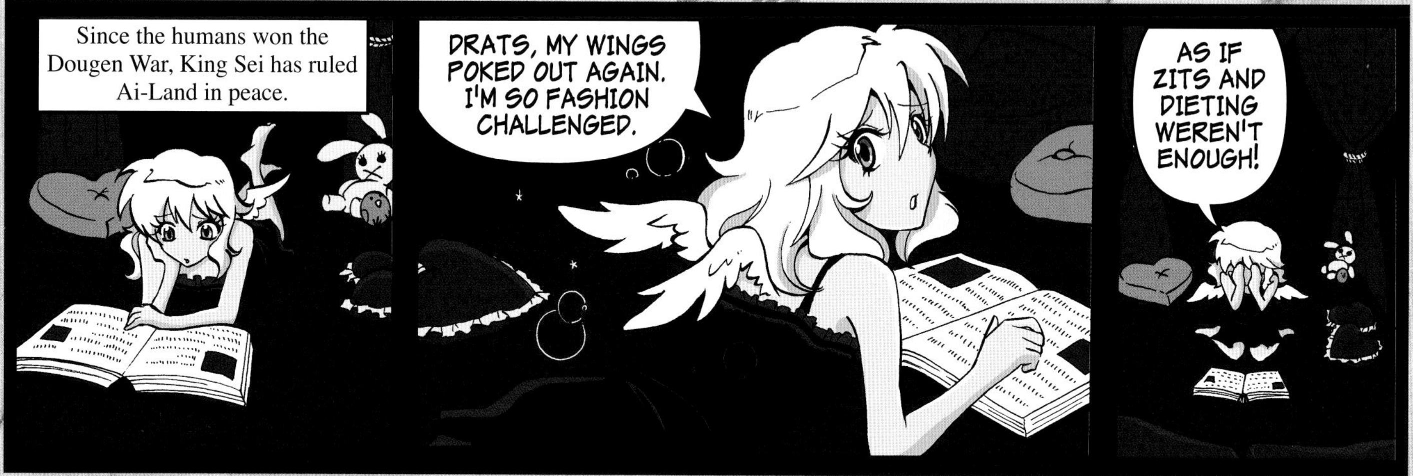

Since the humans won the Dougen War, King Sei has ruled Ai-Land in peace.
DRATS, MY WINGS POKED OUT AGAIN. I'M SO FASHION CHALLENGED.
AS IF ZITS AND DIETING WEREN'T ENOUGH!

Can't Fly

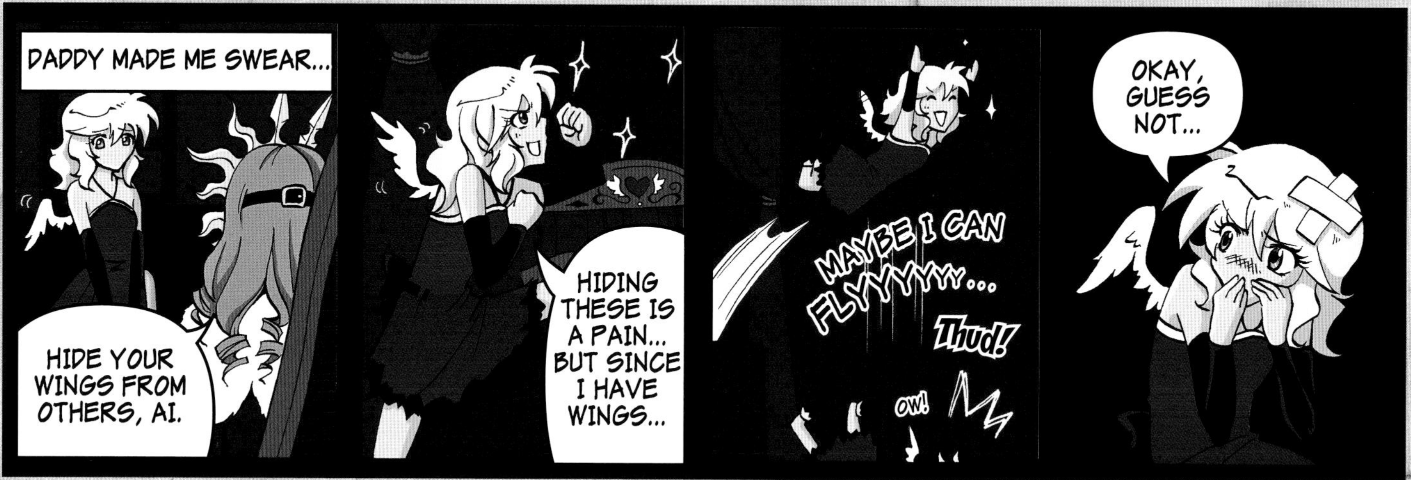

DADDY MADE ME SWEAR...
HIDE YOUR WINGS FROM OTHERS, AI.
HIDING THESE IS A PAIN... BUT SINCE I HAVE WINGS...
MAYBE I CAN FLYYYYYY...
Thud!
OW!
OKAY, GUESS NOT...

Secret

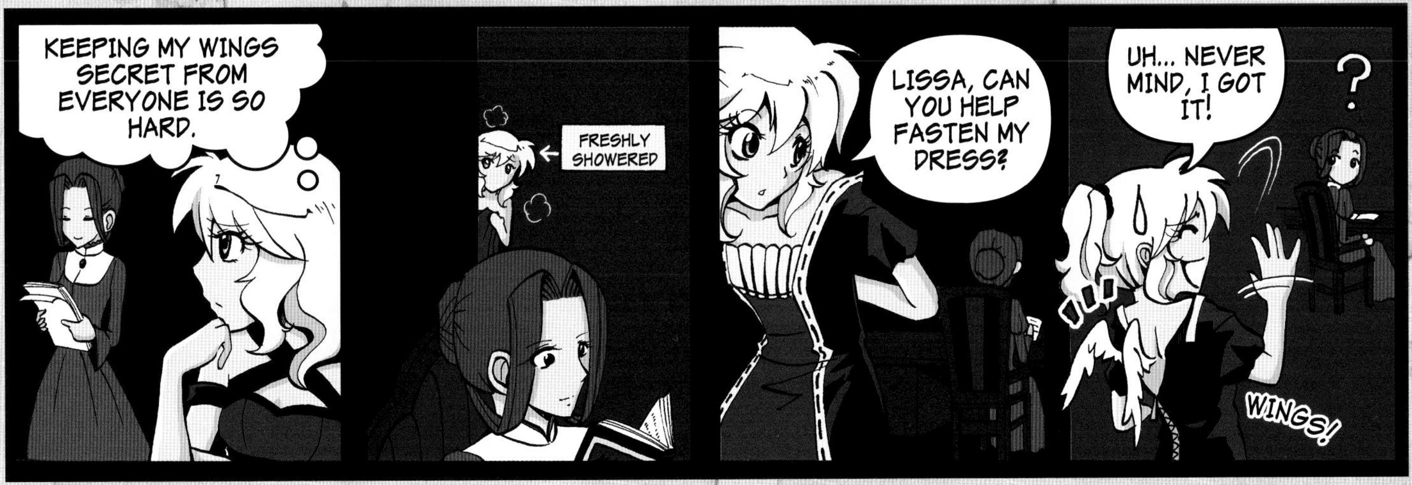
KEEPING MY WINGS SECRET FROM EVERYONE IS SO HARD.
FRESHLY SHOWERED
LISSA, CAN YOU HELP FASTEN MY DRESS?
UH... NEVER MIND, I GOT IT!
?
WINGS!

King Sei

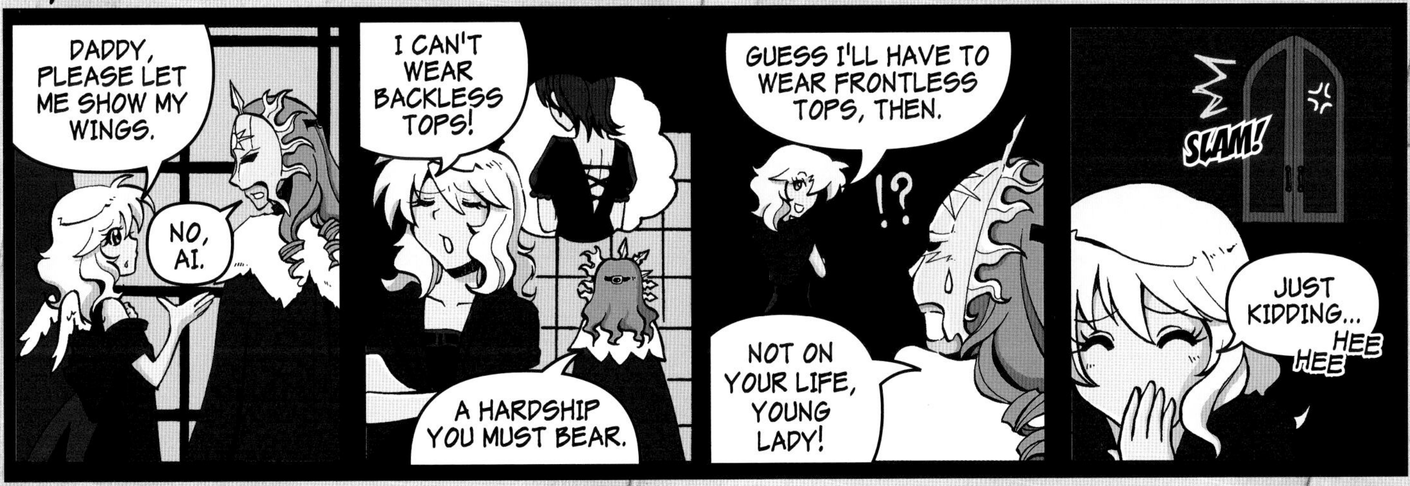
DADDY, PLEASE LET ME SHOW MY WINGS.
NO, AI.
I CAN'T WEAR BACKLESS TOPS!
A HARDSHIP YOU MUST BEAR.
GUESS I'LL HAVE TO WEAR FRONTLESS TOPS, THEN.
!?
NOT ON YOUR LIFE, YOUNG LADY!
SLAM!
JUST KIDDING...
HEE HEE

Practice Flying

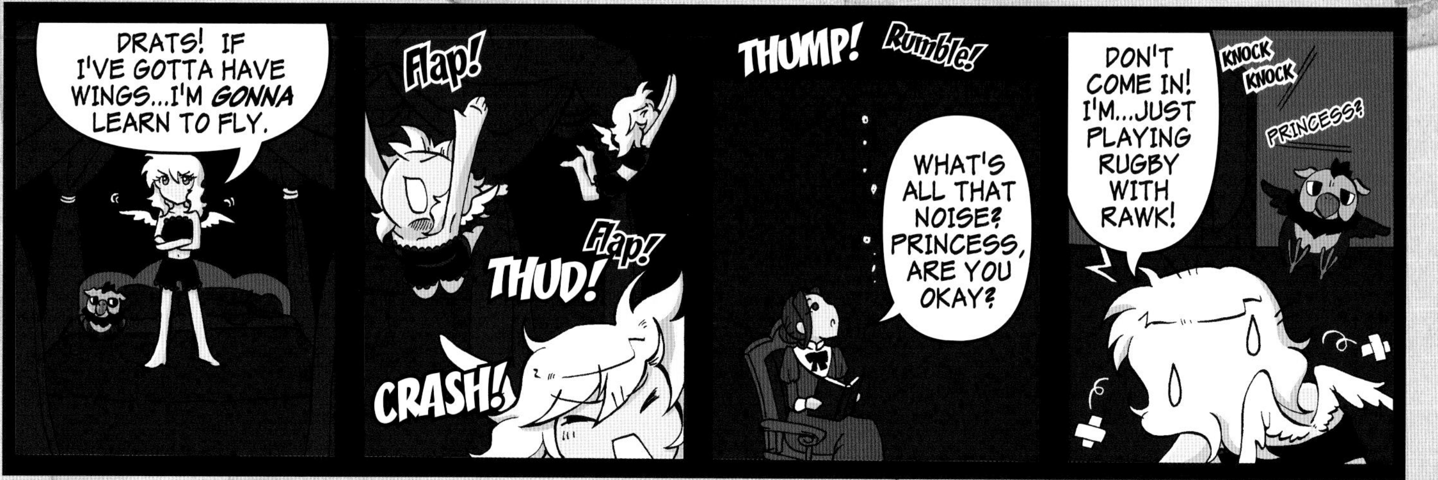
DRATS! IF I'VE GOTTA HAVE WINGS...I'M *GONNA* LEARN TO FLY.
Flap!
Flap!
THUD!
CRASH!
THUMP!
Rumble!
WHAT'S ALL THAT NOISE? PRINCESS, ARE YOU OKAY?
KNOCK
KNOCK
PRINCESS?
DON'T COME IN! I'M...JUST PLAYING RUGBY WITH RAWK!

Cosplay

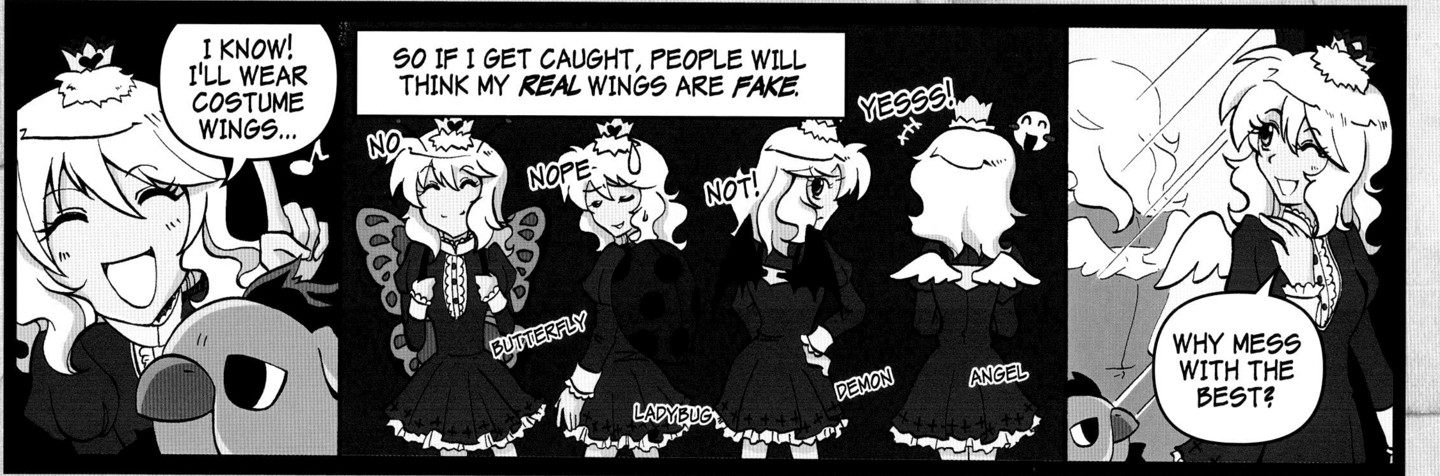
I KNOW! I'LL WEAR COSTUME WINGS...
SO IF I GET CAUGHT, PEOPLE WILL THINK MY *REAL* WINGS ARE *FAKE*.
NO
NOPE
NOT!
YESSS!
BUTTERFLY
LADYBUG
DEMON
ANGEL
WHY MESS WITH THE BEST?

dear d*Ai*ry

Life as the sole Princess of Ai-Land is so full of trials and tribulations. Sure, the shopping sprees are fun, but why am I the only human stuck with wings? I feel like a freak! Worse yet, Daddy insists I never reveal them to another soul--not even my best friend and tutor Lissa. So hopefully my little "fake wings" scheme will work...

love always

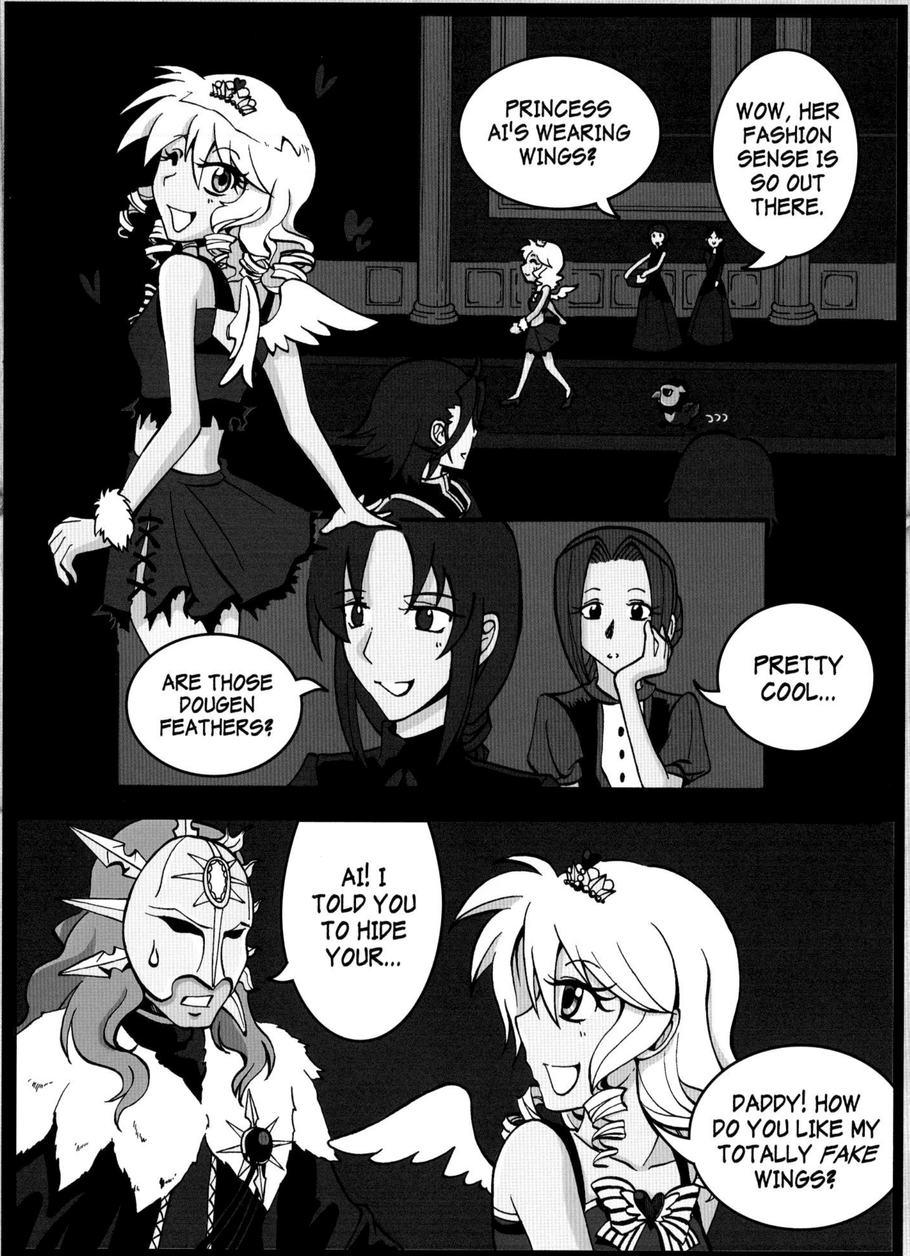
PRINCESS AI'S WEARING WINGS?
WOW, HER FASHION SENSE IS SO OUT THERE.
ARE THOSE DOUGEN FEATHERS?
PRETTY COOL...
AI! I TOLD YOU TO HIDE YOUR...
DADDY! HOW DO YOU LIKE MY TOTALLY *FAKE* WINGS?

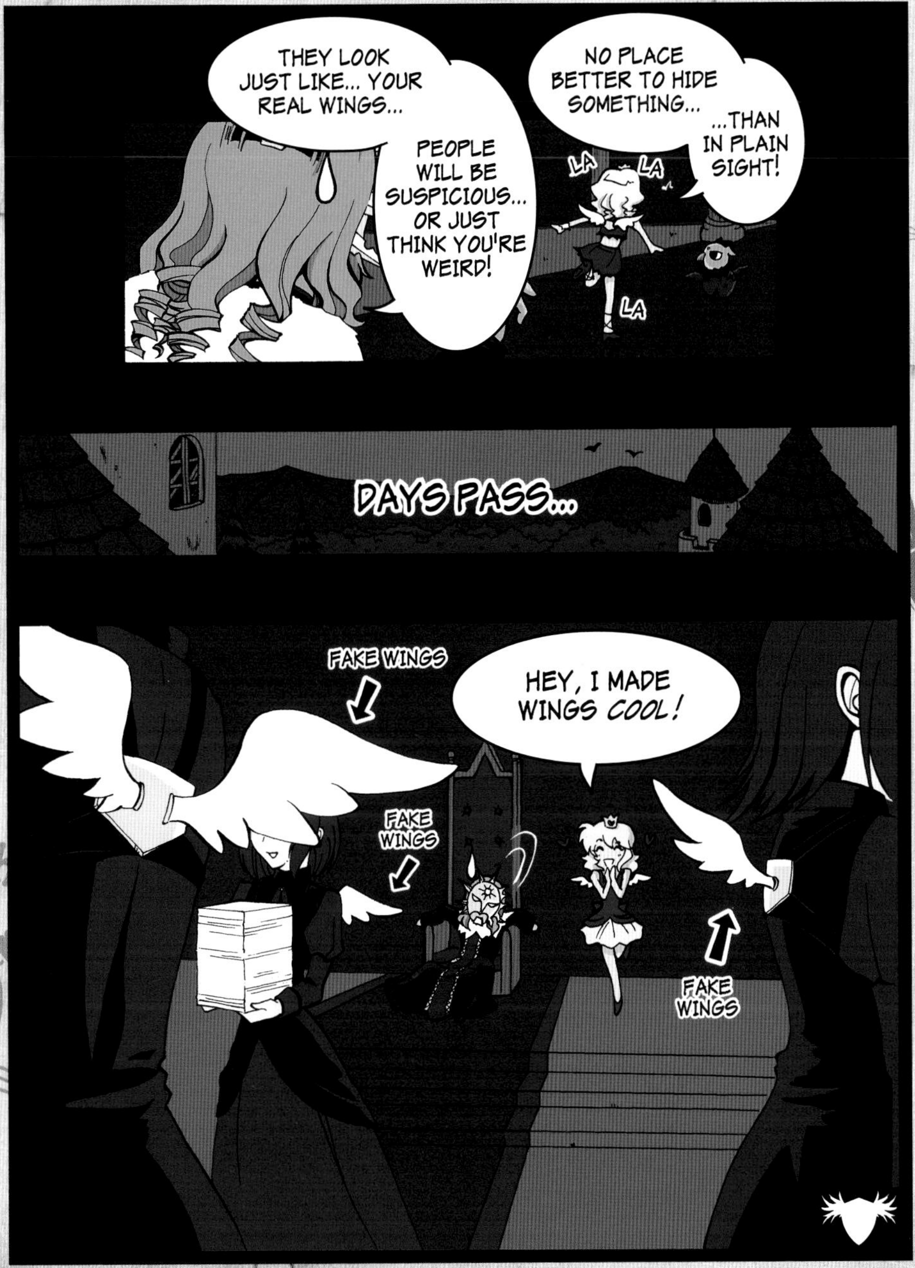
THEY LOOK JUST LIKE... YOUR REAL WINGS...
PEOPLE WILL BE SUSPICIOUS... OR JUST THINK YOU'RE WEIRD!
NO PLACE BETTER TO HIDE SOMETHING...
...THAN IN PLAIN SIGHT!
LA
LA
LA
DAYS PASS...
FAKE WINGS
HEY, I MADE WINGS *COOL*!
FAKE WINGS
FAKE WINGS

Not a Princess?!

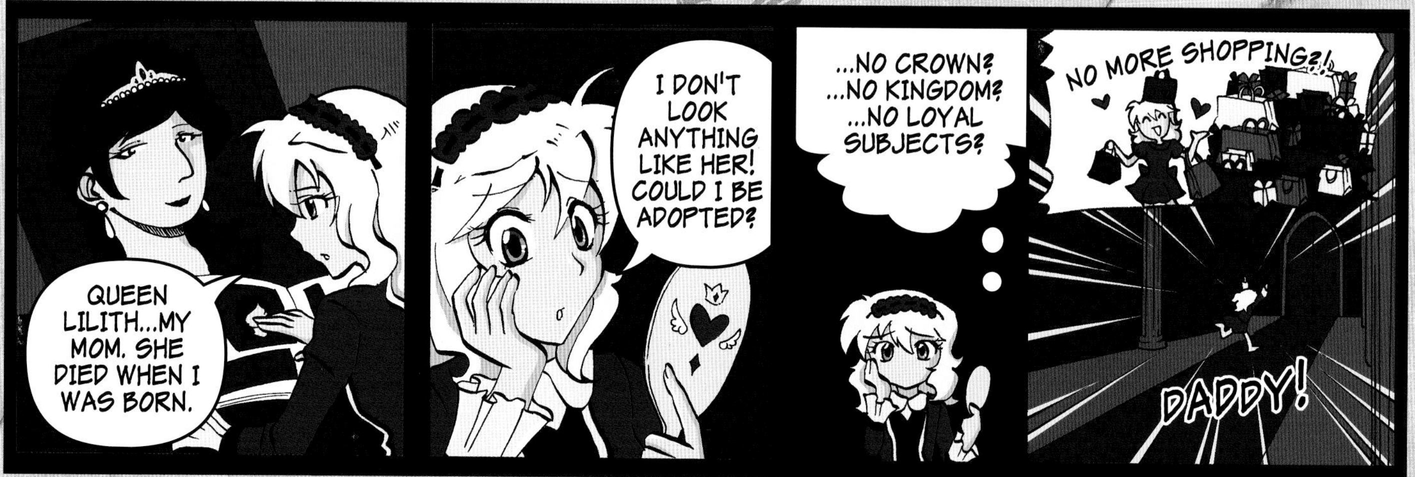
QUEEN LILITH...MY MOM. SHE DIED WHEN I WAS BORN.
I DON'T LOOK ANYTHING LIKE HER! COULD I BE ADOPTED?
...NO CROWN? ...NO KINGDOM? ...NO LOYAL SUBJECTS?
NO MORE SHOPPING?!
DADDY!

Adopted?

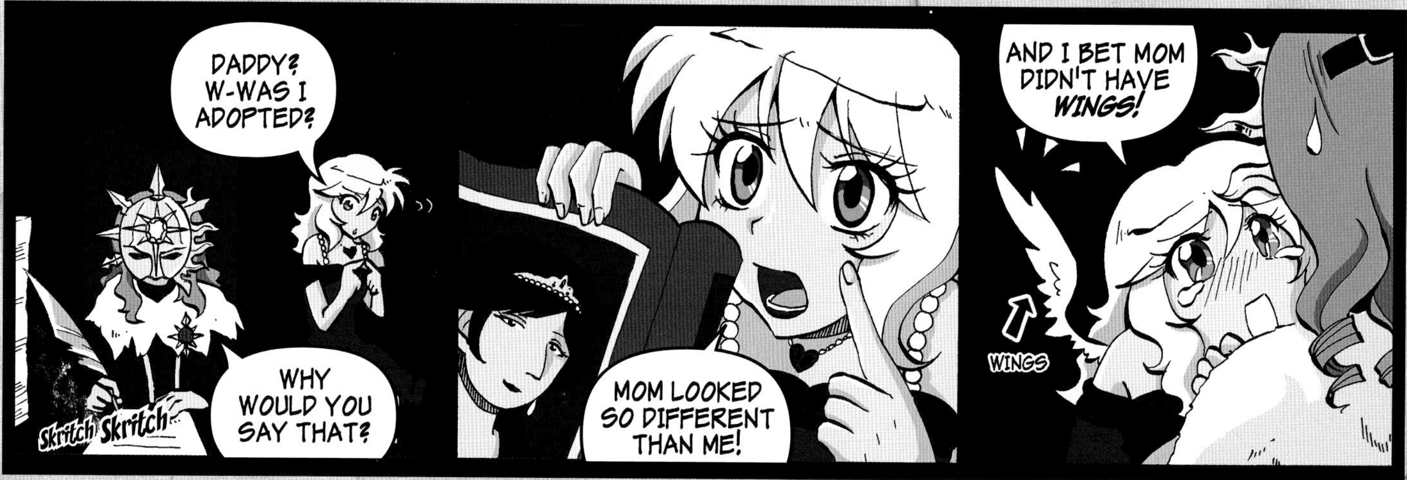
DADDY? W-WAS I ADOPTED?
WHY WOULD YOU SAY THAT?
Skritch Skritch
MOM LOOKED SO DIFFERENT THAN ME!
AND I BET MOM DIDN'T HAVE WINGS!
WINGS

Fatherly Love

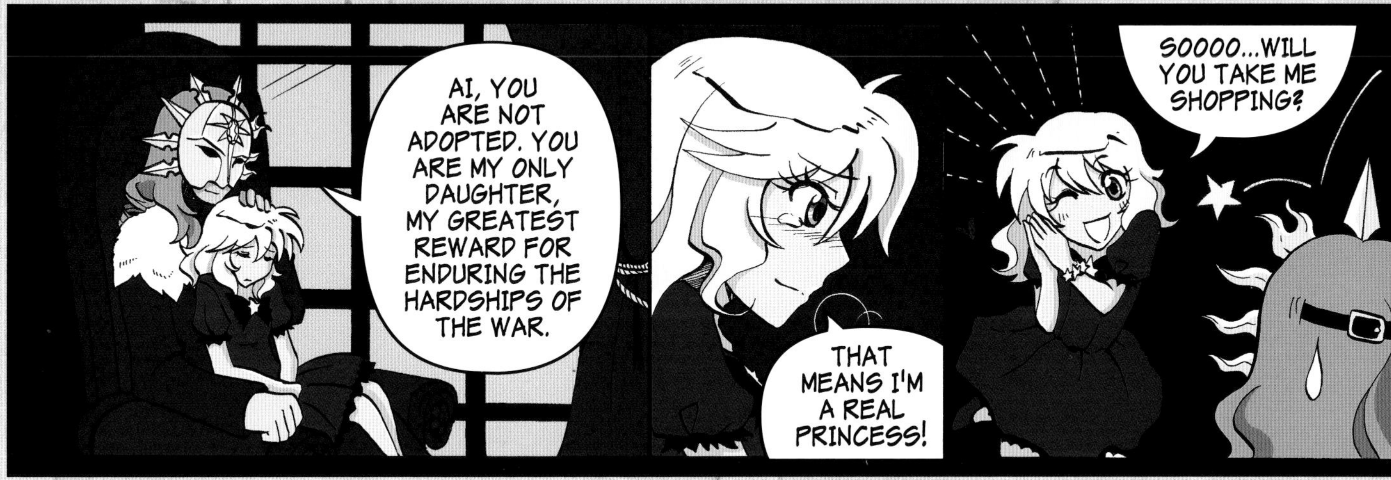
AI, YOU ARE NOT ADOPTED. YOU ARE MY ONLY DAUGHTER, MY GREATEST REWARD FOR ENDURING THE HARDSHIPS OF THE WAR.
THAT MEANS I'M A REAL PRINCESS!
SOOOO...WILL YOU TAKE ME SHOPPING?

Evil Ruler

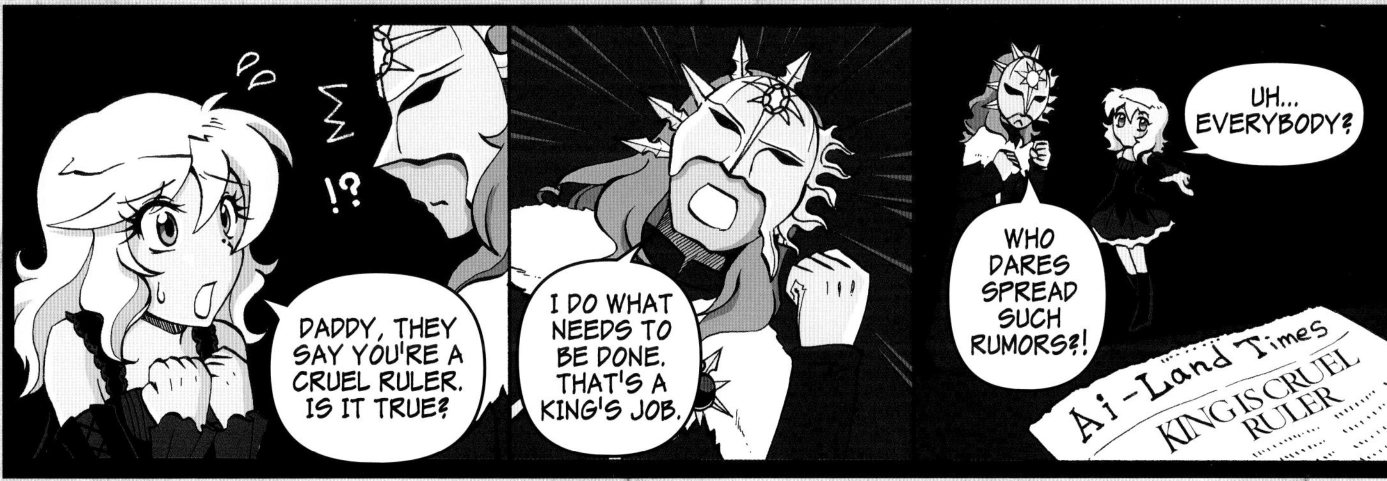
!?
DADDY, THEY SAY YOU'RE A CRUEL RULER. IS IT TRUE?
I DO WHAT NEEDS TO BE DONE. THAT'S A KING'S JOB.
UH... EVERYBODY?
WHO DARES SPREAD SUCH RUMORS?!
Ai-Land Times
KING IS CRUEL RULER

Dating

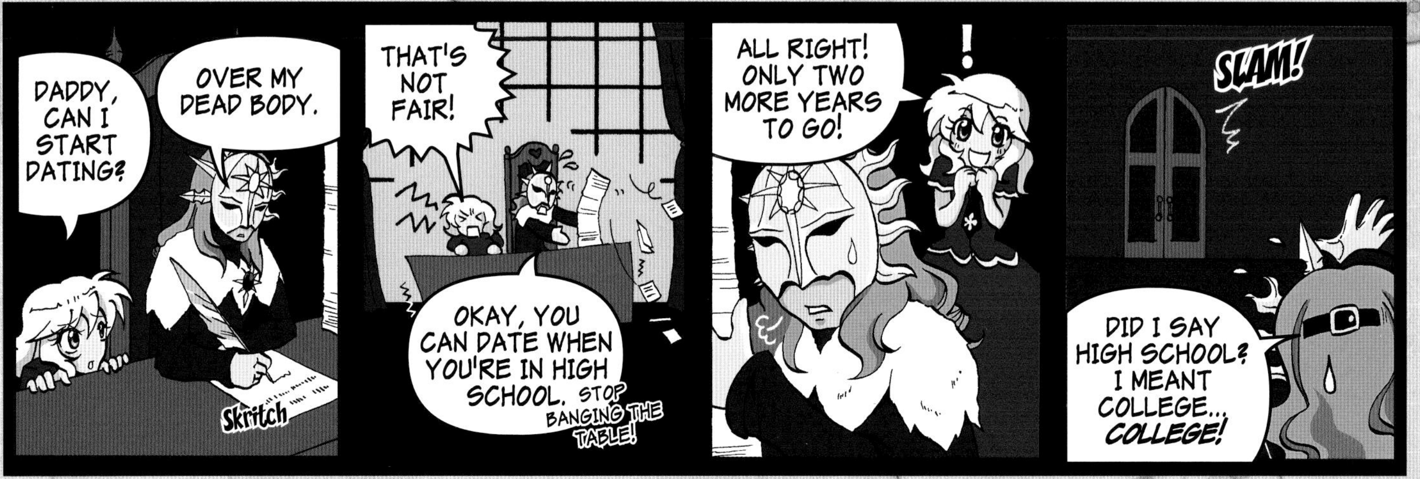
DADDY, CAN I START DATING?
OVER MY DEAD BODY.
Skritch
THAT'S NOT FAIR!
OKAY, YOU CAN DATE WHEN YOU'RE IN HIGH SCHOOL.
STOP BANGING THE TABLE!
ALL RIGHT! ONLY TWO MORE YEARS TO GO!
!
SLAM!
DID I SAY HIGH SCHOOL? I MEANT COLLEGE... ***COLLEGE!***

Dad's Job

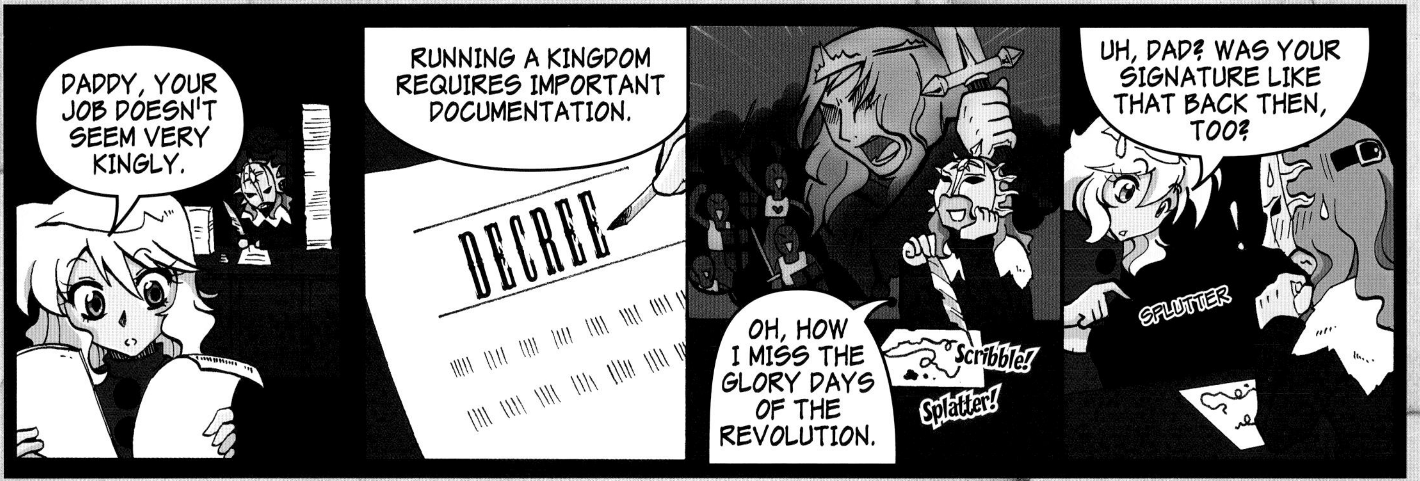
DADDY, YOUR JOB DOESN'T SEEM VERY KINGLY.
RUNNING A KINGDOM REQUIRES IMPORTANT DOCUMENTATION.
DECREE
OH, HOW I MISS THE GLORY DAYS OF THE REVOLUTION.
Scribble!
Splatter!
UH, DAD? WAS YOUR SIGNATURE LIKE THAT BACK THEN, TOO?
SPLUTTER

dear d*Ai*ry

Ai-Land is a special place, and I'm lucky to be Princess, but sometimes I feel so different than everyone else. My dad's not only a king, but he always wears a mask. Mom died as I was born--so I never even saw her. And of course, there are my wings-- No human has wings! I can't help but wonder who I really am...

love always

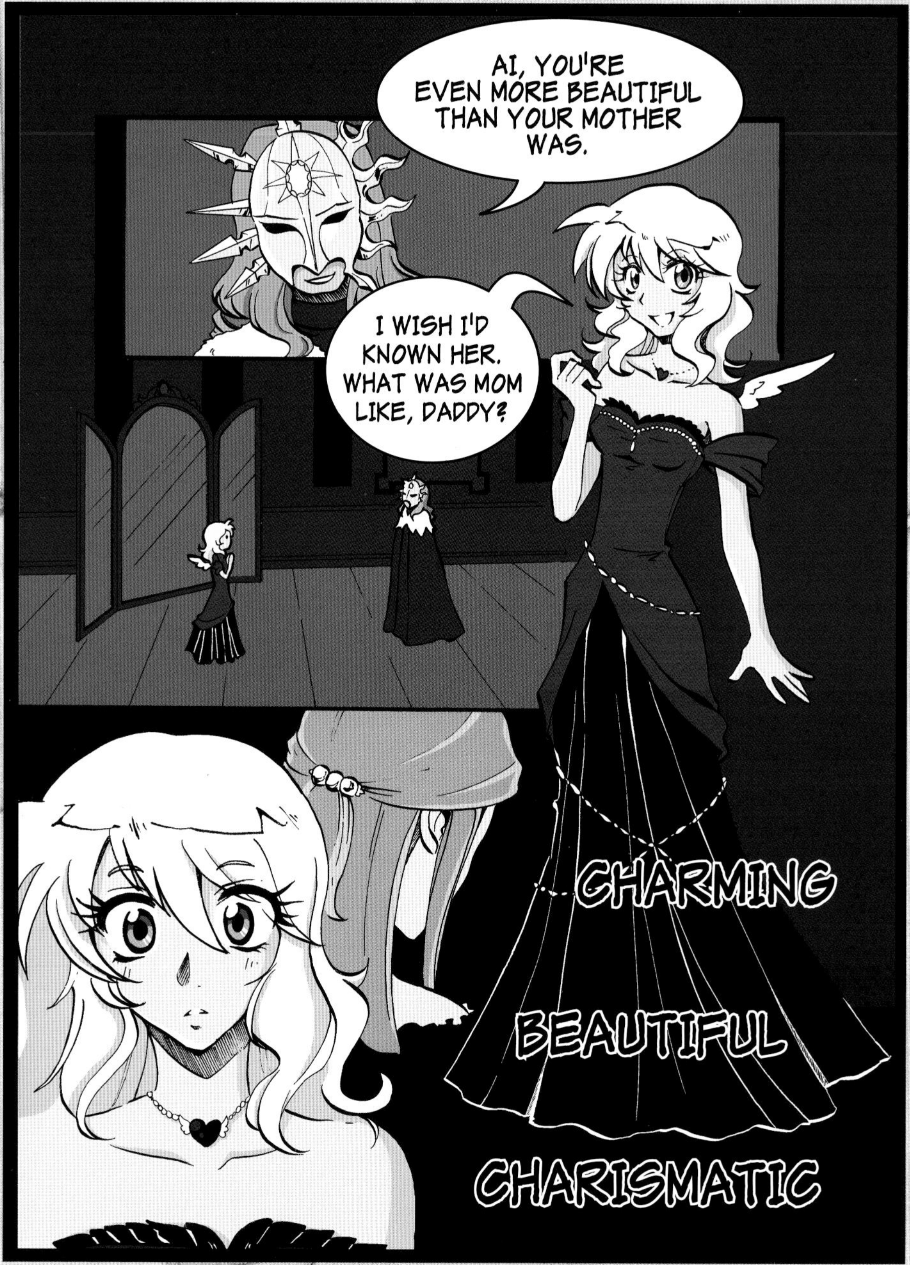
AI, YOU'RE EVEN MORE BEAUTIFUL THAN YOUR MOTHER WAS.
I WISH I'D KNOWN HER. WHAT WAS MOM LIKE, DADDY?
CHARMING
BEAUTIFUL
CHARISMATIC

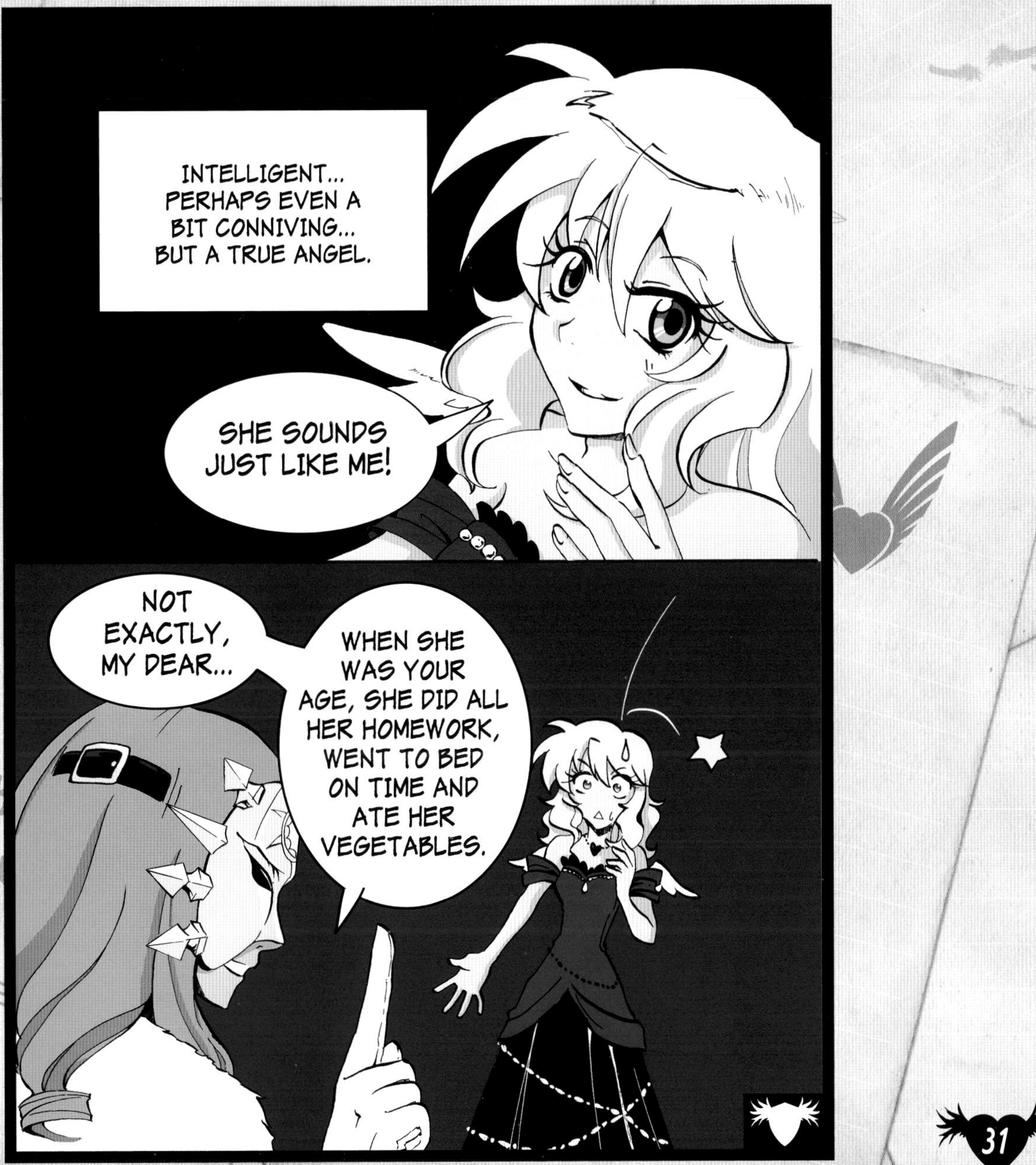
INTELLIGENT... PERHAPS EVEN A BIT CONNIVING... BUT A TRUE ANGEL.
SHE SOUNDS JUST LIKE ME!
NOT EXACTLY, MY DEAR...
WHEN SHE WAS YOUR AGE, SHE DID ALL HER HOMEWORK, WENT TO BED ON TIME AND ATE HER VEGETABLES.

Fashion Mags

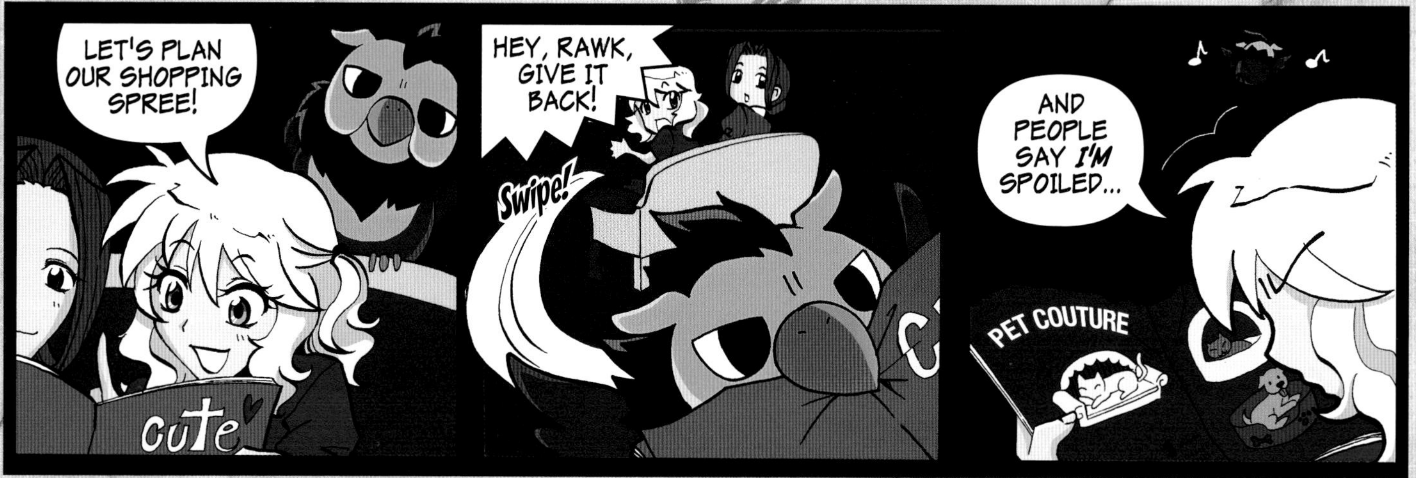
LET'S PLAN OUR SHOPPING SPREE!
CUTE
HEY, RAWK, GIVE IT BACK!
Swipe!
AND PEOPLE SAY *I'M* SPOILED...
PET COUTURE

Lissa's Outfit

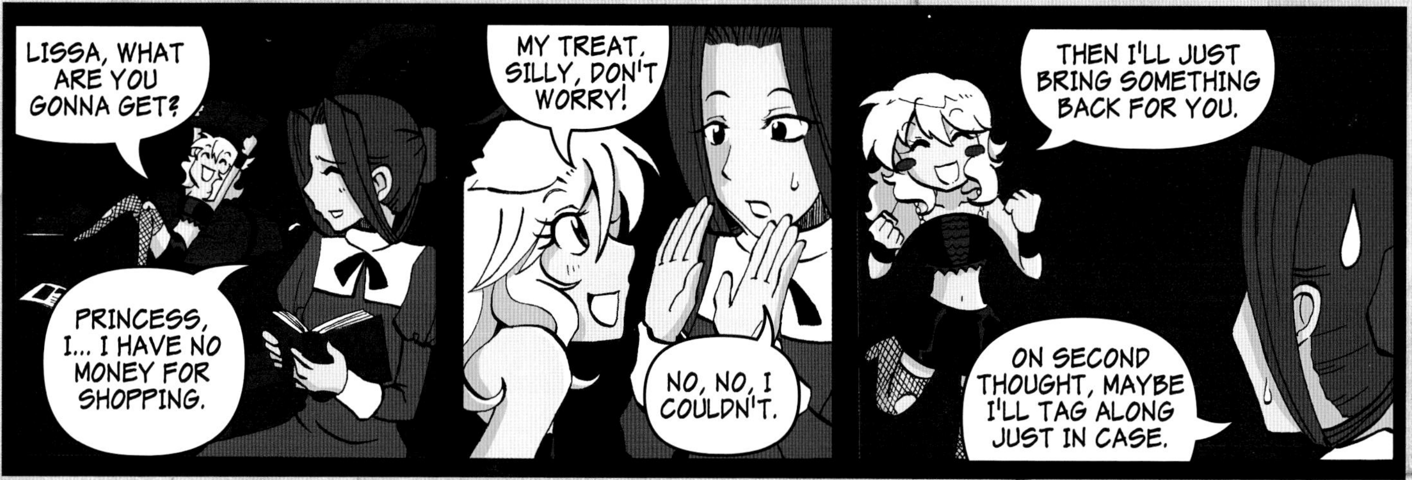
LISSA, WHAT ARE YOU GONNA GET?
PRINCESS, I... I HAVE NO MONEY FOR SHOPPING.
MY TREAT, SILLY, DON'T WORRY!
NO, NO, I COULDN'T.
THEN I'LL JUST BRING SOMETHING BACK FOR YOU.
ON SECOND THOUGHT, MAYBE I'LL TAG ALONG JUST IN CASE.

In the Mall

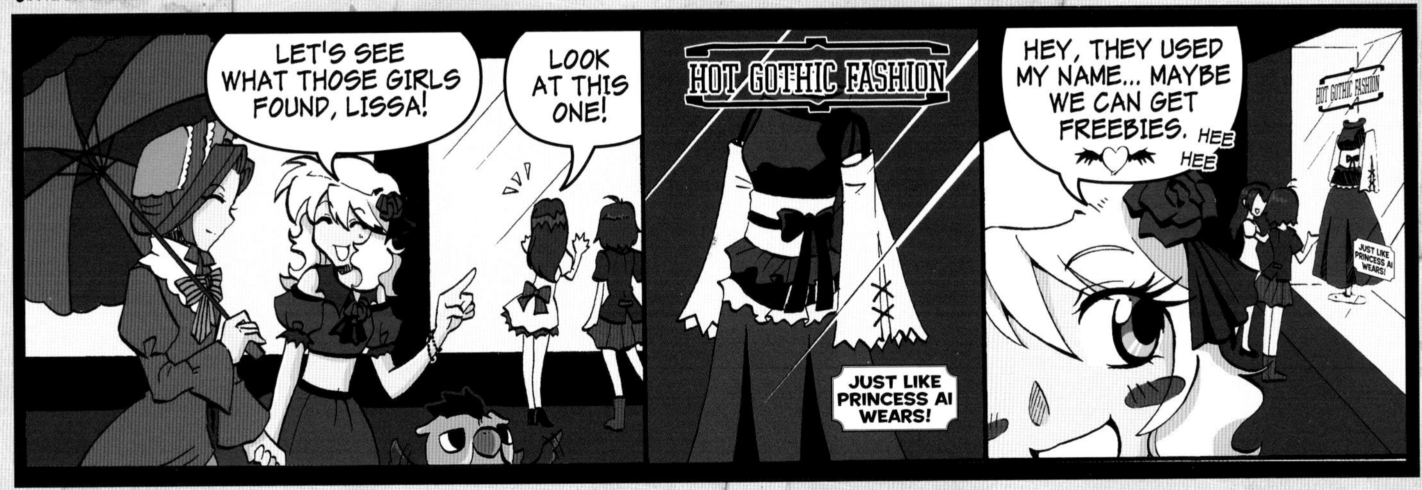

LET'S SEE WHAT THOSE GIRLS FOUND, LISSA!
LOOK AT THIS ONE!
HOT GOTHIC FASHION
JUST LIKE PRINCESS AI WEARS!
HEY, THEY USED MY NAME... MAYBE WE CAN GET FREEBIES.
HEE HEE
HOT GOTHIC FASHION
JUST LIKE PRINCESS AI WEARS!

Shopping Break

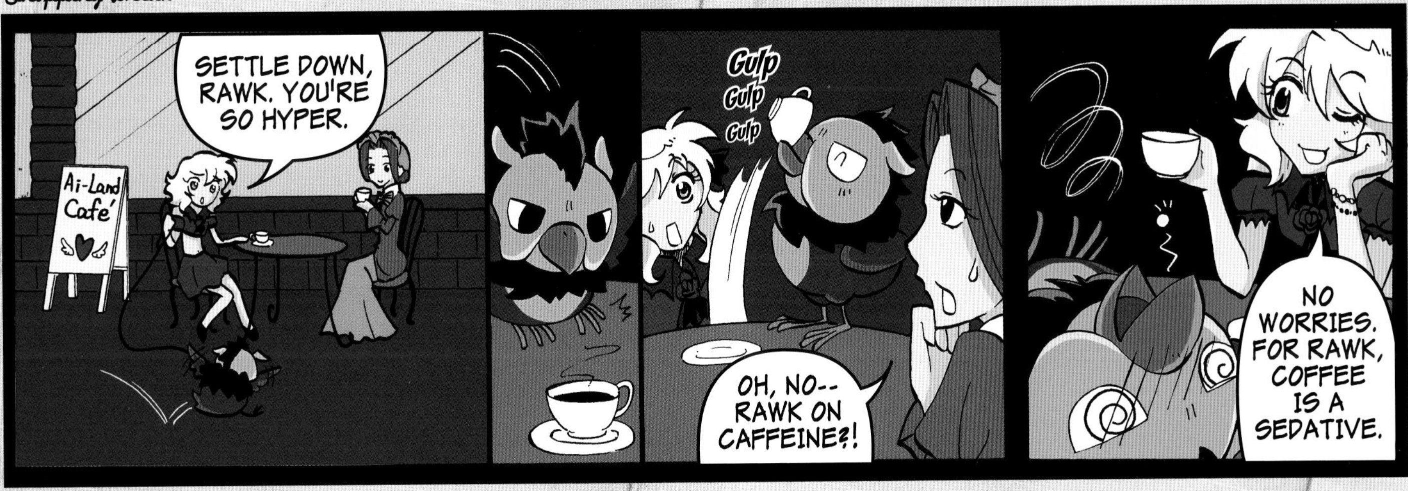

SETTLE DOWN, RAWK. YOU'RE SO HYPER.
Ai-Land Café
Gulp
Gulp
Gulp
OH, NO--RAWK ON CAFFEINE?!
NO WORRIES. FOR RAWK, COFFEE IS A SEDATIVE.

Shoes

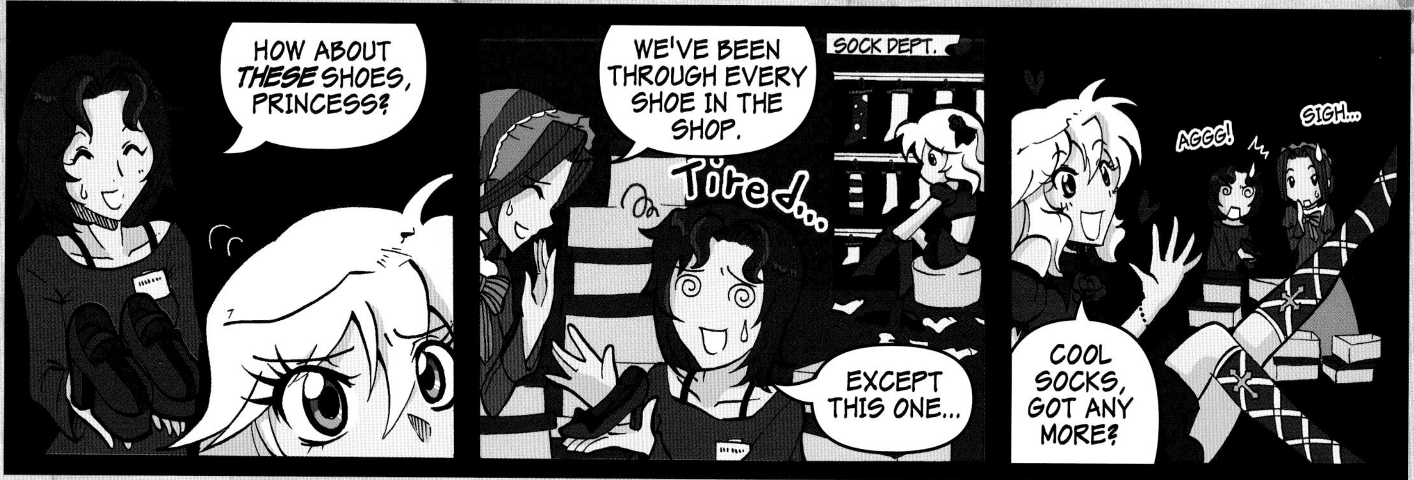
HOW ABOUT *THESE* SHOES, PRINCESS?
WE'VE BEEN THROUGH EVERY SHOE IN THE SHOP.
SOCK DEPT.
Tired...
EXCEPT THIS ONE...
AGGG!
SIGH...
COOL SOCKS, GOT ANY MORE?

Guys

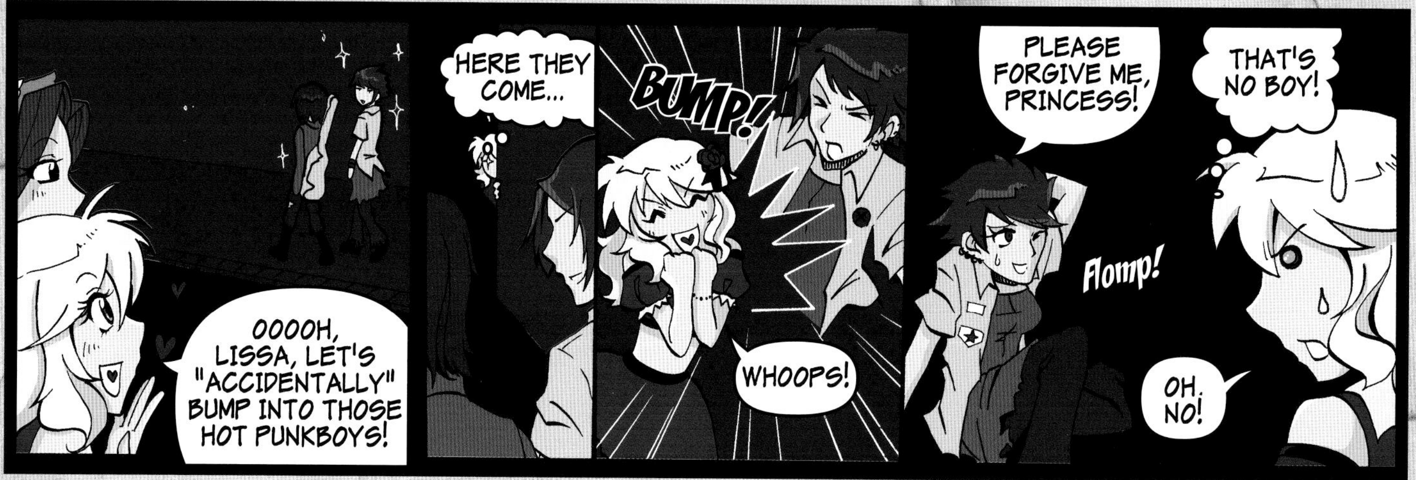
OOOOH, LISSA, LET'S "ACCIDENTALLY" BUMP INTO THOSE HOT PUNKBOYS!
HERE THEY COME...
BUMP!!
WHOOPS!
PLEASE FORGIVE ME, PRINCESS!
Flomp!
THAT'S NO BOY!
OH. NO!

dear d**Ai**ry

Shopping is by far the
best perk I get for being
Princess of Ai-Land.
Of course, Daddy rarely lets
me leave the castle. He's
way too overprotective, even
though I'm already 13. But
every now and then
I get my way.

love always

Ai

35

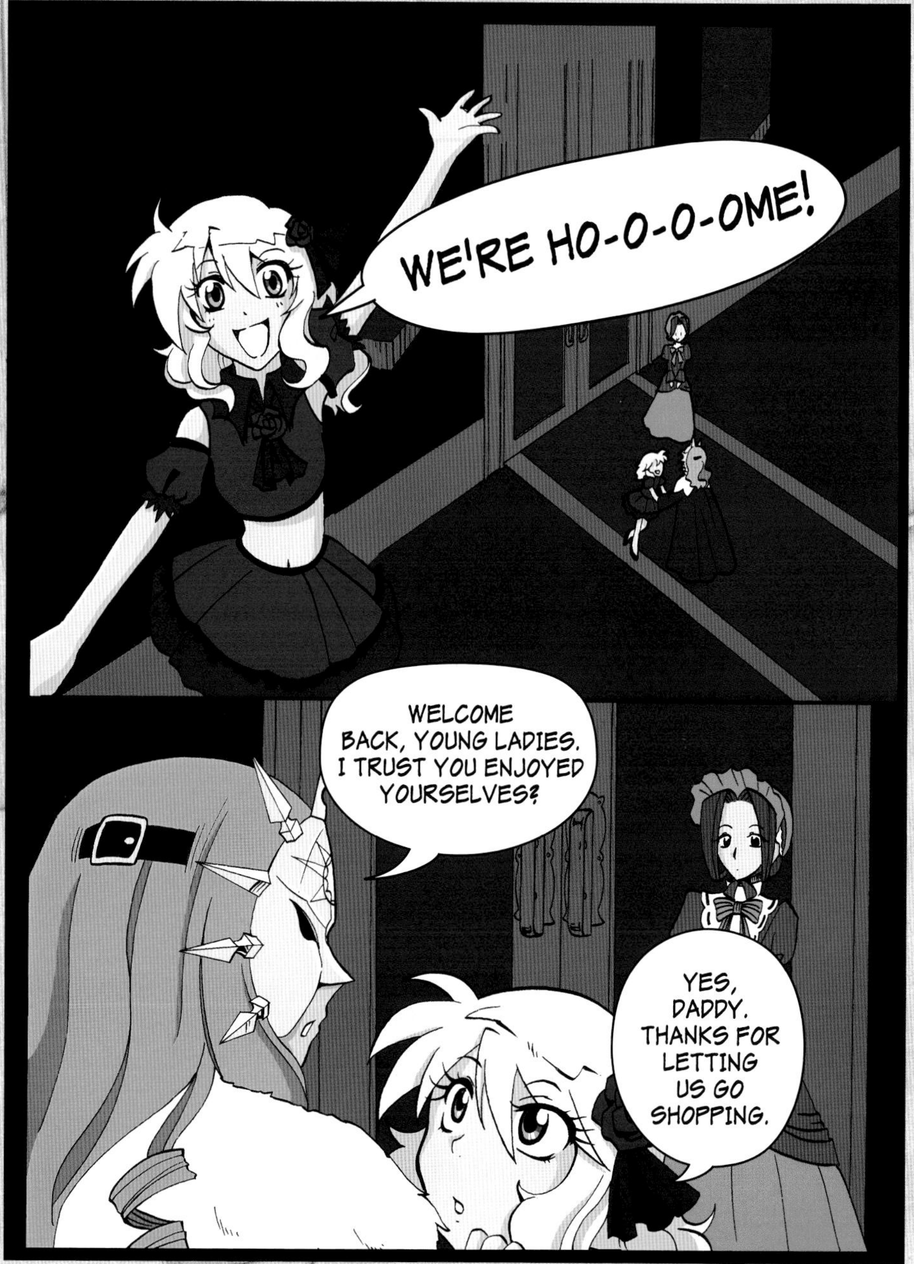
WE'RE HO-O-O-OME!
WELCOME BACK, YOUNG LADIES. I TRUST YOU ENJOYED YOURSELVES?
YES, DADDY. THANKS FOR LETTING US GO SHOPPING.

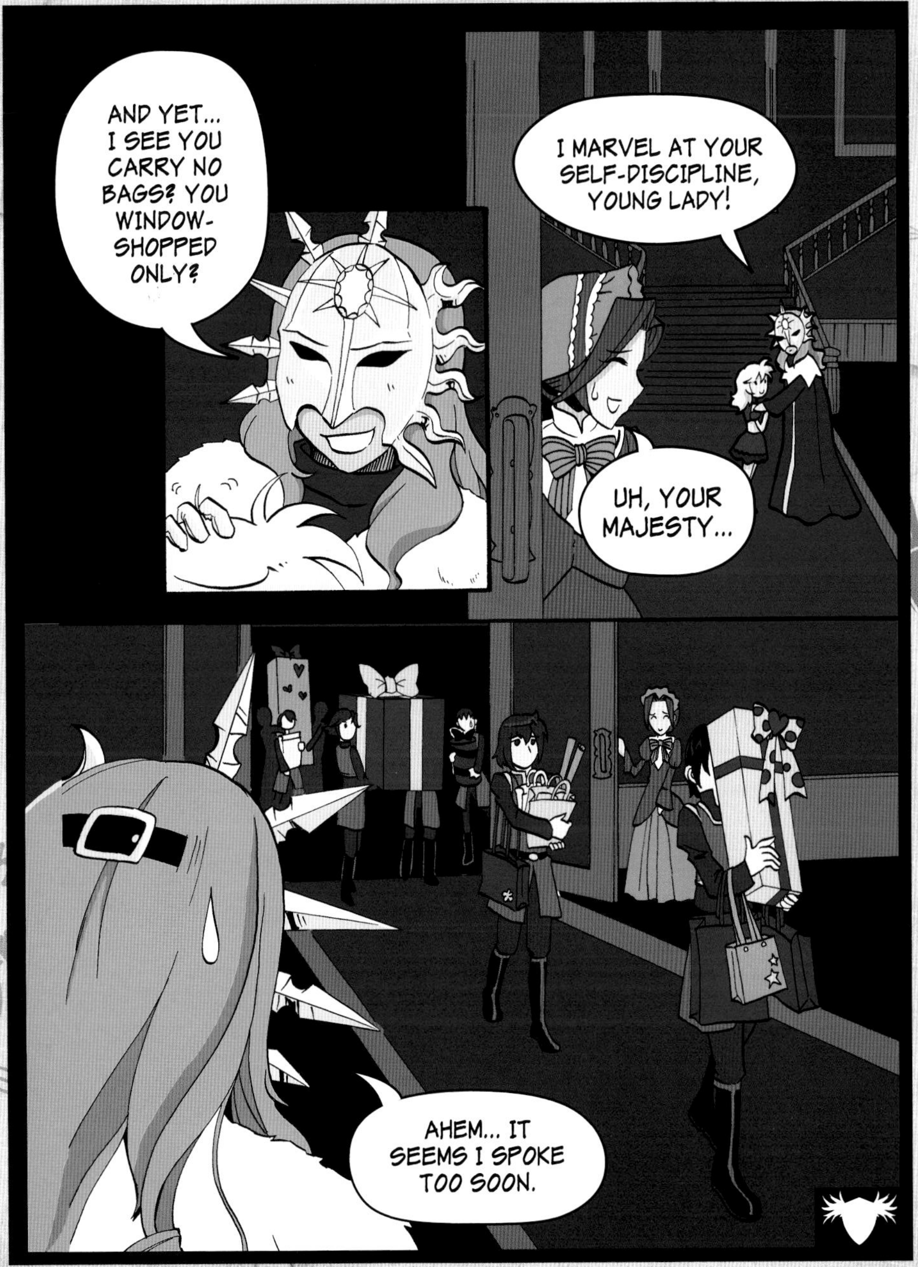
AND YET... I SEE YOU CARRY NO BAGS? YOU WINDOW-SHOPPED ONLY?
I MARVEL AT YOUR SELF-DISCIPLINE, YOUNG LADY!
UH, YOUR MAJESTY...
AHEM... IT SEEMS I SPOKE TOO SOON.

Homework

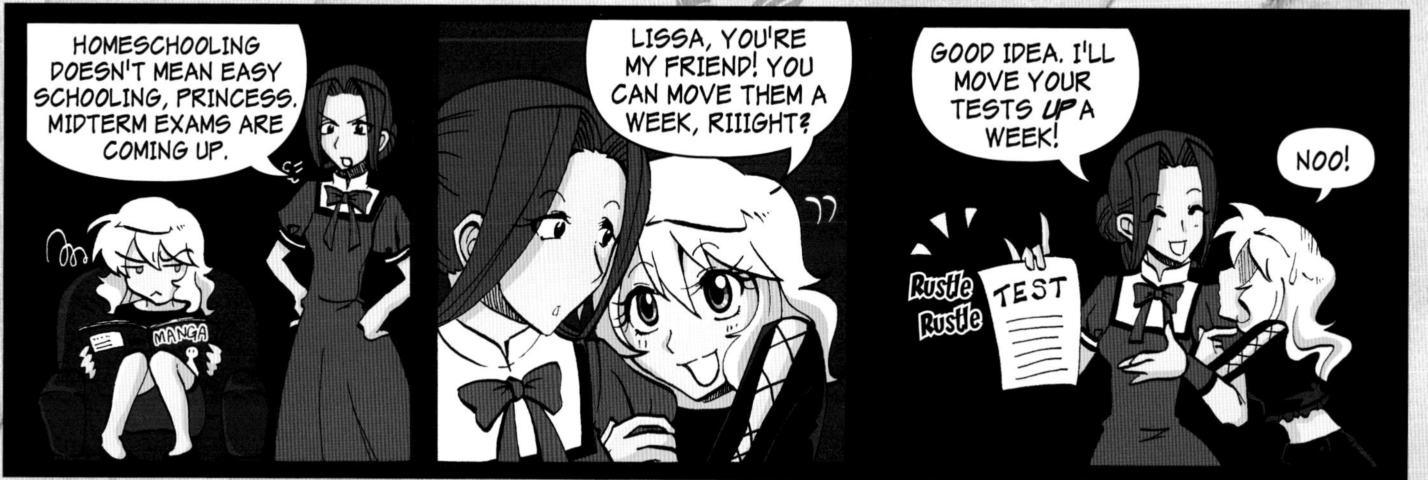
HOMESCHOOLING DOESN'T MEAN EASY SCHOOLING, PRINCESS. MIDTERM EXAMS ARE COMING UP.
MANGA
LISSA, YOU'RE MY FRIEND! YOU CAN MOVE THEM A WEEK, RIIIGHT?
GOOD IDEA. I'LL MOVE YOUR TESTS *UP* A WEEK!
Rustle Rustle
TEST
NOO!

Studying

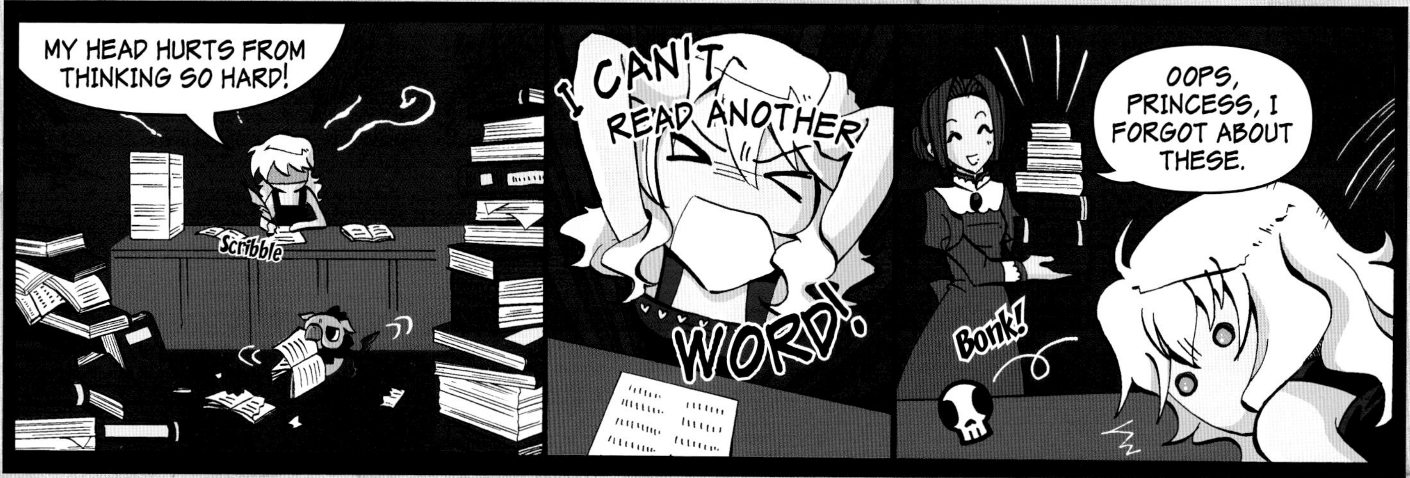
MY HEAD HURTS FROM THINKING SO HARD!
Scribble
I CAN'T READ ANOTHER WORD!
Bonk!
OOPS, PRINCESS, I FORGOT ABOUT THESE.

Music & Arts

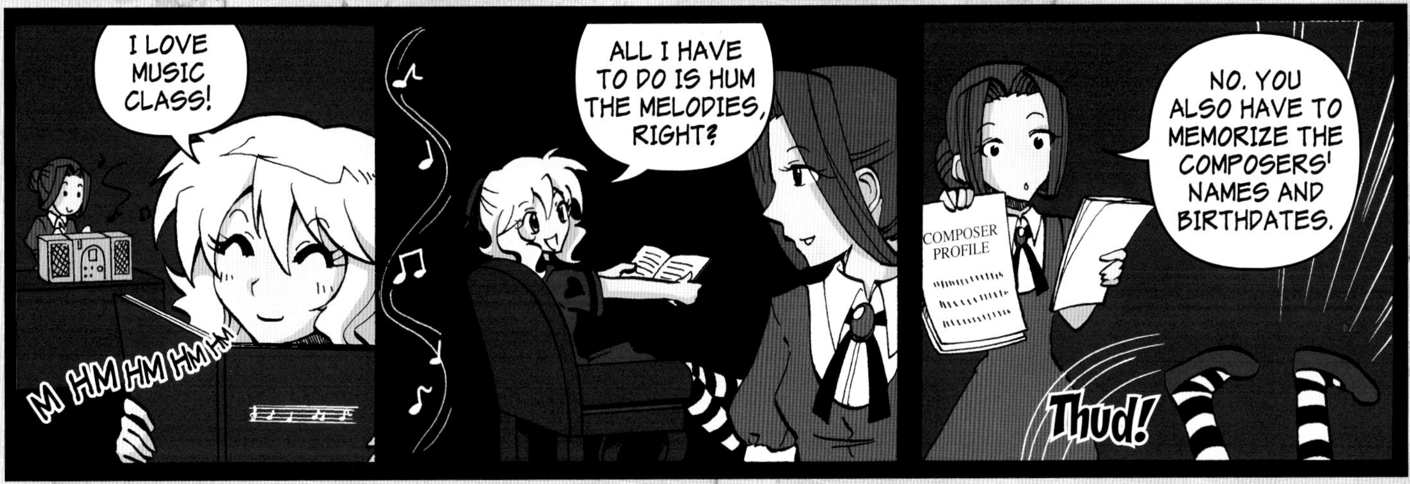
I LOVE MUSIC CLASS!
M HM HM HM HM HM
ALL I HAVE TO DO IS HUM THE MELODIES, RIGHT?
COMPOSER PROFILE
NO. YOU ALSO HAVE TO MEMORIZE THE COMPOSERS' NAMES AND BIRTHDATES.
Thud!

History

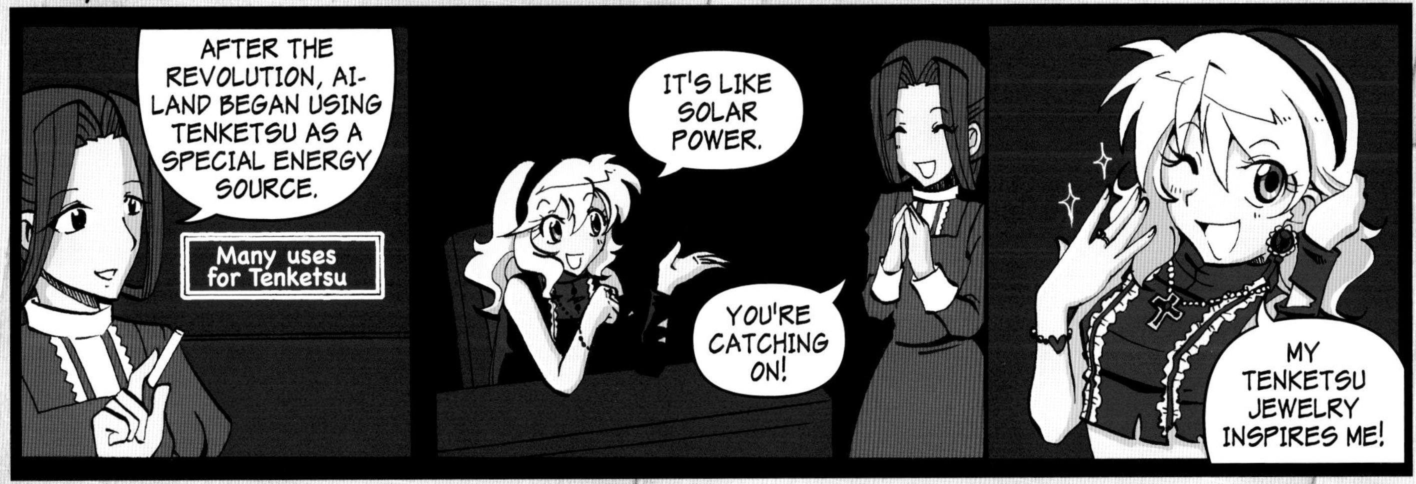
AFTER THE REVOLUTION, AI-LAND BEGAN USING TENKETSU AS A SPECIAL ENERGY SOURCE.
Many uses for Tenketsu
IT'S LIKE SOLAR POWER.
YOU'RE CATCHING ON!
MY TENKETSU JEWELRY INSPIRES ME!

Sleeping Beauty

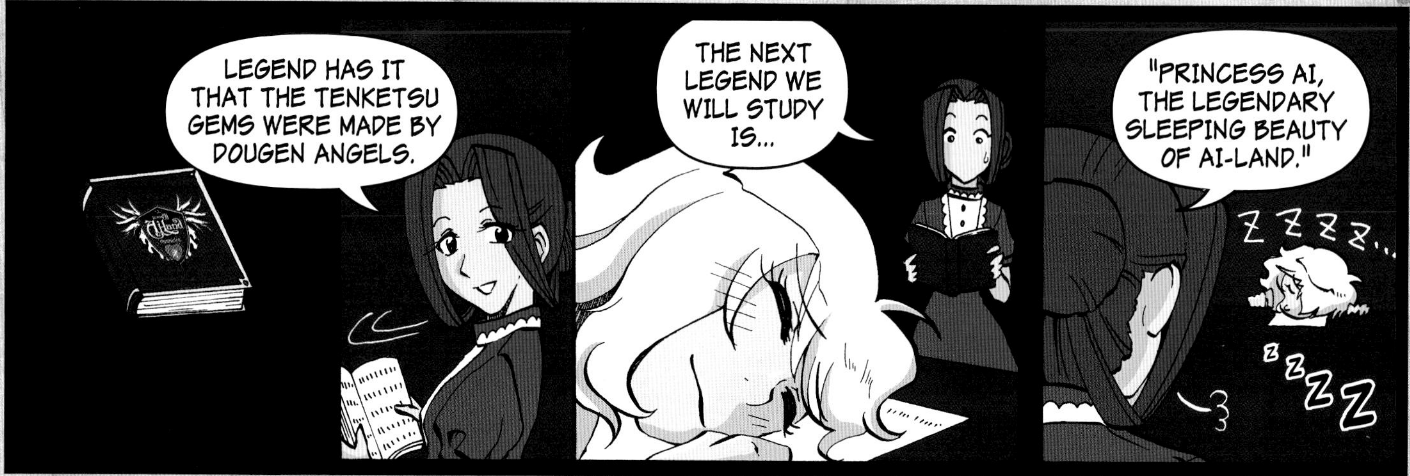
LEGEND HAS IT THAT THE TENKETSU GEMS WERE MADE BY DOUGEN ANGELS.
THE NEXT LEGEND WE WILL STUDY IS...
"PRINCESS AI, THE LEGENDARY SLEEPING BEAUTY OF AI-LAND."
ZZZZ...
ZZZZ

Report Due

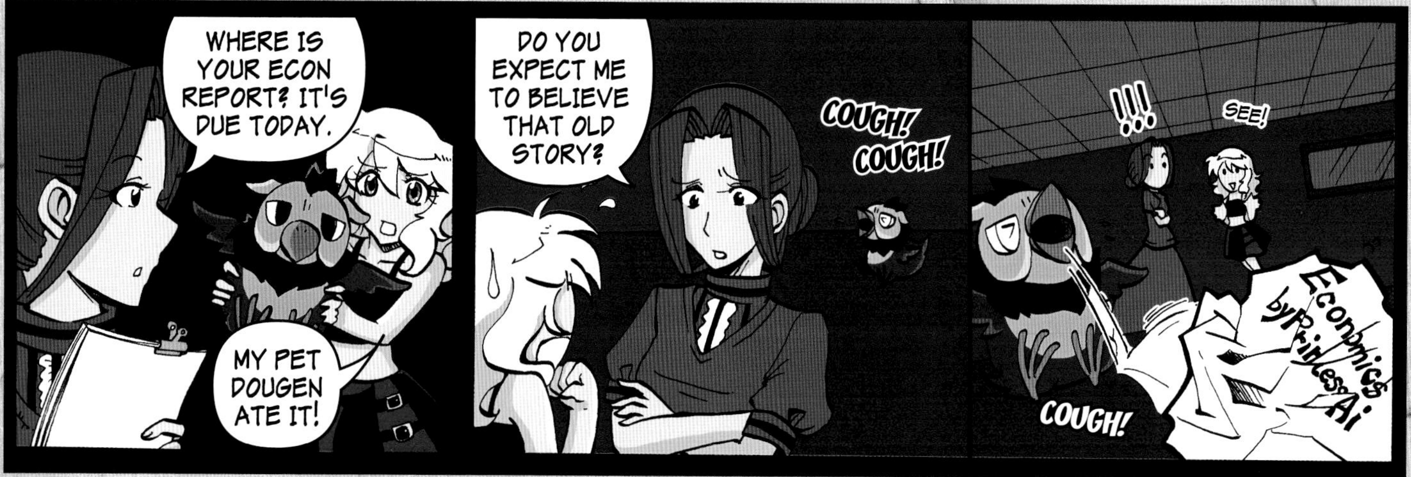
WHERE IS YOUR ECON REPORT? IT'S DUE TODAY.
MY PET DOUGEN ATE IT!
DO YOU EXPECT ME TO BELIEVE THAT OLD STORY?
COUGH! COUGH!
!!!
SEE!
Economics by Princess Ai
COUGH!

dear d**Ai**ry

I can't complain too much about growing up as the Princess of Ai-Land, but homeschooling isn't really what it's cracked up to be. Sure, Lissa is not just my tutor--she's also my best friend. So, why does she have to be so intense about homework and exams?

Well, this time I'm ready--for all aces.

love forever

Ai

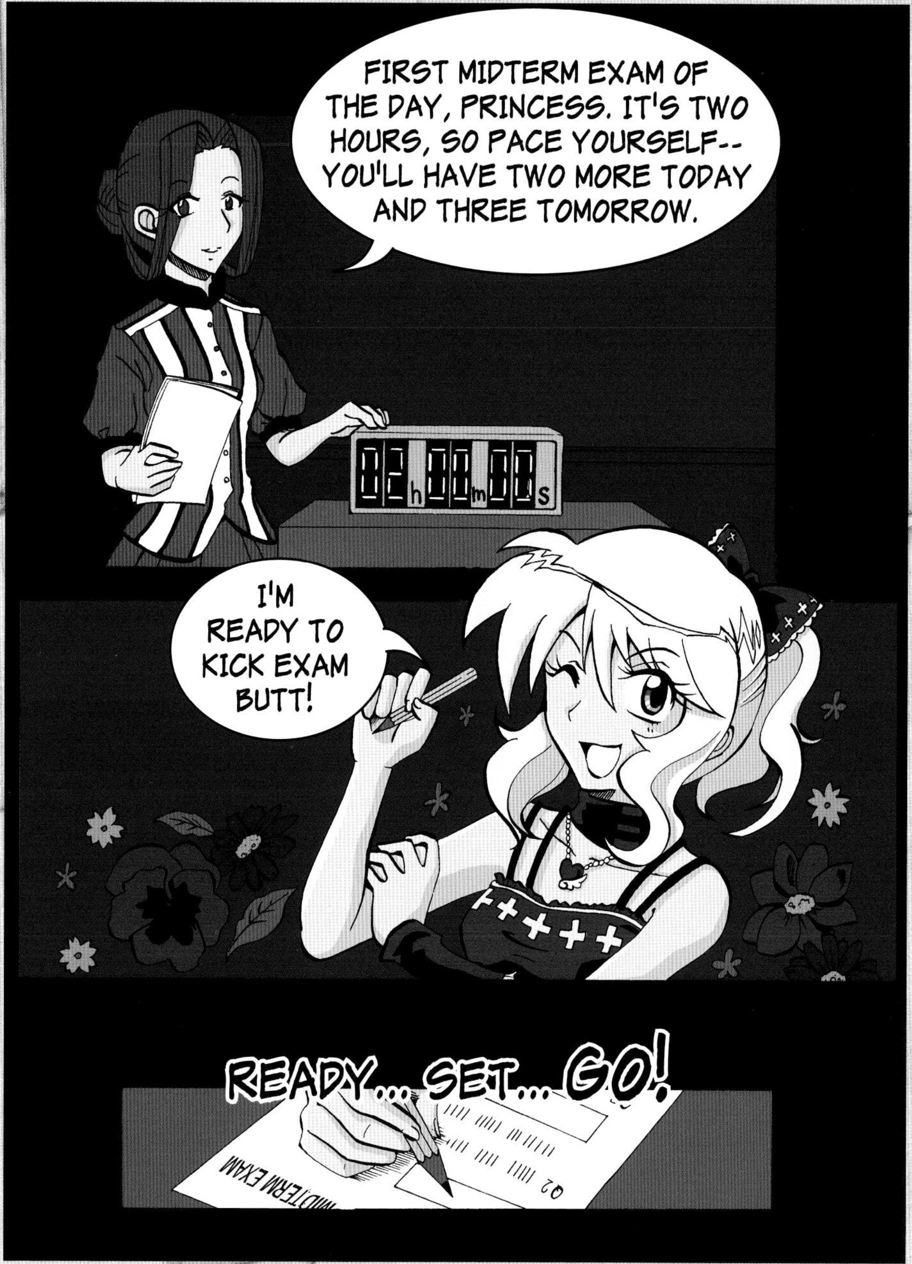
FIRST MIDTERM EXAM OF THE DAY, PRINCESS. IT'S TWO HOURS, SO PACE YOURSELF-- YOU'LL HAVE TWO MORE TODAY AND THREE TOMORROW.
02h00m00s
I'M READY TO KICK EXAM BUTT!
READY... SET... GO!
MIDTERM EXAM

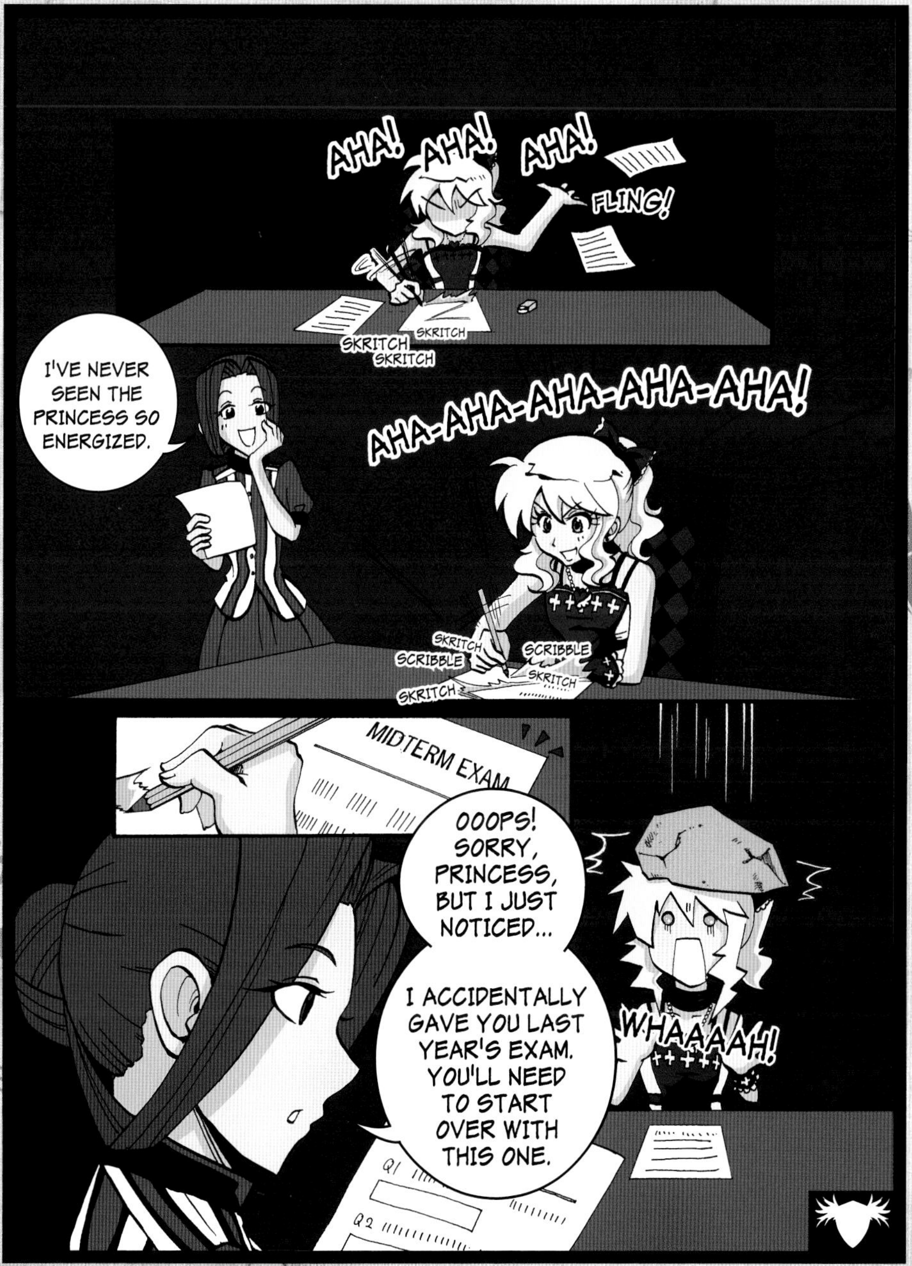
AHA! AHA! AHA!
FLING!
SKRITCH
SKRITCH
SKRITCH
I'VE NEVER SEEN THE PRINCESS SO ENERGIZED.
AHA-AHA-AHA-AHA-AHA!
SKRITCH
SCRIBBLE
SCRIBBLE
SKRITCH
SKRITCH
MIDTERM EXAM
OOOPS! SORRY, PRINCESS, BUT I JUST NOTICED...
I ACCIDENTALLY GAVE YOU LAST YEAR'S EXAM. YOU'LL NEED TO START OVER WITH THIS ONE.
WHAAAAAH!
Q1
Q2

Tickets

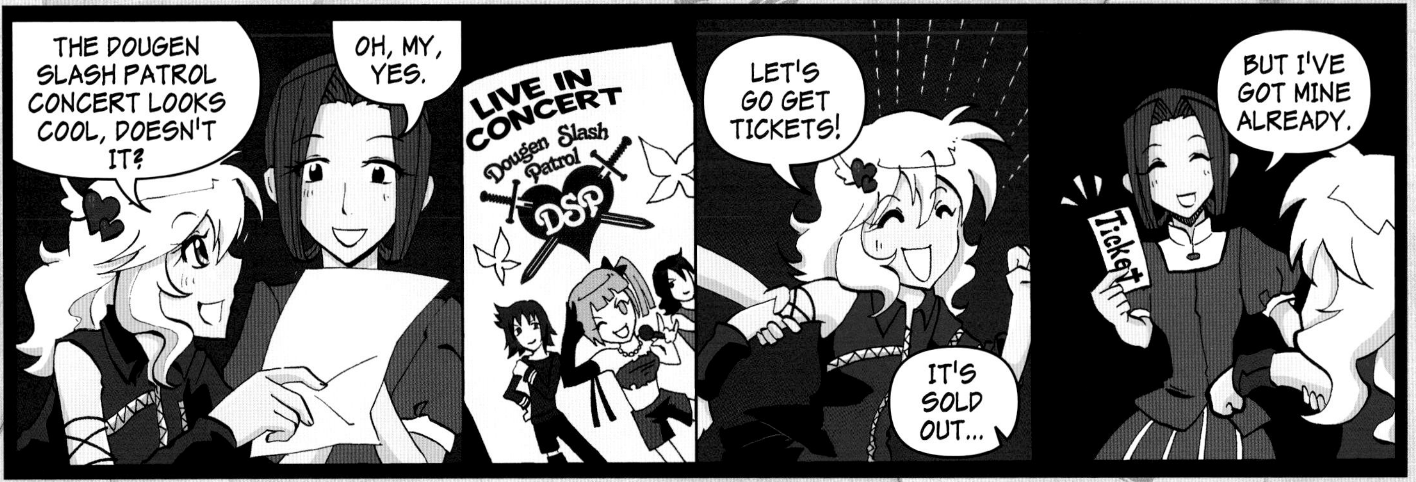
THE DOUGEN SLASH PATROL CONCERT LOOKS COOL, DOESN'T IT?
OH, MY, YES.
LIVE IN CONCERT
Dougen Slash Patrol
DSP
LET'S GO GET TICKETS!
IT'S SOLD OUT...
BUT I'VE GOT MINE ALREADY.
Ticket

Together

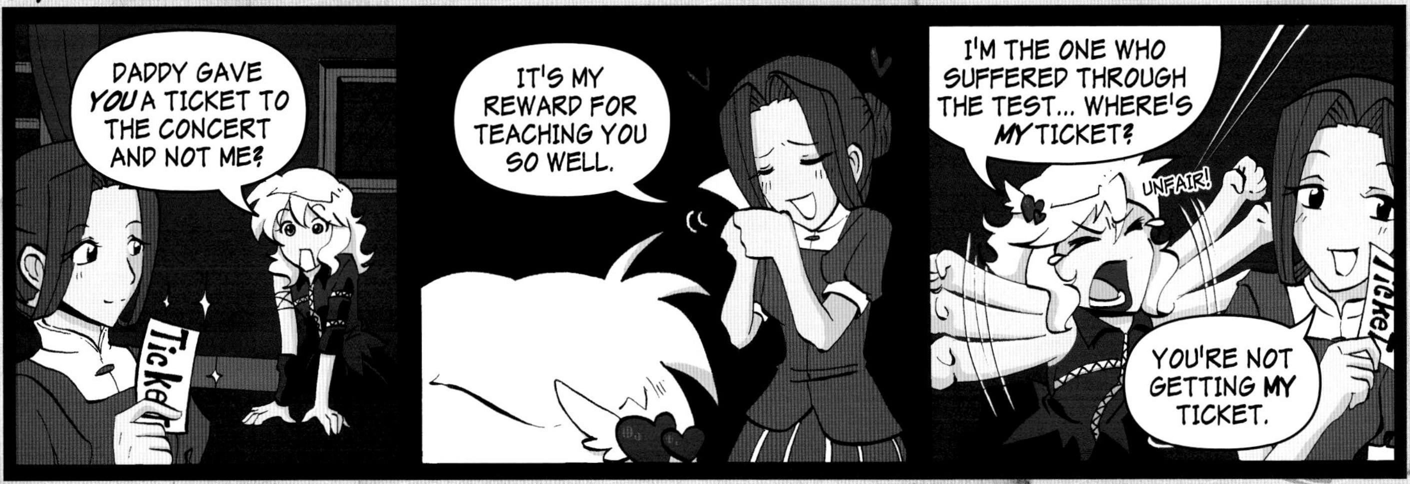
DADDY GAVE YOU A TICKET TO THE CONCERT AND NOT ME?
Ticket
IT'S MY REWARD FOR TEACHING YOU SO WELL.
I'M THE ONE WHO SUFFERED THROUGH THE TEST... WHERE'S MY TICKET?
UNFAIR!
Ticket
YOU'RE NOT GETTING MY TICKET.

Results

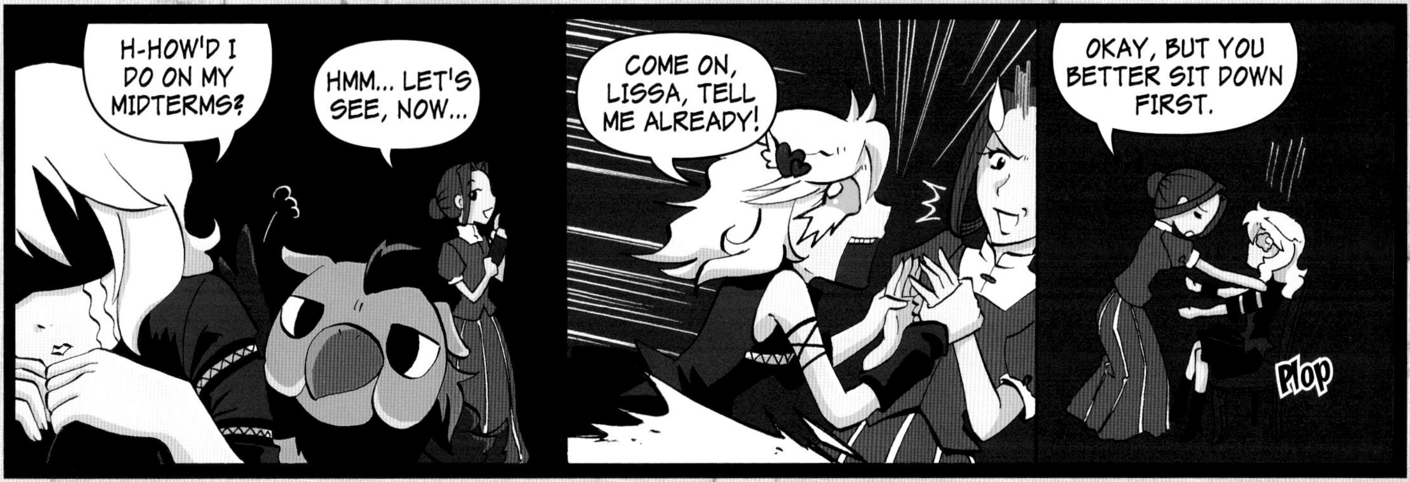

H-HOW'D I DO ON MY MIDTERMS?
HMM... LET'S SEE, NOW...
COME ON, LISSA, TELL ME ALREADY!
OKAY, BUT YOU BETTER SIT DOWN FIRST.
Plop

Reward

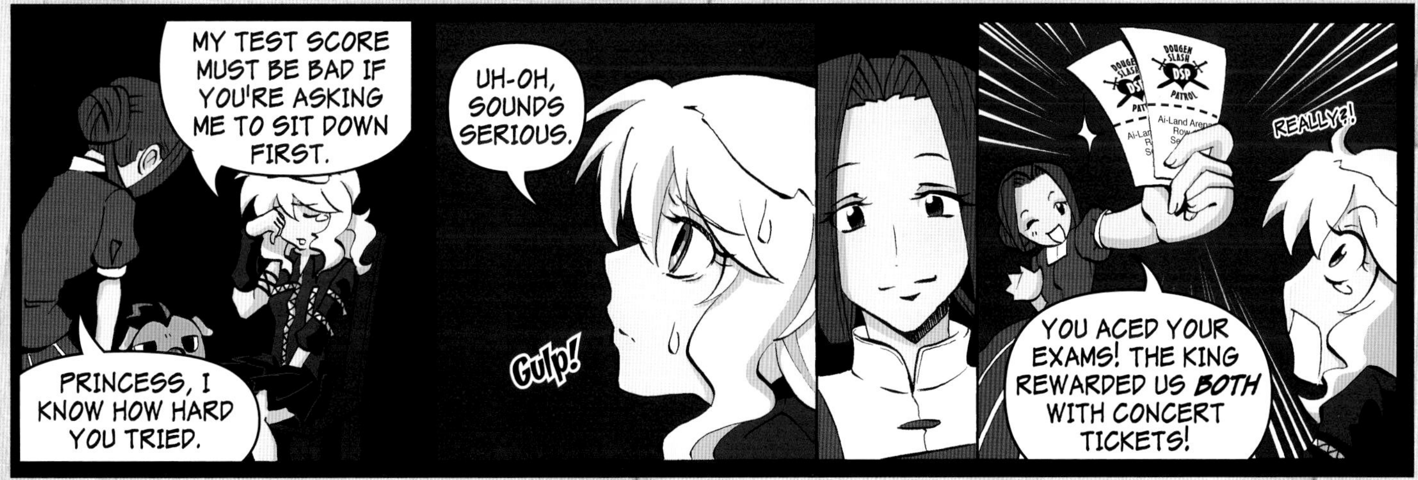

MY TEST SCORE MUST BE BAD IF YOU'RE ASKING ME TO SIT DOWN FIRST.
PRINCESS, I KNOW HOW HARD YOU TRIED.
UH-OH, SOUNDS SERIOUS.
Gulp!
DOUGEN SLASH DSP PATROL
Ai-Land Arena
REALLY?!
YOU ACED YOUR EXAMS! THE KING REWARDED US *BOTH* WITH CONCERT TICKETS!

We're Going!

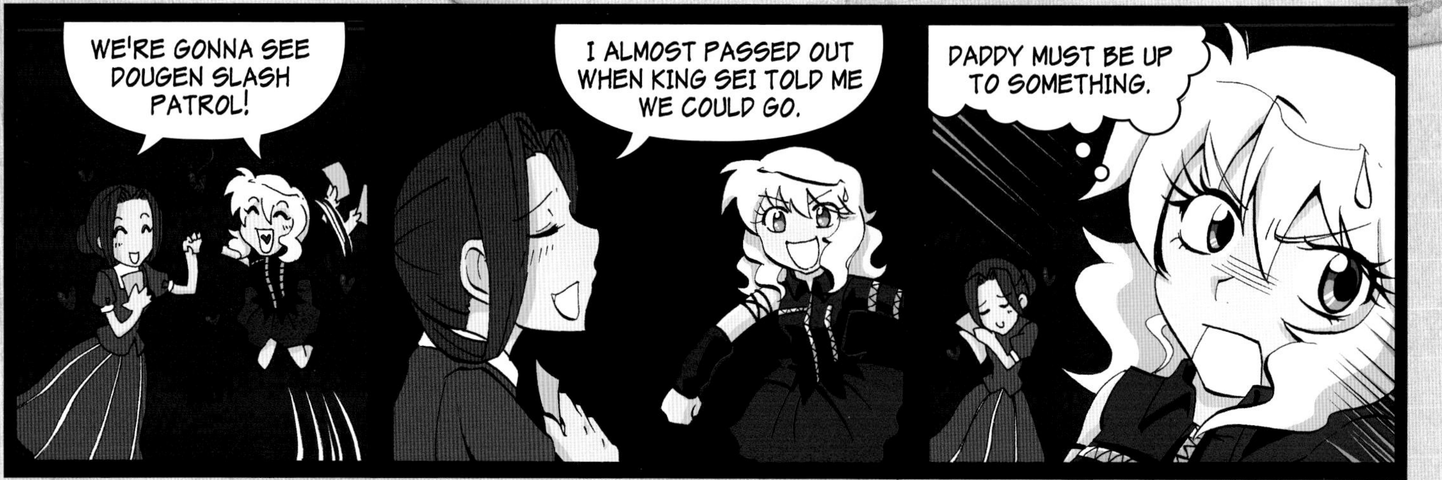
WE'RE GONNA SEE DOUGEN SLASH PATROL!
I ALMOST PASSED OUT WHEN KING SEI TOLD ME WE COULD GO.
DADDY MUST BE UP TO SOMETHING.

Suspicious

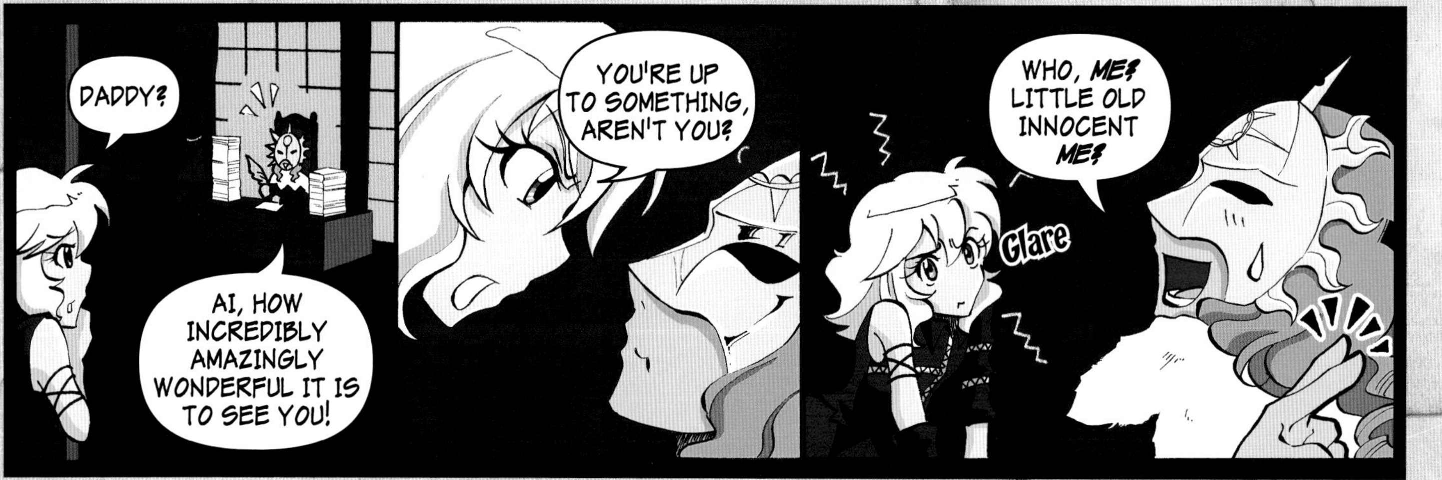
DADDY?
AI, HOW INCREDIBLY AMAZINGLY WONDERFUL IT IS TO SEE YOU!
YOU'RE UP TO SOMETHING, AREN'T YOU?
WHO, ME? LITTLE OLD INNOCENT ME?
Glare

dear dry

Sometimes I just don't understand Daddy. He can be a real jerk--Almost like it's on purpose. Then, out of the blue, he's the sweetest guy in the whole world. This week, though, he's treating me way beyond normal. Beyond *Princess* normal!

I guess I got the "scheme" gene from him.

love forever

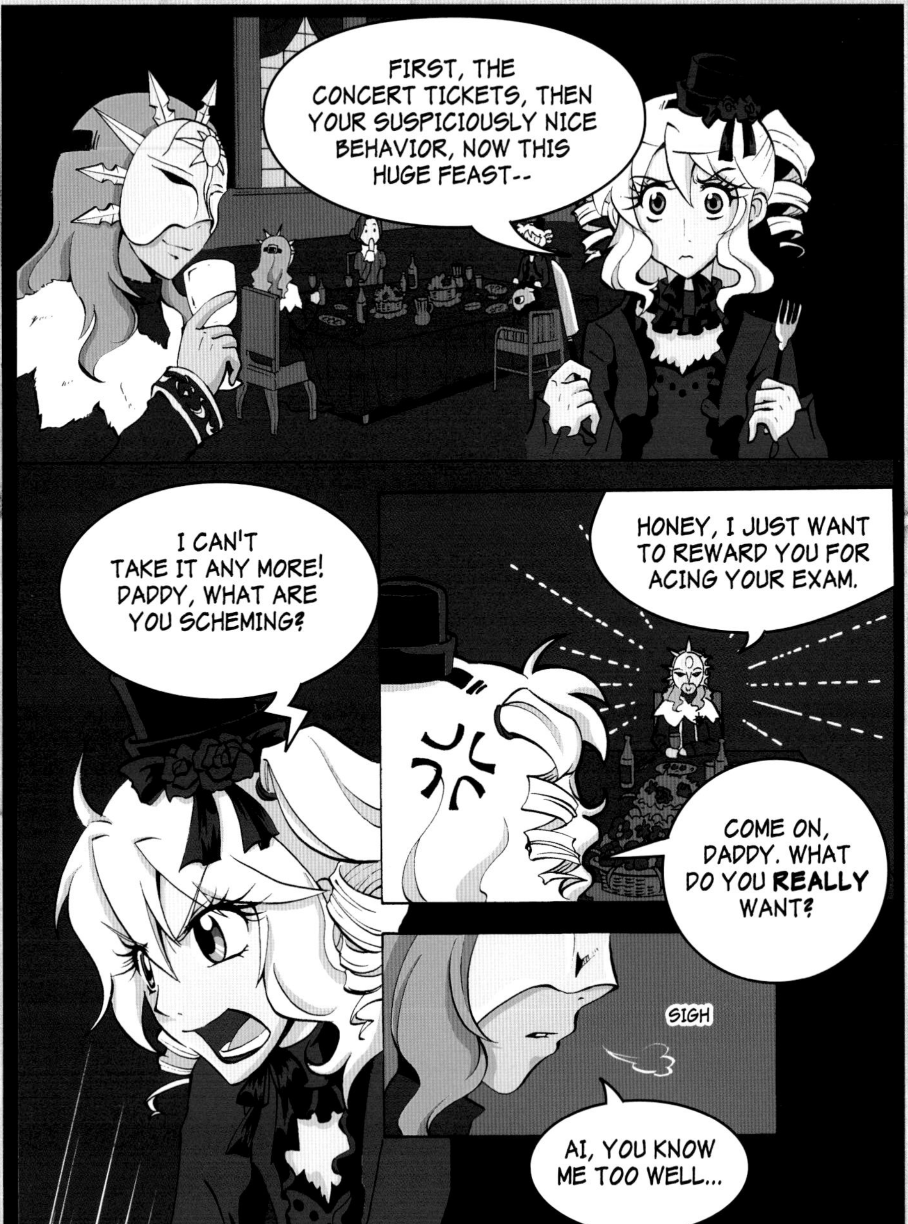
FIRST, THE CONCERT TICKETS, THEN YOUR SUSPICIOUSLY NICE BEHAVIOR, NOW THIS HUGE FEAST--
I CAN'T TAKE IT ANY MORE! DADDY, WHAT ARE YOU SCHEMING?
HONEY, I JUST WANT TO REWARD YOU FOR ACING YOUR EXAM.
COME ON, DADDY. WHAT DO YOU **REALLY** WANT?
SIGH
AI, YOU KNOW ME TOO WELL...

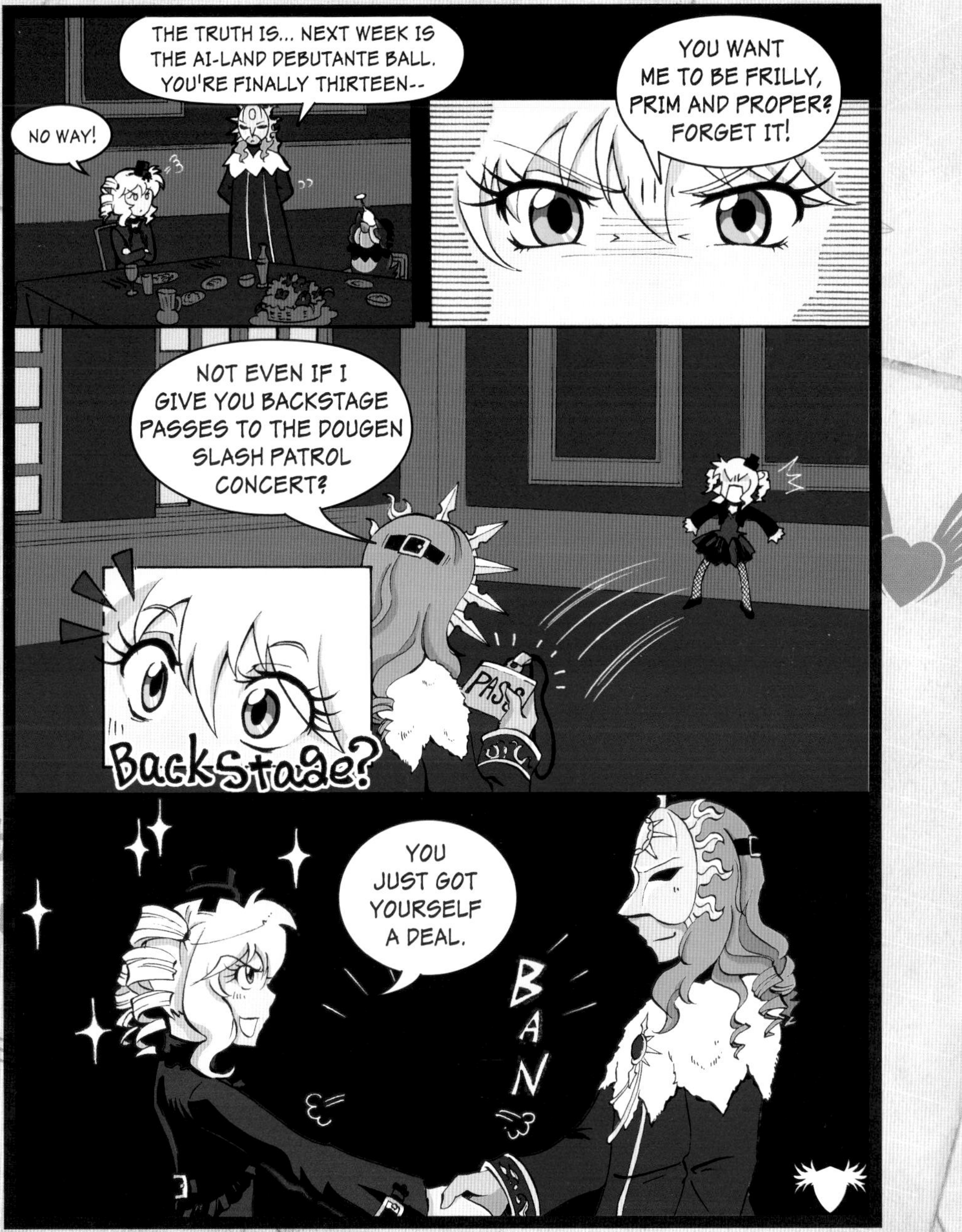
THE TRUTH IS... NEXT WEEK IS THE AI-LAND DEBUTANTE BALL. YOU'RE FINALLY THIRTEEN--
NO WAY!
YOU WANT ME TO BE FRILLY, PRIM AND PROPER? FORGET IT!
NOT EVEN IF I GIVE YOU BACKSTAGE PASSES TO THE DOUGEN SLASH PATROL CONCERT?
Backstage?
YOU JUST GOT YOURSELF A DEAL.
BAN

Concert Plans

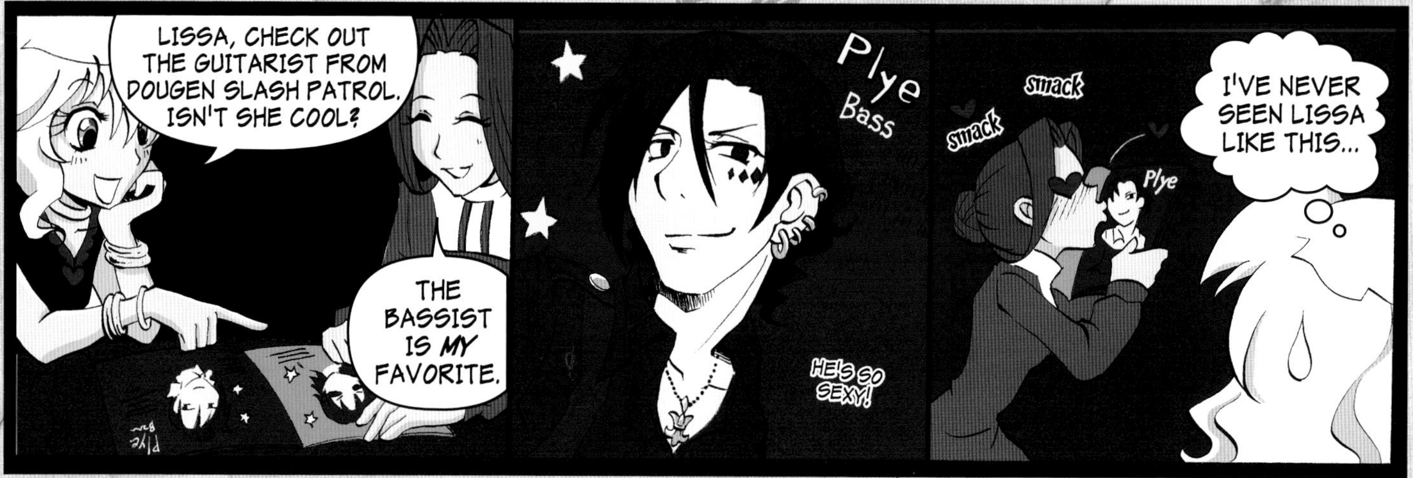

LISSA, CHECK OUT THE GUITARIST FROM DOUGEN SLASH PATROL. ISN'T SHE COOL?
THE BASSIST IS *MY* FAVORITE.
Plye
Bass
HE'S SO SEXY!
smack
smack
Plye
I'VE NEVER SEEN LISSA LIKE THIS...

Concert Outfits

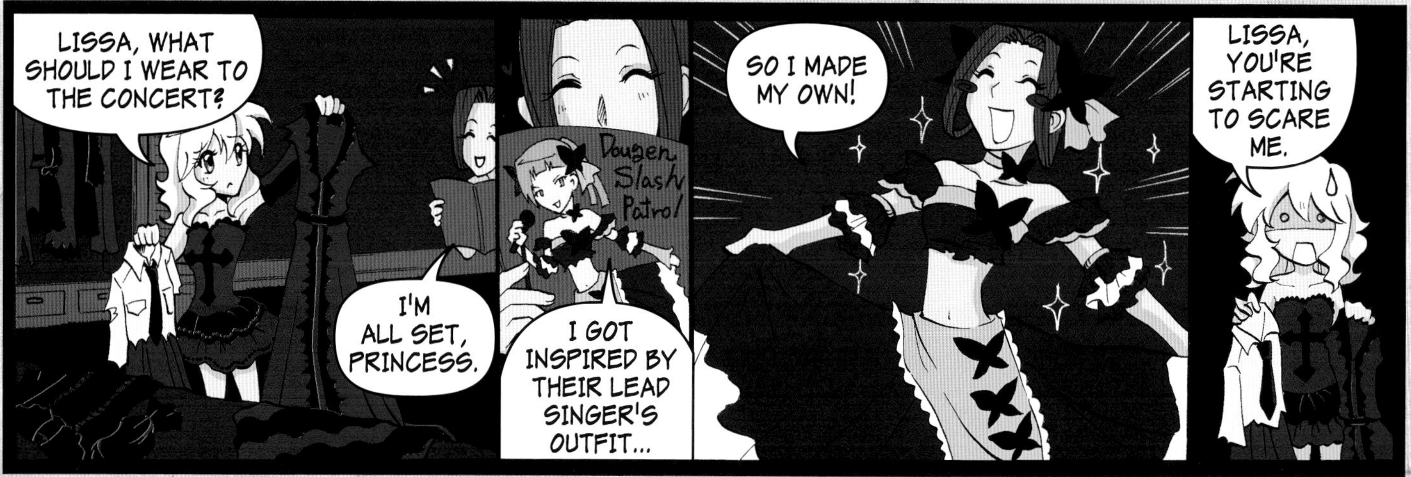

LISSA, WHAT SHOULD I WEAR TO THE CONCERT?
I'M ALL SET, PRINCESS.
Dougen Slash Patrol
I GOT INSPIRED BY THEIR LEAD SINGER'S OUTFIT...
SO I MADE MY OWN!
LISSA, YOU'RE STARTING TO SCARE ME.

Concert Night

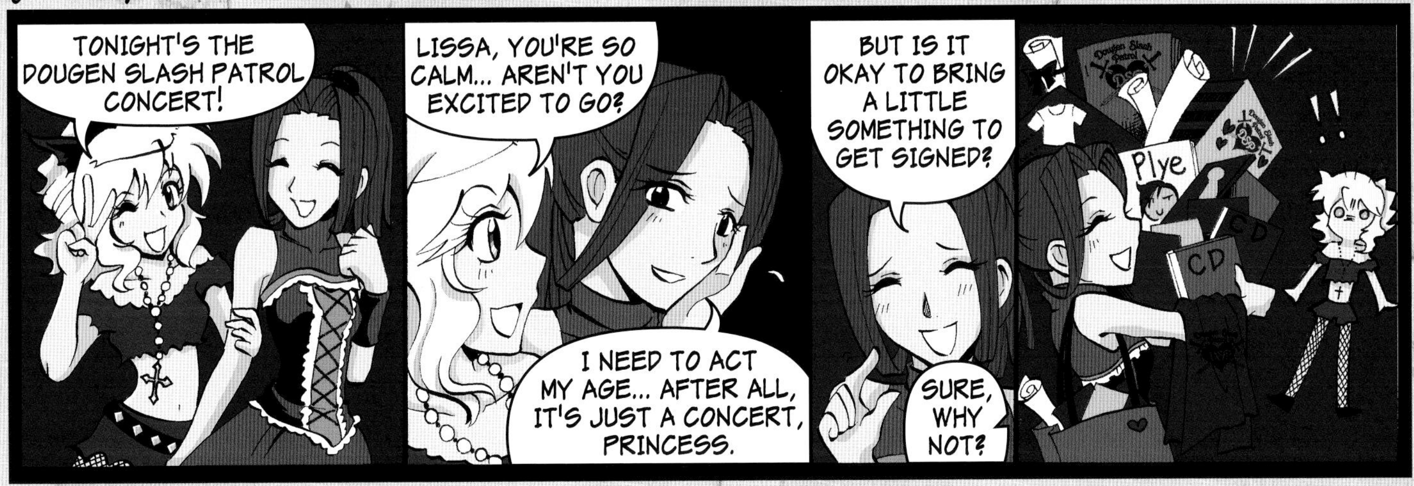
TONIGHT'S THE DOUGEN SLASH PATROL CONCERT!
LISSA, YOU'RE SO CALM... AREN'T YOU EXCITED TO GO?
I NEED TO ACT MY AGE... AFTER ALL, IT'S JUST A CONCERT, PRINCESS.
BUT IS IT OKAY TO BRING A LITTLE SOMETHING TO GET SIGNED?
SURE, WHY NOT?
Dougen Slash Patrol
!!
Plye
CD
CD

Groupie on a Rampage

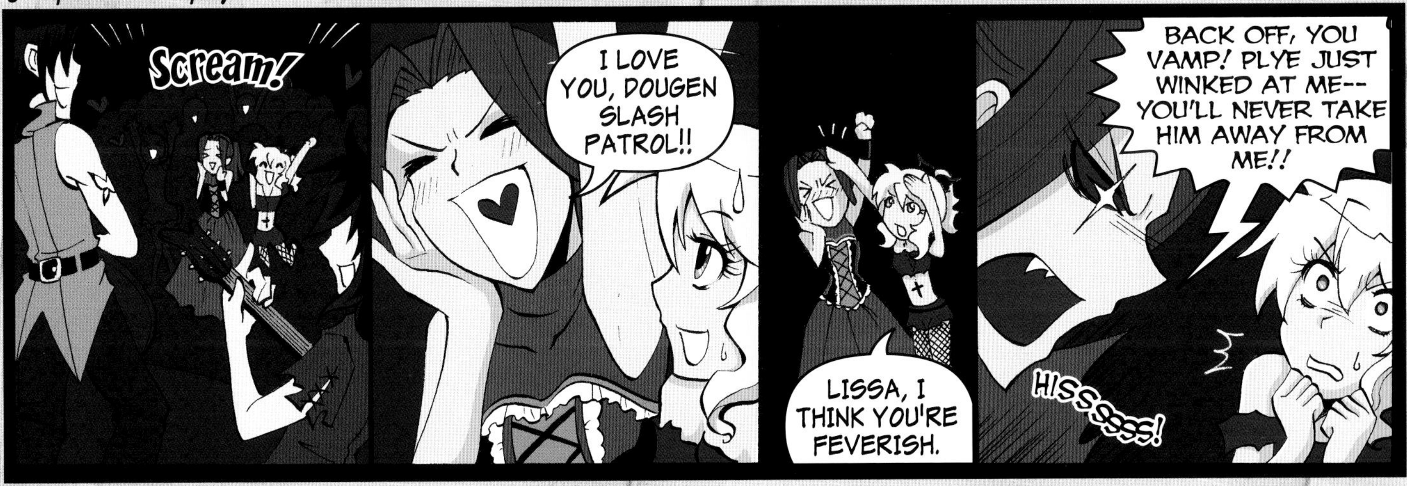
Scream!
I LOVE YOU, DOUGEN SLASH PATROL!!
LISSA, I THINK YOU'RE FEVERISH.
BACK OFF, YOU VAMP! PLYE JUST WINKED AT ME-- YOU'LL NEVER TAKE HIM AWAY FROM ME!!
HISSSSSS!

After the Show

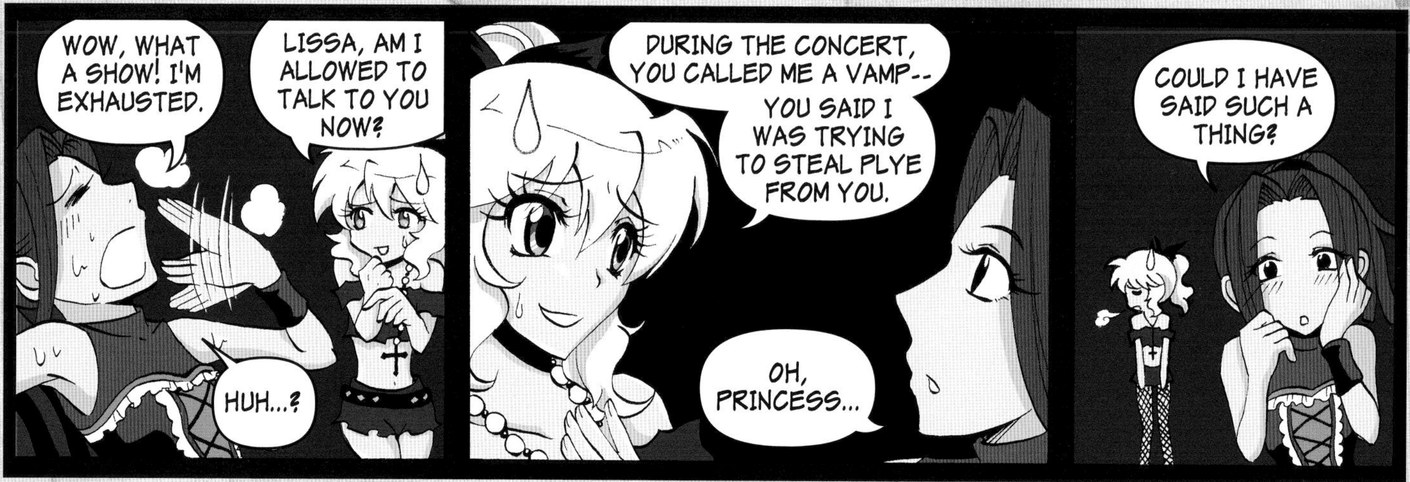
WOW, WHAT A SHOW! I'M EXHAUSTED.
LISSA, AM I ALLOWED TO TALK TO YOU NOW?
HUH...?
DURING THE CONCERT, YOU CALLED ME A VAMP--
YOU SAID I WAS TRYING TO STEAL PLYE FROM YOU.
OH, PRINCESS...
COULD I HAVE SAID SUCH A THING?

Backstage

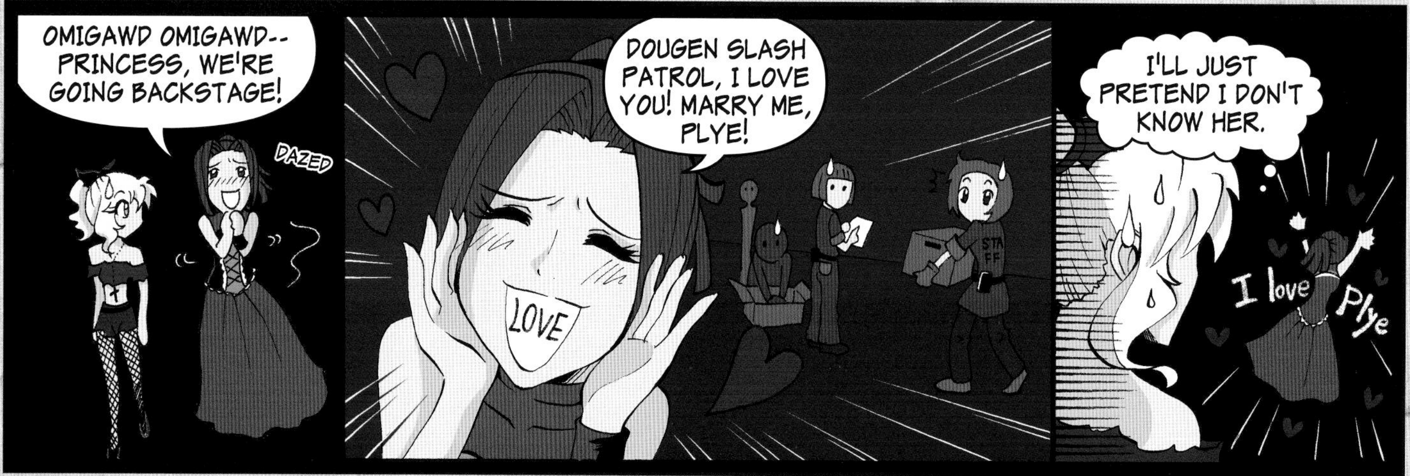
OMIGAWD OMIGAWD-- PRINCESS, WE'RE GOING BACKSTAGE!
DAZED
DOUGEN SLASH PATROL, I LOVE YOU! MARRY ME, PLYE!
LOVE
STAFF
I'LL JUST PRETEND I DON'T KNOW HER.
I love Plye

dear dry

Wow. That's a one-word summary of my current state of mind. What a night! Being a princess is harder than everyone must think--Daddy **never** lets me go anywhere. But this time I really lucked out. My first concert! And it was Dougen Slash Patrol--the hottest band on Ai-Land! It was amazing...except for Lissa. I never knew she had such an extreme side to her. Prim and proper Lissa, a.k.a. "Groupie From Hell."

love forever

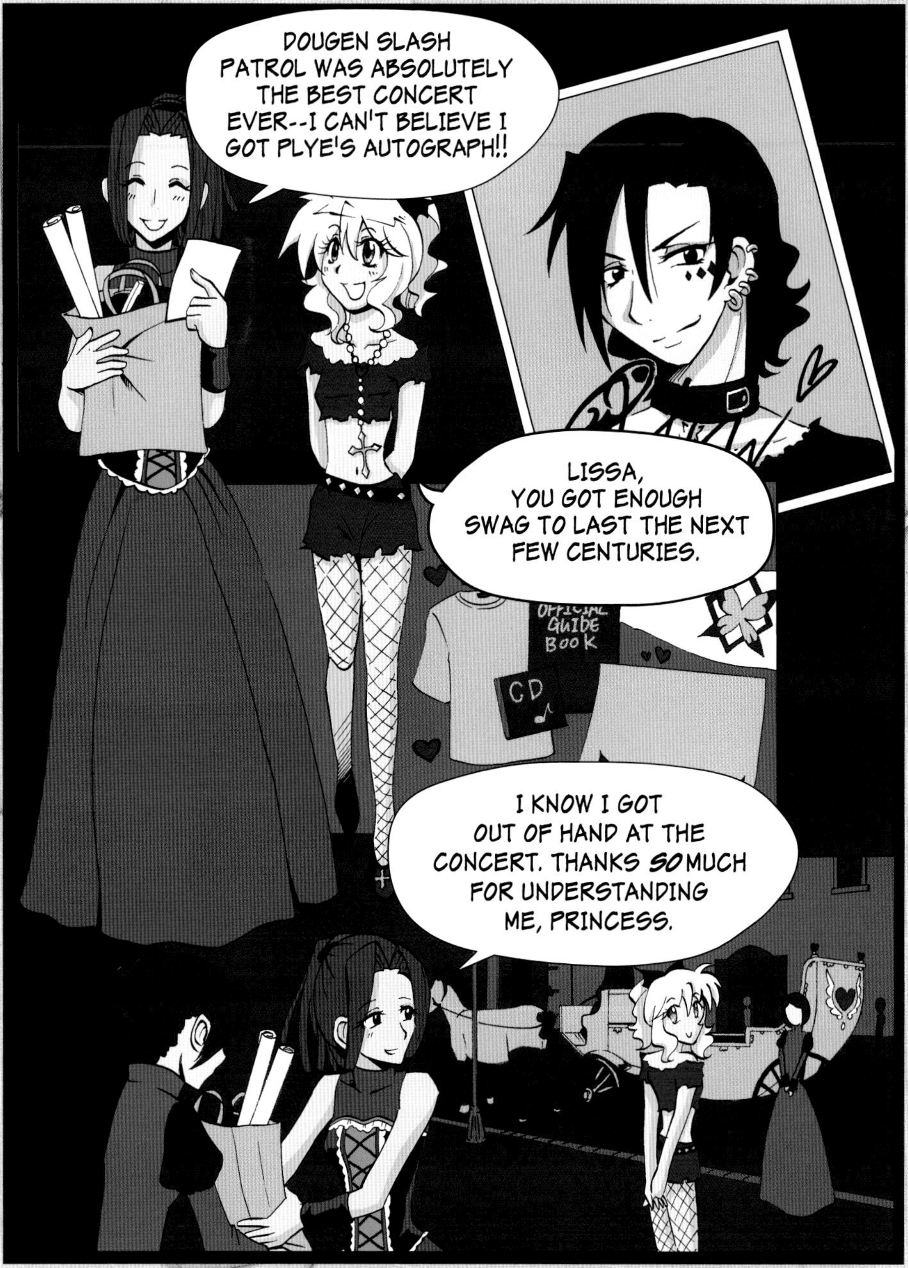
DOUGEN SLASH PATROL WAS ABSOLUTELY THE BEST CONCERT EVER--I CAN'T BELIEVE I GOT PLYE'S AUTOGRAPH!!
LISSA, YOU GOT ENOUGH SWAG TO LAST THE NEXT FEW CENTURIES.
OFFICIAL GUIDE BOOK
CD
I KNOW I GOT OUT OF HAND AT THE CONCERT. THANKS *SO* MUCH FOR UNDERSTANDING ME, PRINCESS.

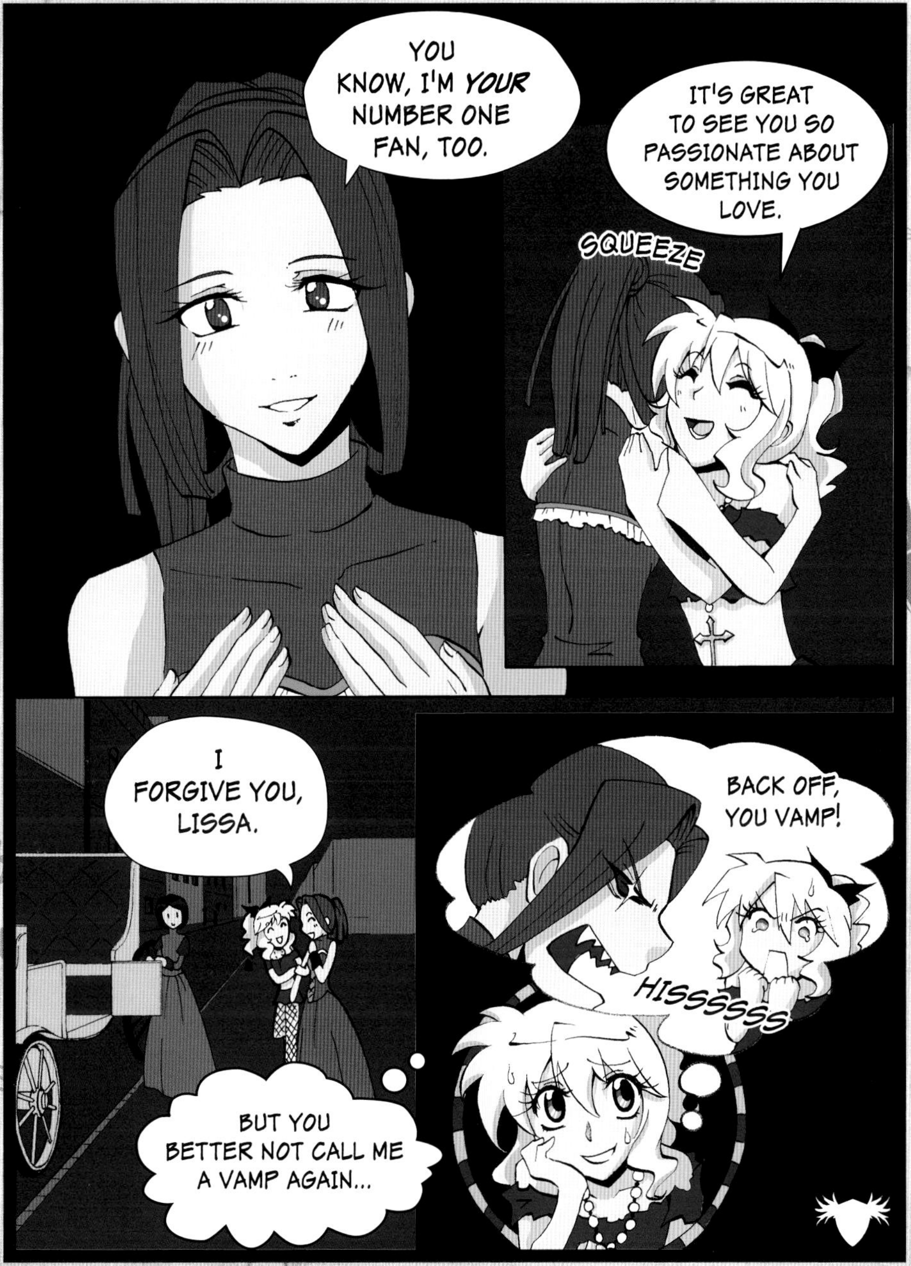
YOU KNOW, I'M *YOUR* NUMBER ONE FAN, TOO.
IT'S GREAT TO SEE YOU SO PASSIONATE ABOUT SOMETHING YOU LOVE.
SQUEEZE
I FORGIVE YOU, LISSA.
BUT YOU BETTER NOT CALL ME A VAMP AGAIN...
BACK OFF, YOU VAMP!
HISSSSSSS

Luv for Music

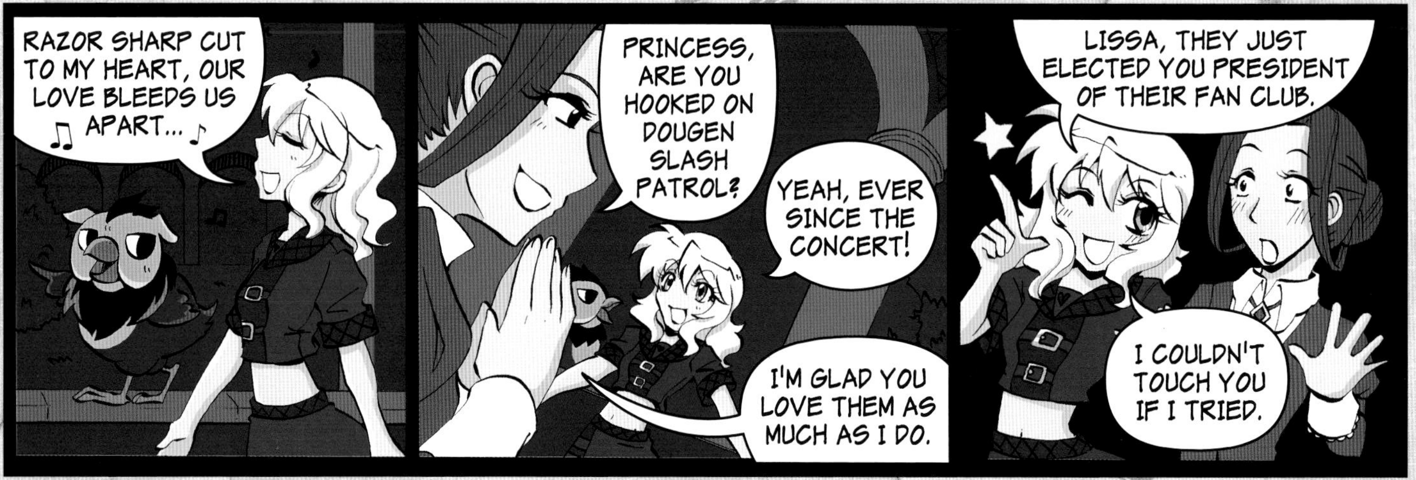

RAZOR SHARP CUT TO MY HEART, OUR LOVE BLEEDS US APART... ♪
PRINCESS, ARE YOU HOOKED ON DOUGEN SLASH PATROL?
YEAH, EVER SINCE THE CONCERT!
I'M GLAD YOU LOVE THEM AS MUCH AS I DO.
LISSA, THEY JUST ELECTED YOU PRESIDENT OF THEIR FAN CLUB.
I COULDN'T TOUCH YOU IF I TRIED.

King's Request

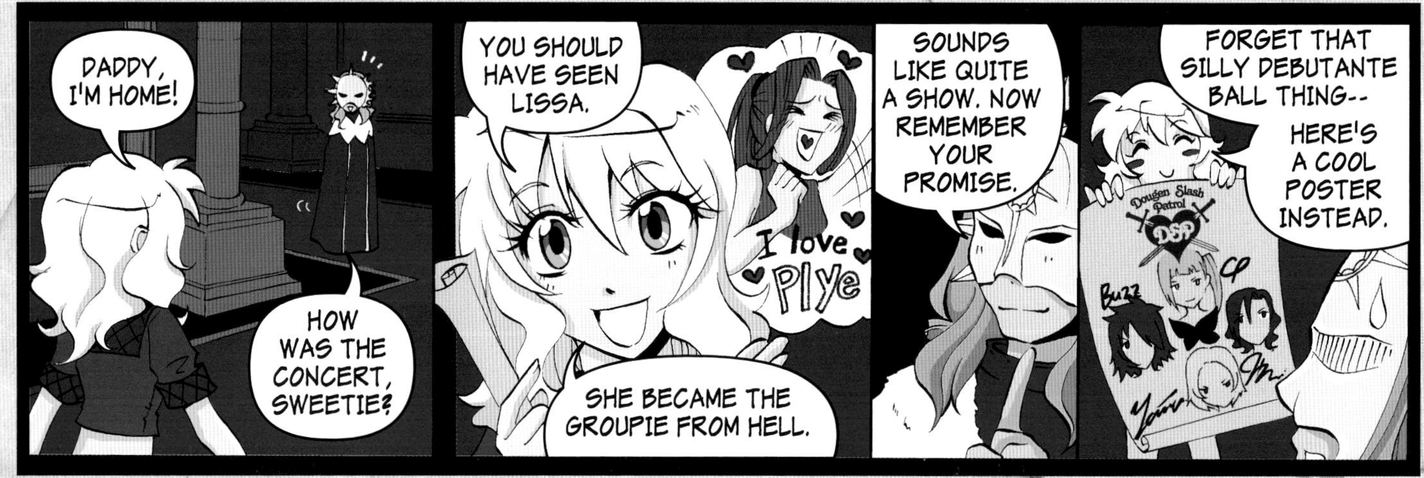

DADDY, I'M HOME!
HOW WAS THE CONCERT, SWEETIE?
YOU SHOULD HAVE SEEN LISSA.
I love Plye
SHE BECAME THE GROUPIE FROM HELL.
SOUNDS LIKE QUITE A SHOW. NOW REMEMBER YOUR PROMISE.
FORGET THAT SILLY DEBUTANTE BALL THING--
HERE'S A COOL POSTER INSTEAD.
Dougen Slash Patrol
DSP
Buzz

Debutante

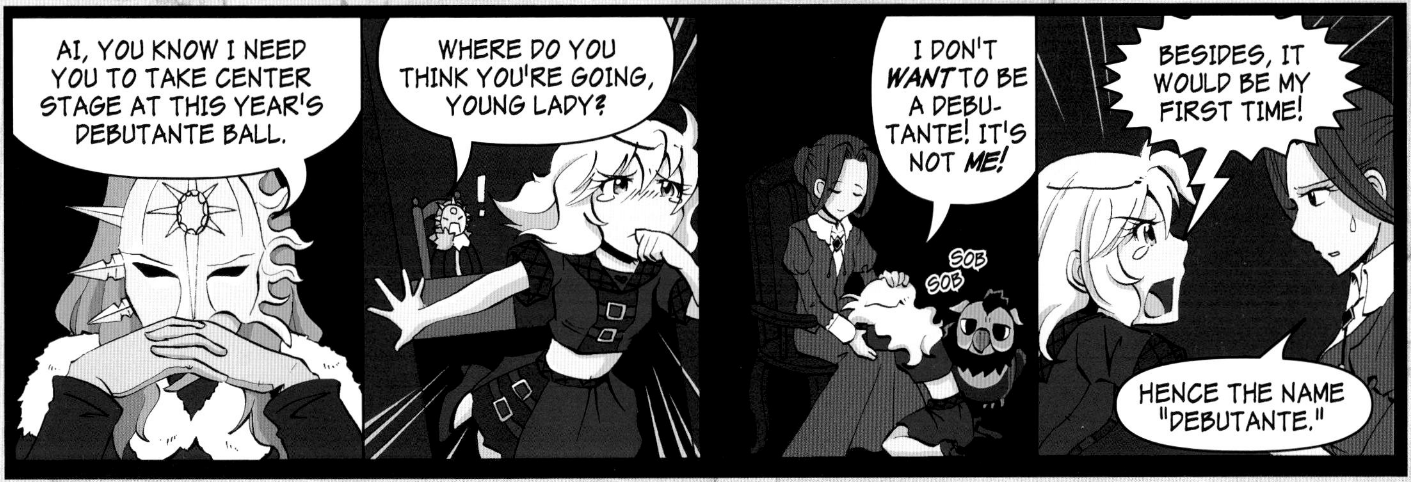
AI, YOU KNOW I NEED YOU TO TAKE CENTER STAGE AT THIS YEAR'S DEBUTANTE BALL.
WHERE DO YOU THINK YOU'RE GOING, YOUNG LADY?
!
I DON'T *WANT* TO BE A DEBU-TANTE! IT'S NOT *ME!*
SOB
SOB
BESIDES, IT WOULD BE MY FIRST TIME!
HENCE THE NAME "DEBUTANTE."

Ai's Plan

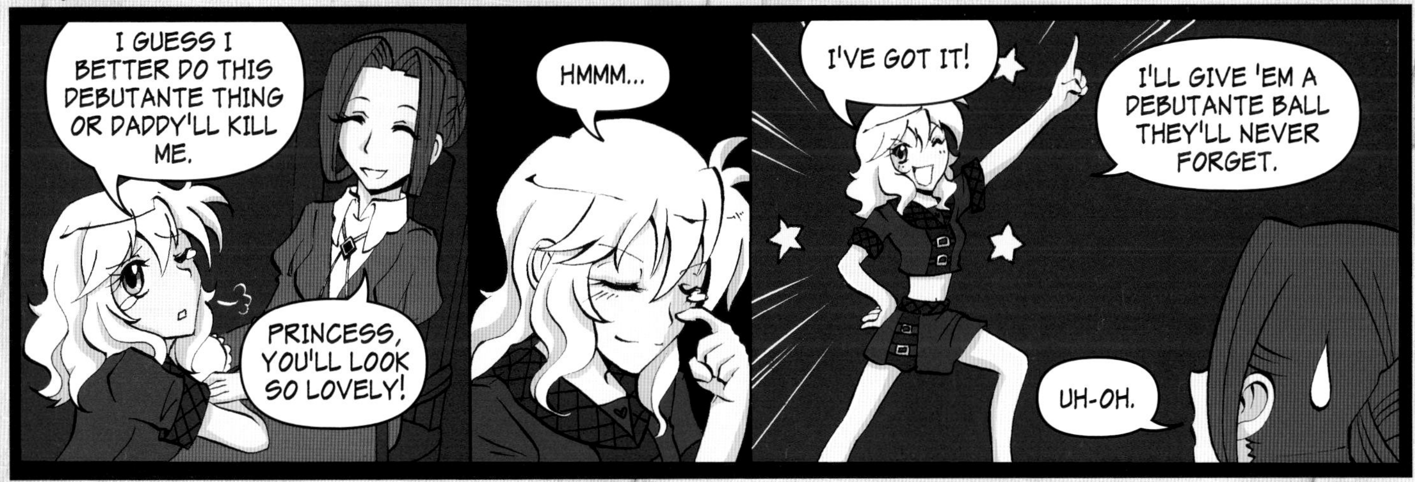
I GUESS I BETTER DO THIS DEBUTANTE THING OR DADDY'LL KILL ME.
PRINCESS, YOU'LL LOOK SO LOVELY!
HMMM...
I'VE GOT IT!
I'LL GIVE 'EM A DEBUTANTE BALL THEY'LL NEVER FORGET.
UH-OH.

Ai Style

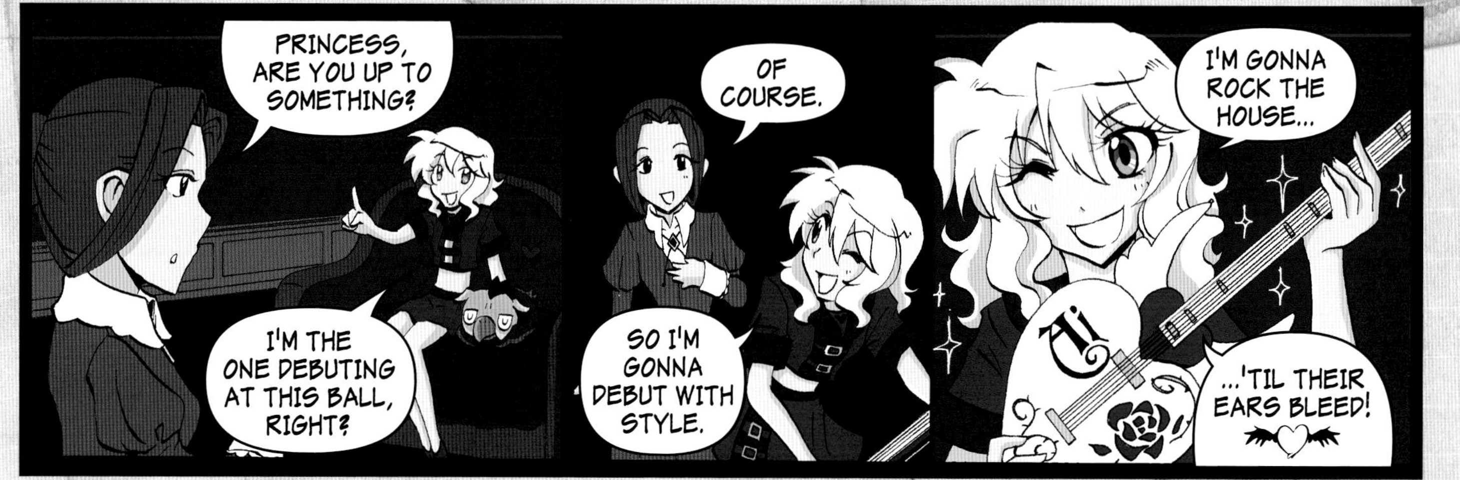
PRINCESS, ARE YOU UP TO SOMETHING?
I'M THE ONE DEBUTING AT THIS BALL, RIGHT?
OF COURSE.
SO I'M GONNA DEBUT WITH STYLE.
I'M GONNA ROCK THE HOUSE...
...'TIL THEIR EARS BLEED!

Guitar

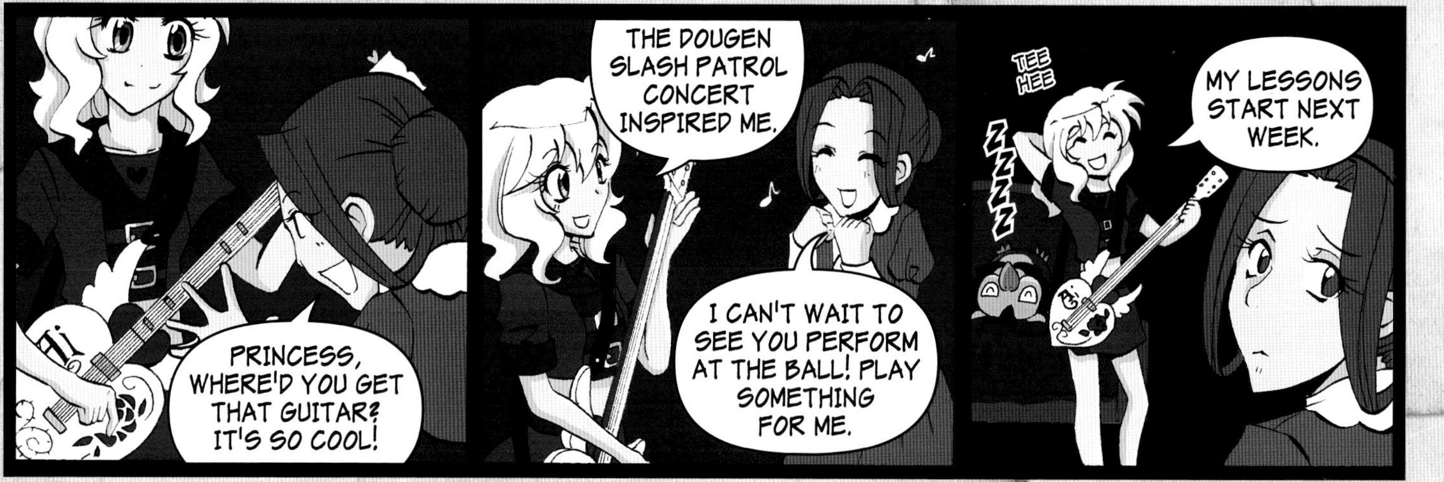
PRINCESS, WHERE'D YOU GET THAT GUITAR? IT'S SO COOL!
THE DOUGEN SLASH PATROL CONCERT INSPIRED ME.
I CAN'T WAIT TO SEE YOU PERFORM AT THE BALL! PLAY SOMETHING FOR ME.
TEE HEE
ZZZZ
MY LESSONS START NEXT WEEK.

dear d A i ry

Honestly, I love Lissa. She's my tutor, my best friend. Really, she's like my big sis. If it weren't for her, I'd be the loneliest girl on the planet. I guess that's why I feel so guilty for getting close to Plye. It was never about hurting Lissa. Does that make me selfish, though? I'm not sure what's right and what's wrong...

love forever

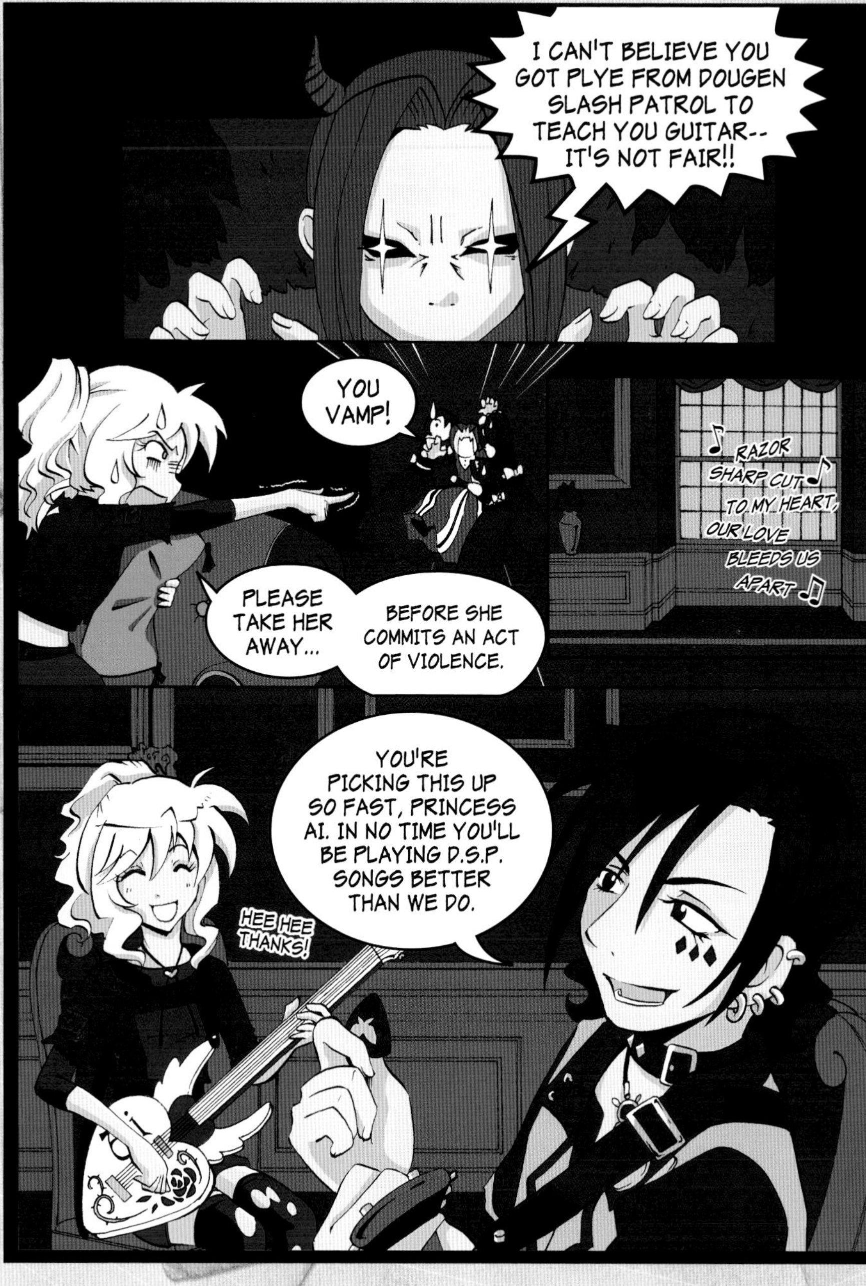
I CAN'T BELIEVE YOU GOT PLYE FROM DOUGEN SLASH PATROL TO TEACH YOU GUITAR-- IT'S NOT FAIR!!
YOU VAMP!
RAZOR SHARP CUT TO MY HEART, OUR LOVE BLEEDS US APART
PLEASE TAKE HER AWAY...
BEFORE SHE COMMITS AN ACT OF VIOLENCE.
HEE HEE THANKS!
YOU'RE PICKING THIS UP SO FAST, PRINCESS AI. IN NO TIME YOU'LL BE PLAYING D.S.P. SONGS BETTER THAN WE DO.

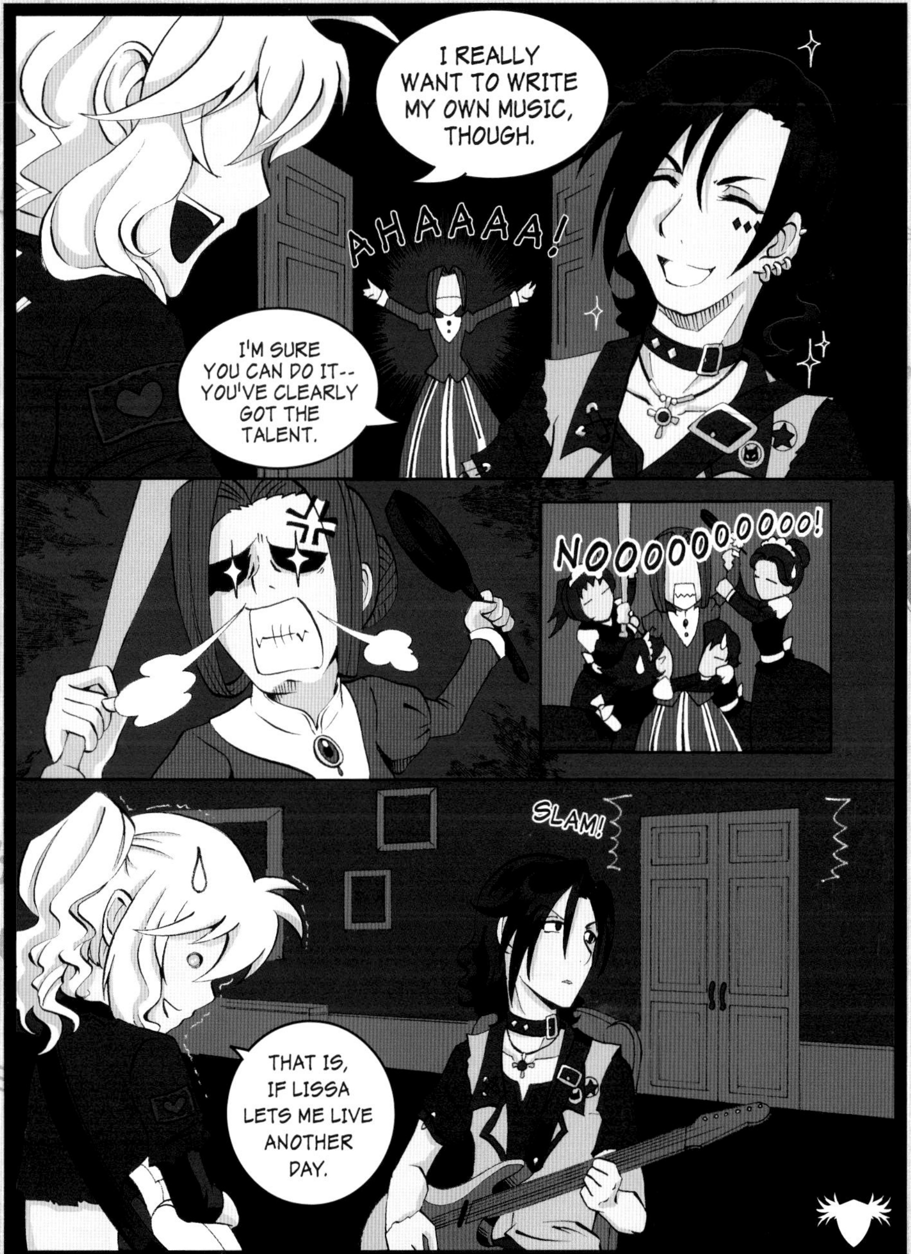
I REALLY WANT TO WRITE MY OWN MUSIC, THOUGH.
AHAAAAA!
I'M SURE YOU CAN DO IT-- YOU'VE CLEARLY GOT THE TALENT.
NOOOOOOOOOOO!
SLAM!
THAT IS, IF LISSA LETS ME LIVE ANOTHER DAY.

Lounging Around

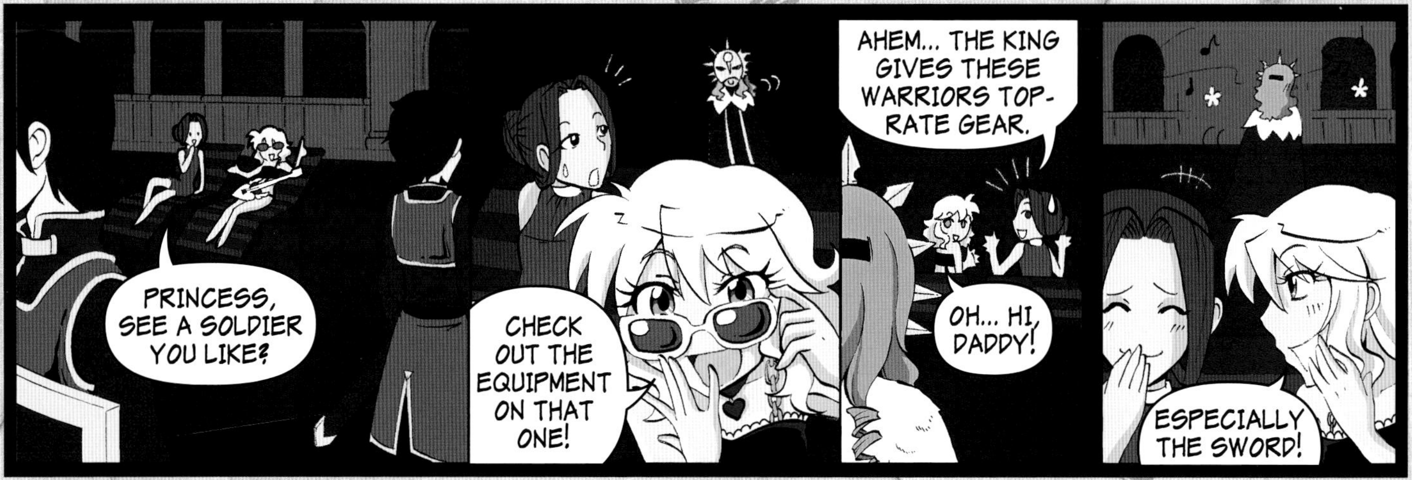
PRINCESS, SEE A SOLDIER YOU LIKE?
CHECK OUT THE EQUIPMENT ON THAT ONE!
AHEM... THE KING GIVES THESE WARRIORS TOP-RATE GEAR.
OH... HI, DADDY!
ESPECIALLY THE SWORD!

Too Serious

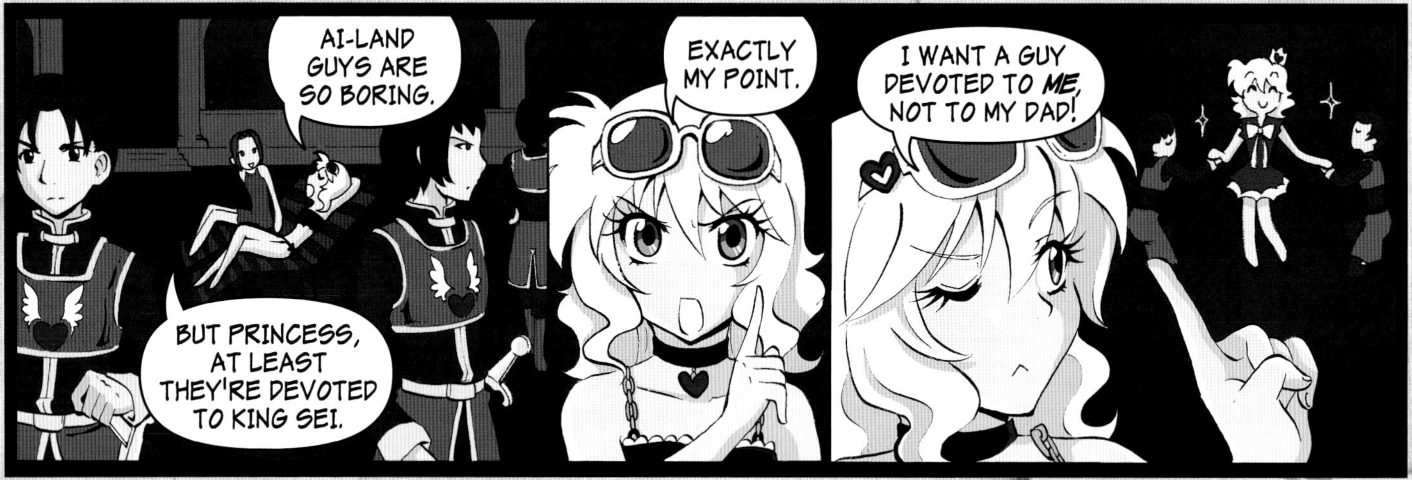
AI-LAND GUYS ARE SO BORING.
BUT PRINCESS, AT LEAST THEY'RE DEVOTED TO KING SEI.
EXACTLY MY POINT.
I WANT A GUY DEVOTED TO *ME*, NOT TO MY DAD!

Damsels in Distress

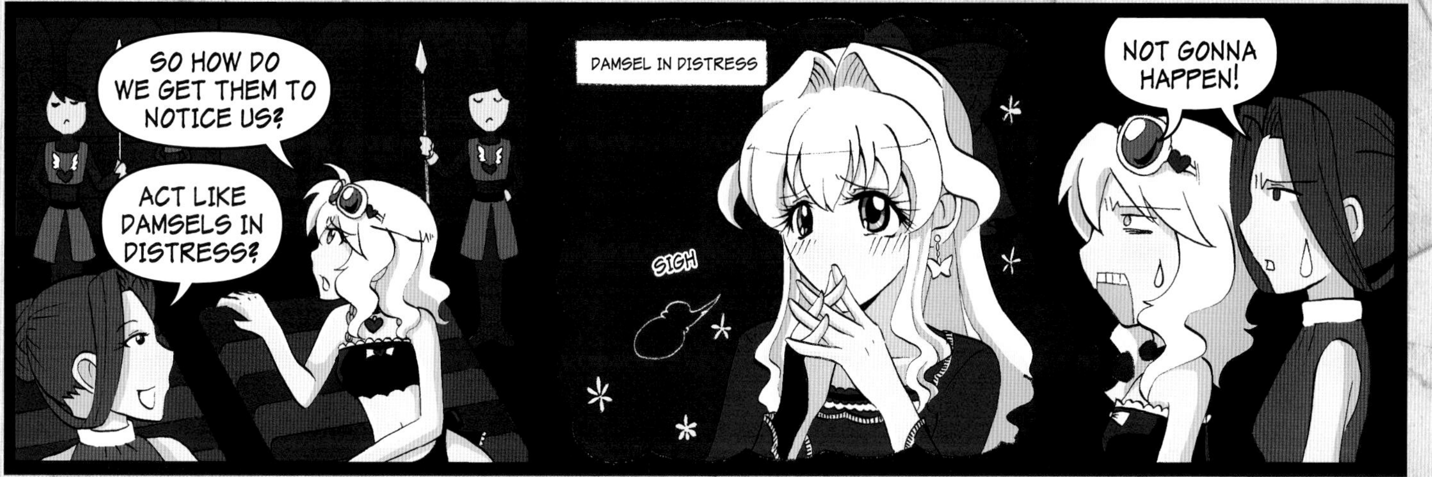
SO HOW DO WE GET THEM TO NOTICE US?
ACT LIKE DAMSELS IN DISTRESS?
DAMSEL IN DISTRESS
SIGH
NOT GONNA HAPPEN!

Playin' Guitar

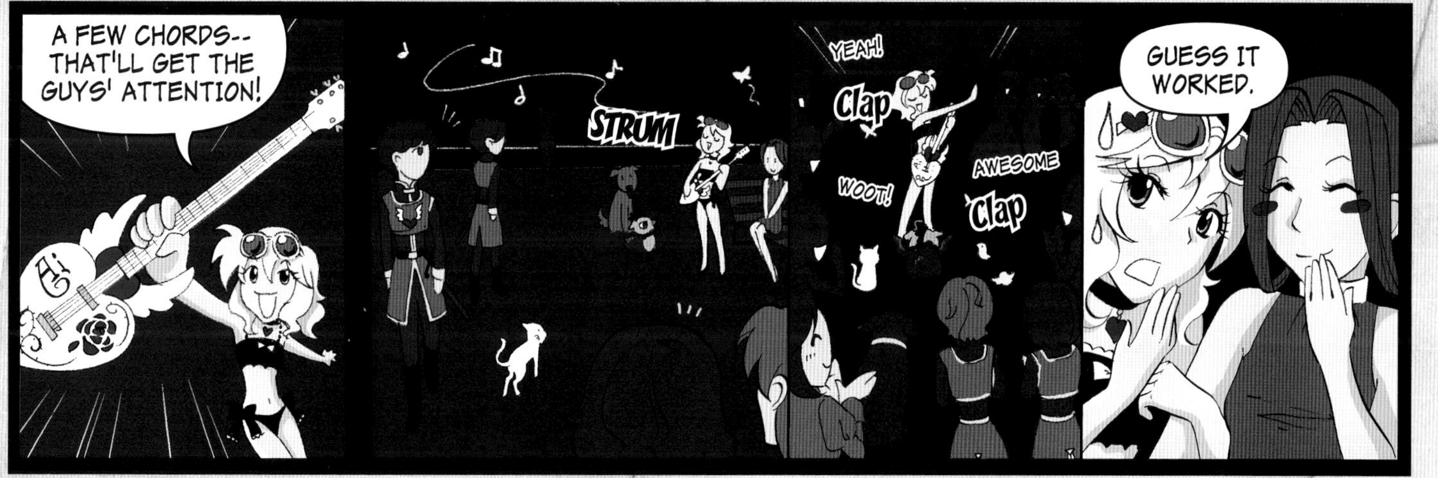
A FEW CHORDS-- THAT'LL GET THE GUYS' ATTENTION!
Hi
STRUM
YEAH!
Clap
WOOT!
AWESOME
Clap
GUESS IT WORKED.

Cards

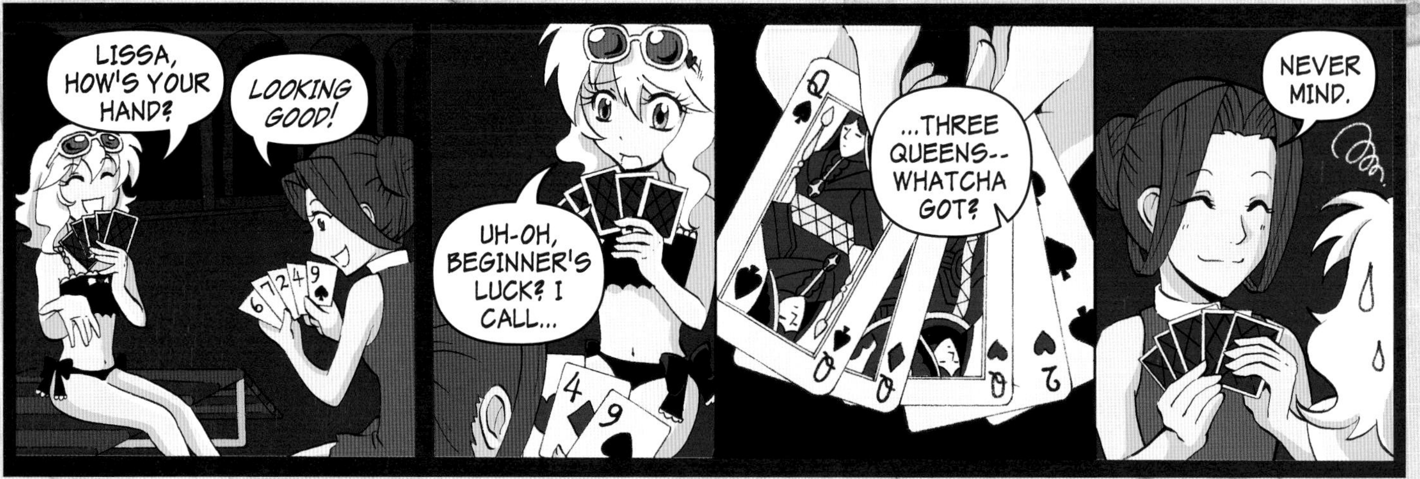
LISSA, HOW'S YOUR HAND?
LOOKING GOOD!
UH-OH, BEGINNER'S LUCK? I CALL...
...THREE QUEENS--WHATCHA GOT?
NEVER MIND.

More Cards

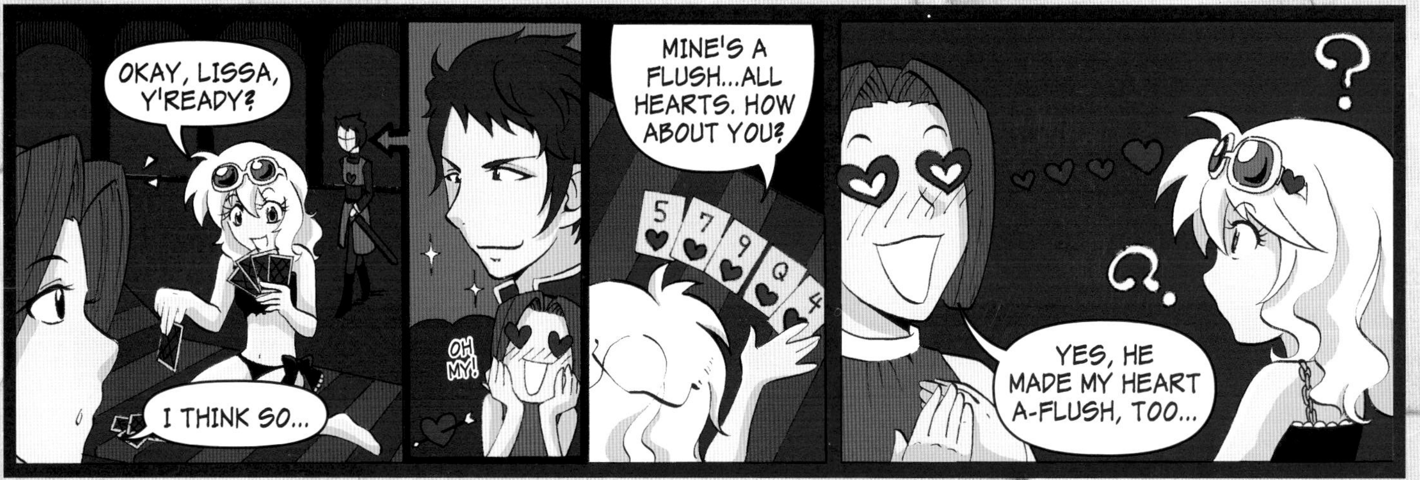
OKAY, LISSA, Y'READY?
I THINK SO...
OH MY!
MINE'S A FLUSH...ALL HEARTS. HOW ABOUT YOU?
YES, HE MADE MY HEART A-FLUSH, TOO...

dear dry

Daddy insists I'm too young to date. I think he wants me to die a virgin. Either that or he wants to choose. Well, no way Jose! I know it's part of my job as a teenager (now that I'm officially one!) to learn about guys. But one thing I'm learning about my "big sis" Lissa--she may act prude but no one loves guys more than her.

love forever

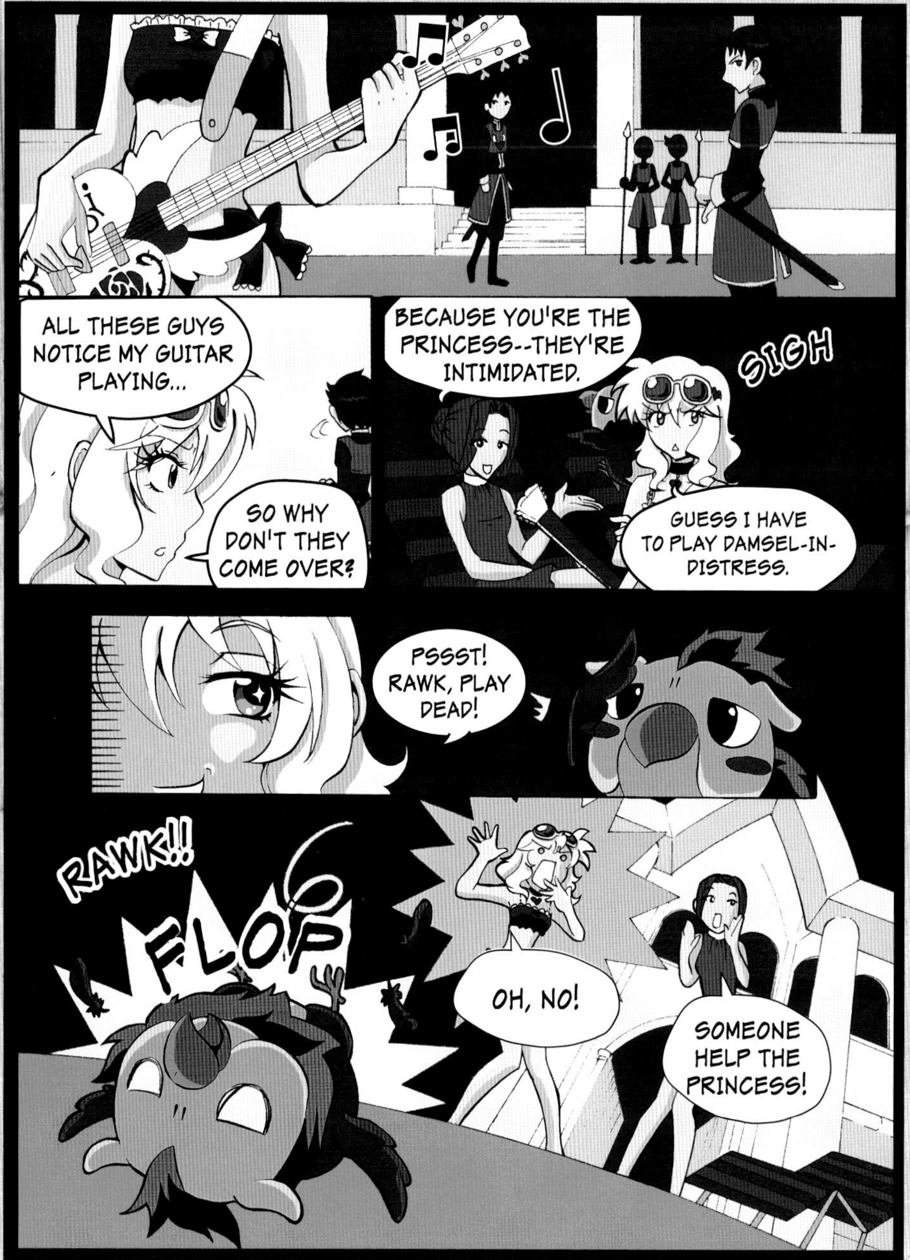
ALL THESE GUYS NOTICE MY GUITAR PLAYING...
SO WHY DON'T THEY COME OVER?
BECAUSE YOU'RE THE PRINCESS--THEY'RE INTIMIDATED.
SIGH
GUESS I HAVE TO PLAY DAMSEL-IN-DISTRESS.
PSSST! RAWK, PLAY DEAD!
RAWK!!
FLOP
OH, NO!
SOMEONE HELP THE PRINCESS!

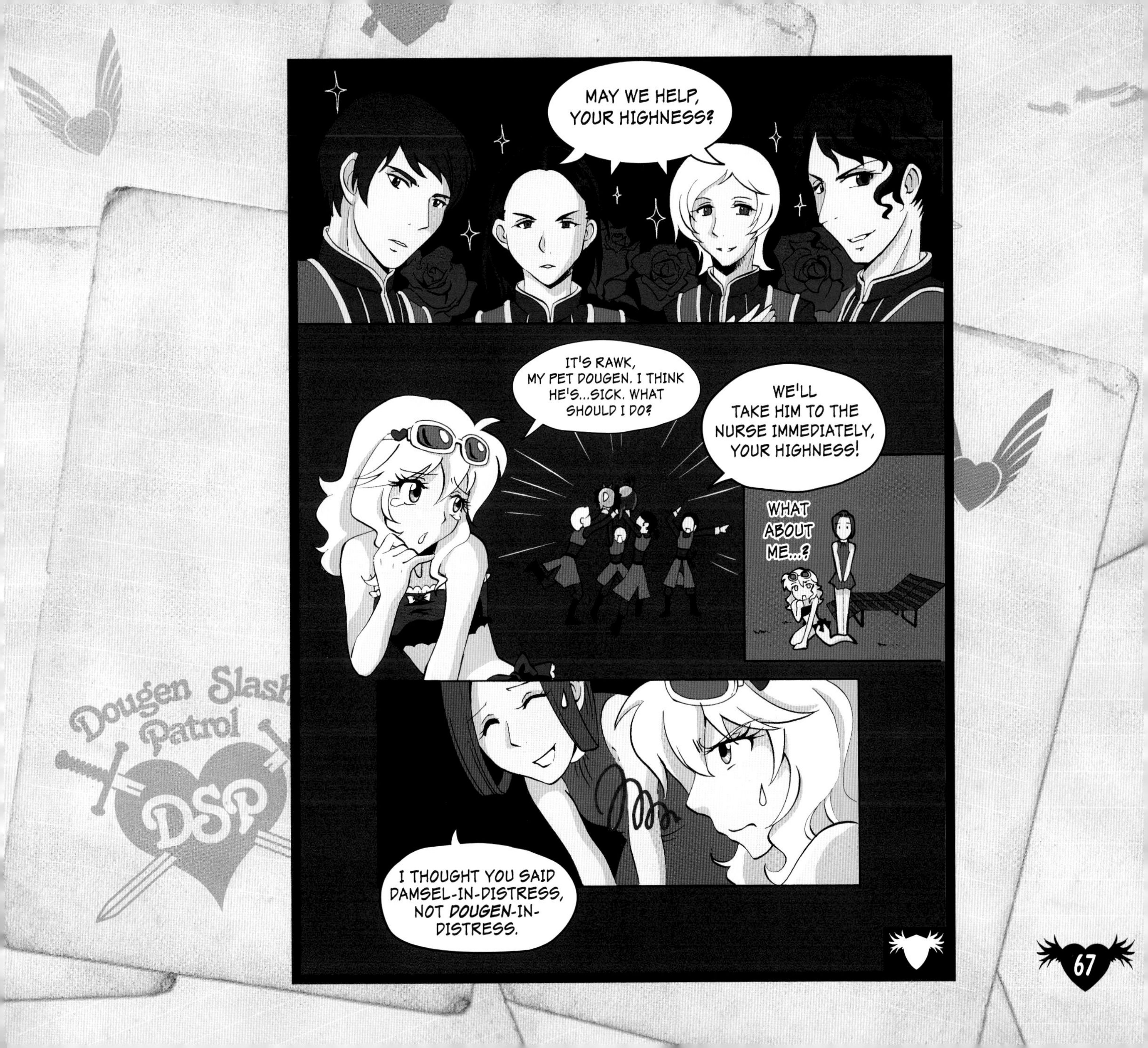

MAY WE HELP, YOUR HIGHNESS?
IT'S RAWK, MY PET DOUGEN. I THINK HE'S...SICK. WHAT SHOULD I DO?
WE'LL TAKE HIM TO THE NURSE IMMEDIATELY, YOUR HIGHNESS!
WHAT ABOUT ME...?
I THOUGHT YOU SAID DAMSEL-IN-DISTRESS, NOT *DOUGEN*-IN-DISTRESS.

What a Pain

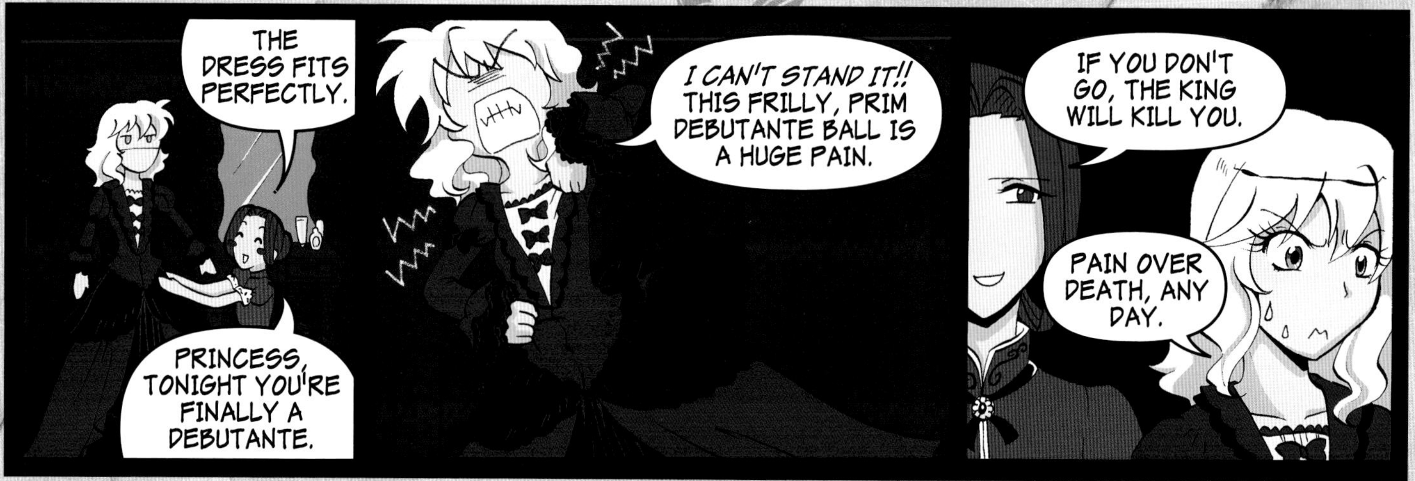
THE DRESS FITS PERFECTLY.
PRINCESS, TONIGHT YOU'RE FINALLY A DEBUTANTE.
I CAN'T STAND IT!! THIS FRILLY, PRIM DEBUTANTE BALL IS A HUGE PAIN.
IF YOU DON'T GO, THE KING WILL KILL YOU.
PAIN OVER DEATH, ANY DAY.

No Breaking Promises

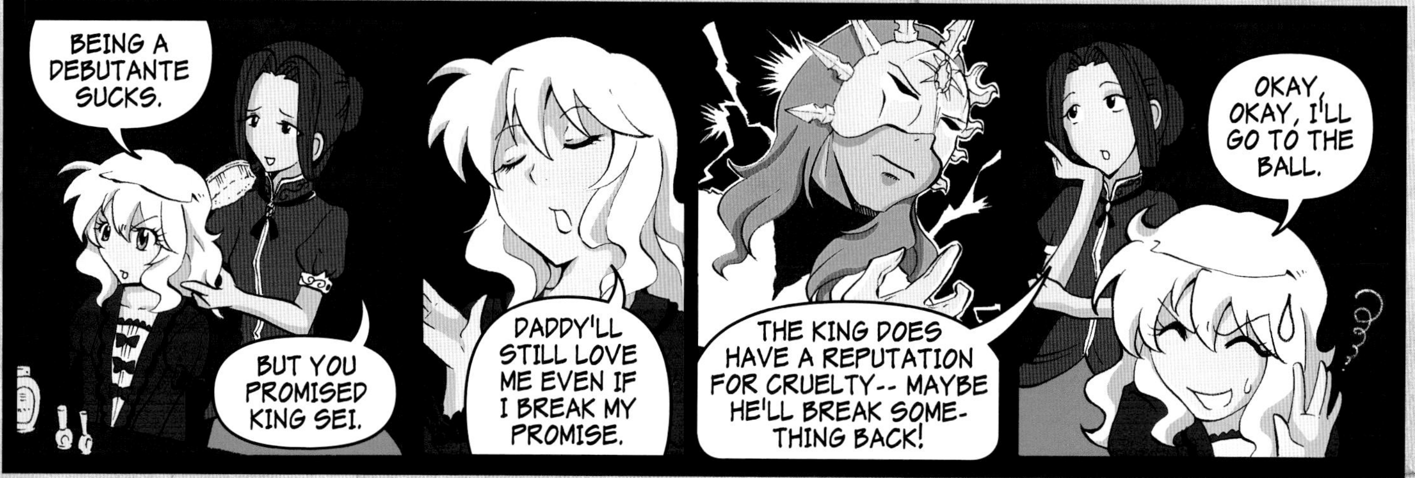
BEING A DEBUTANTE SUCKS.
BUT YOU PROMISED KING SEI.
DADDY'LL STILL LOVE ME EVEN IF I BREAK MY PROMISE.
THE KING DOES HAVE A REPUTATION FOR CRUELTY-- MAYBE HE'LL BREAK SOME-THING BACK!
OKAY, OKAY, I'LL GO TO THE BALL.

Cut Down to Size

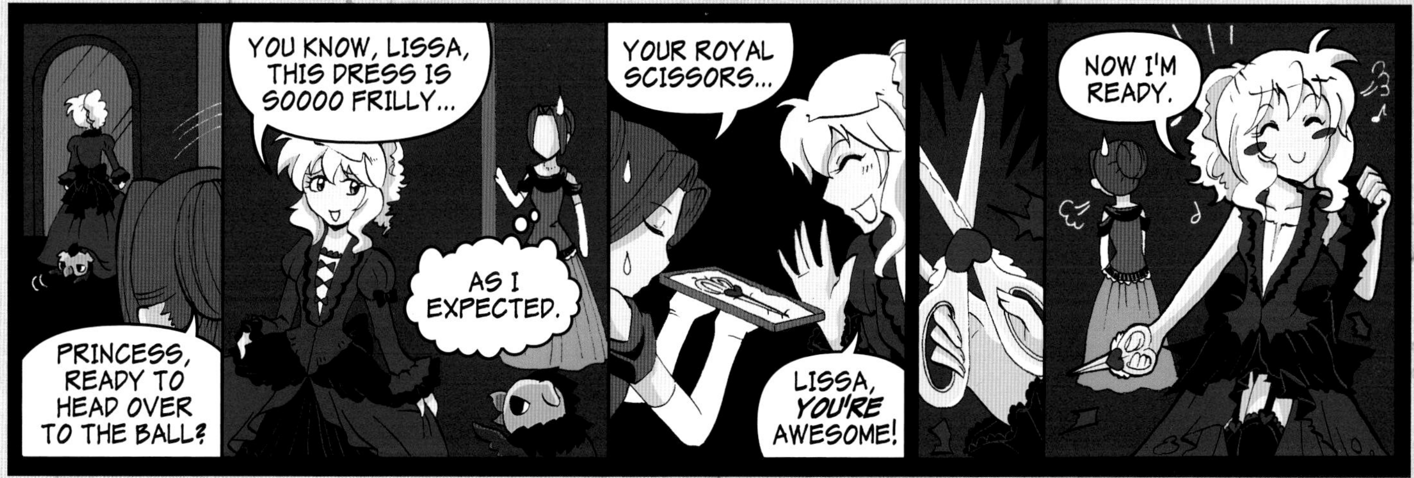
PRINCESS, READY TO HEAD OVER TO THE BALL?
YOU KNOW, LISSA, THIS DRESS IS SOOOO FRILLY...
AS I EXPECTED.
YOUR ROYAL SCISSORS...
LISSA, *YOU'RE* AWESOME!
NOW I'M READY.

Hot Guys

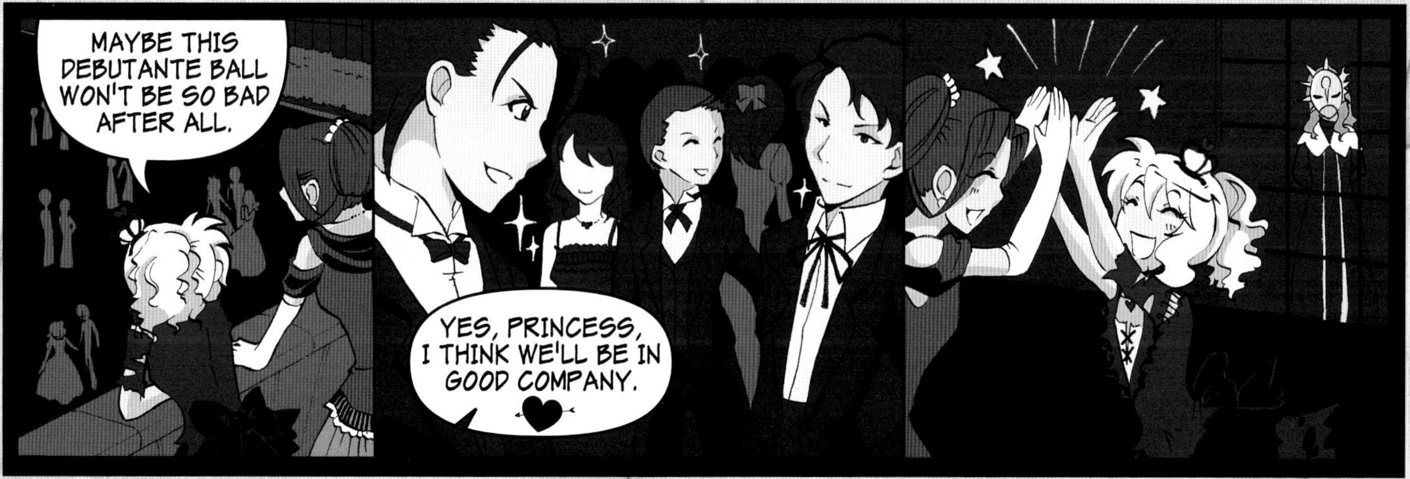
MAYBE THIS DEBUTANTE BALL WON'T BE SO BAD AFTER ALL.
YES, PRINCESS, I THINK WE'LL BE IN GOOD COMPANY.

Escort Patrol

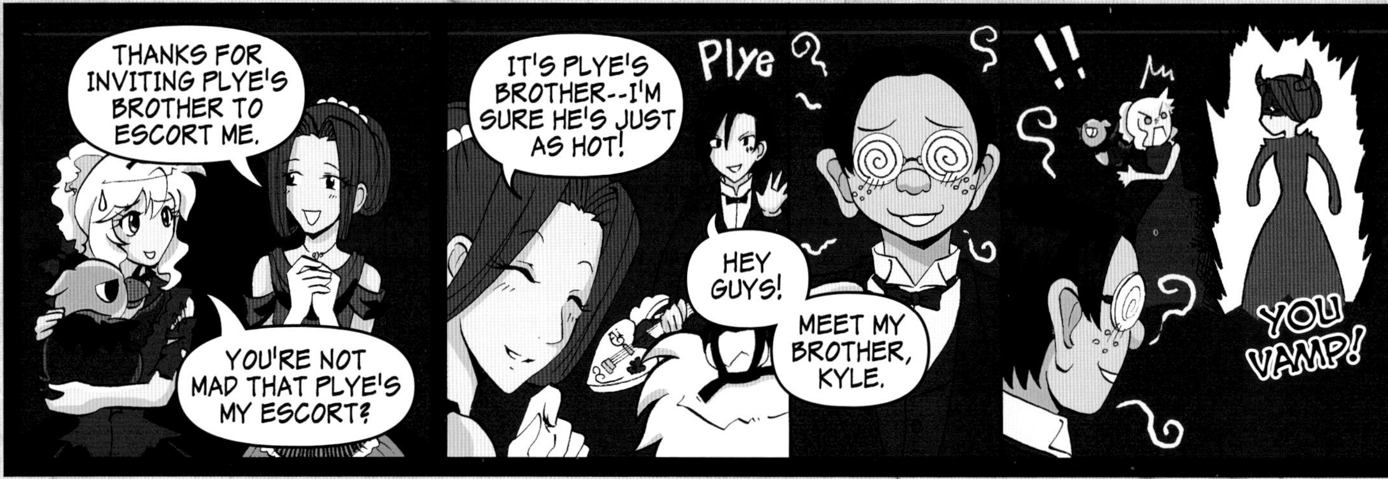
THANKS FOR INVITING PLYE'S BROTHER TO ESCORT ME.
YOU'RE NOT MAD THAT PLYE'S MY ESCORT?
IT'S PLYE'S BROTHER--I'M SURE HE'S JUST AS HOT!
Plye
HEY GUYS!
MEET MY BROTHER, KYLE.
!!
YOU VAMP!

Debu-Taunt

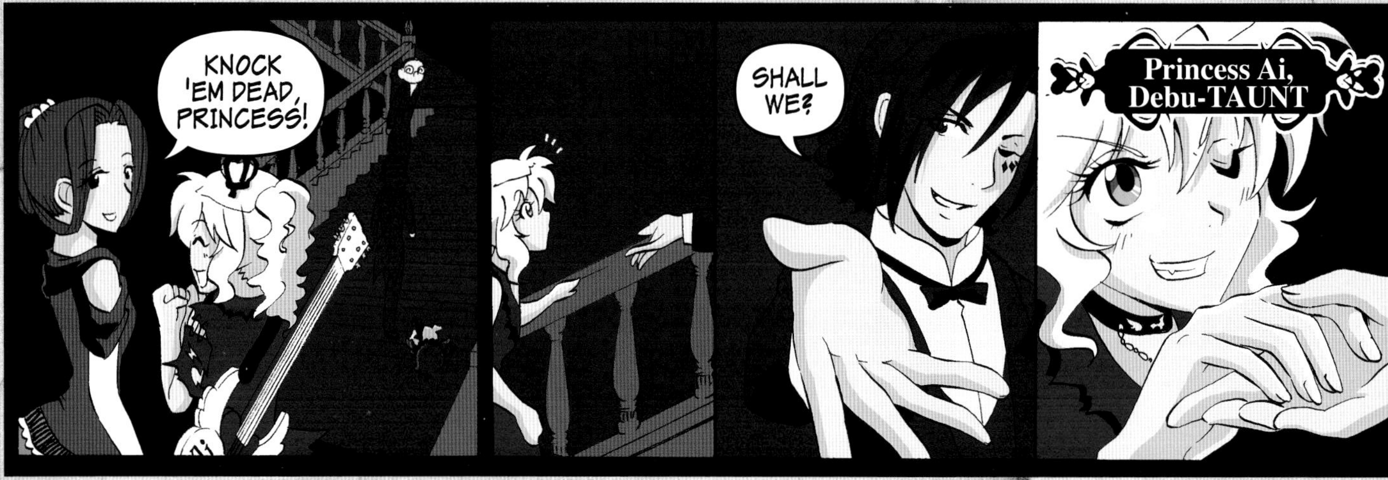
KNOCK 'EM DEAD, PRINCESS!
SHALL WE?
Princess Ai, Debu-TAUNT

dear d**Ai**ry

What is it about me that drives me to rebel? I can't help myself--all I want to do is shock everyone, especially Daddy. Am I mental? It's just so fun to see people's faces when I'm not the Princess they expect me to be (or want me to be). I can't help it, though--the more I'm supposed to act good, the more I want to be bad.
Poor Daddy.

love forever

Ai

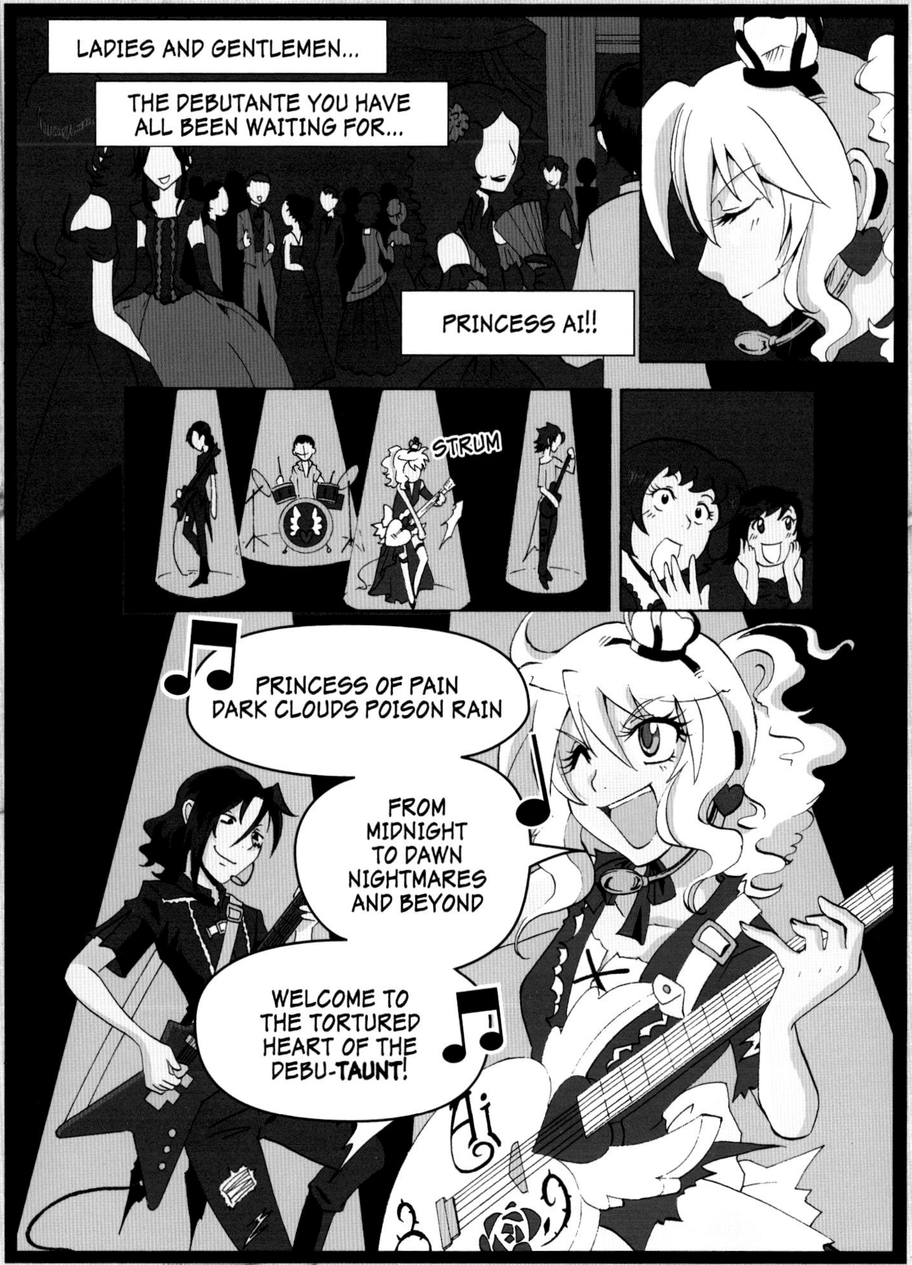
LADIES AND GENTLEMEN...
THE DEBUTANTE YOU HAVE ALL BEEN WAITING FOR...
PRINCESS AI!!
STRUM
PRINCESS OF PAIN DARK CLOUDS POISON RAIN
FROM MIDNIGHT TO DAWN NIGHTMARES AND BEYOND
WELCOME TO THE TORTURED HEART OF THE DEBU-TAUNT!
Ai

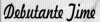

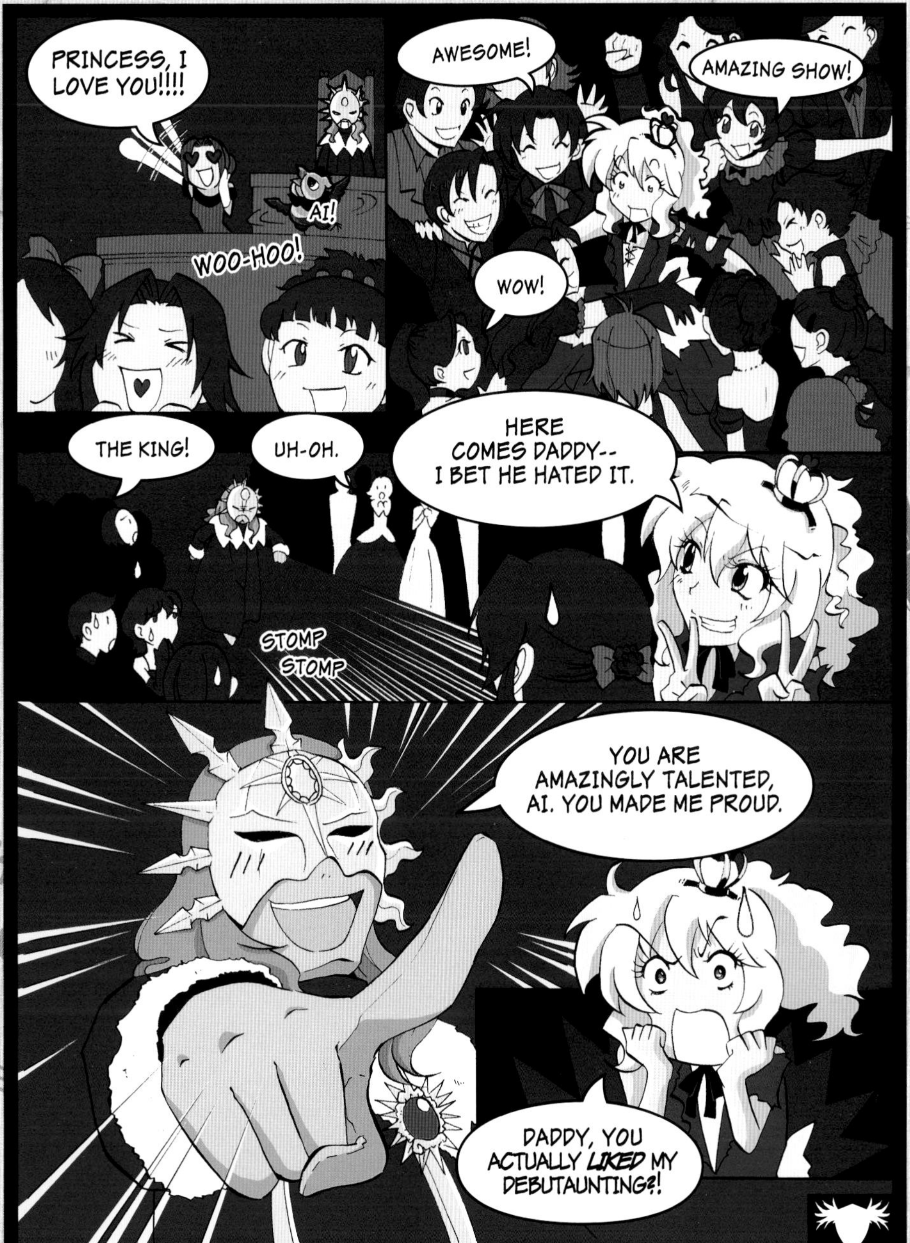
PRINCESS, I LOVE YOU!!!!
AI!
WOO-HOO!
AWESOME!
AMAZING SHOW!
WOW!
THE KING!
UH-OH.
HERE COMES DADDY-- I BET HE HATED IT.
STOMP
STOMP
YOU ARE AMAZINGLY TALENTED, AI. YOU MADE ME PROUD.
DADDY, YOU ACTUALLY *LIKED* MY DEBUTAUNTING?!

Drinks From the Other Side

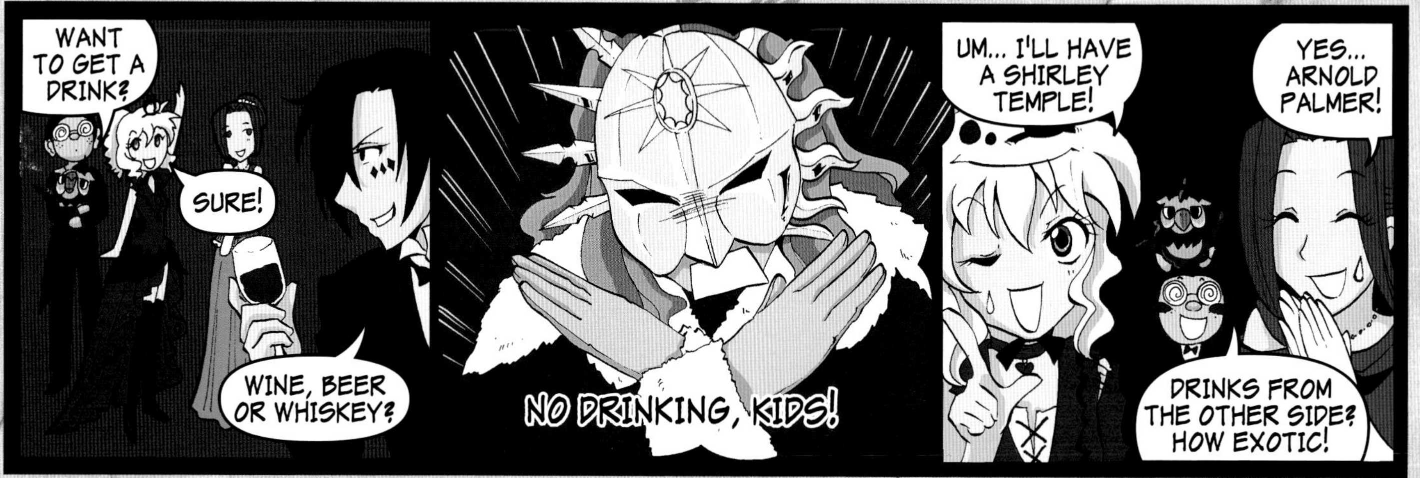
WANT TO GET A DRINK?
SURE!
WINE, BEER OR WHISKEY?
NO DRINKING, KIDS!
UM... I'LL HAVE A SHIRLEY TEMPLE!
YES... ARNOLD PALMER!
DRINKS FROM THE OTHER SIDE? HOW EXOTIC!

Two to Tango

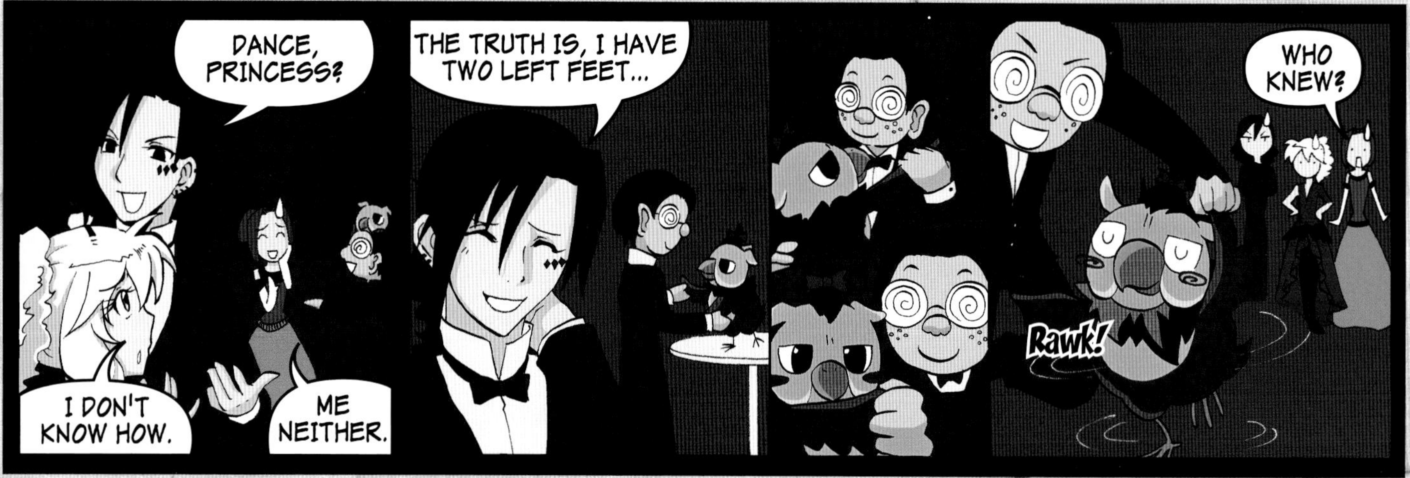
DANCE, PRINCESS?
I DON'T KNOW HOW.
ME NEITHER.
THE TRUTH IS, I HAVE TWO LEFT FEET...
WHO KNEW?
Rawk!

Stepping

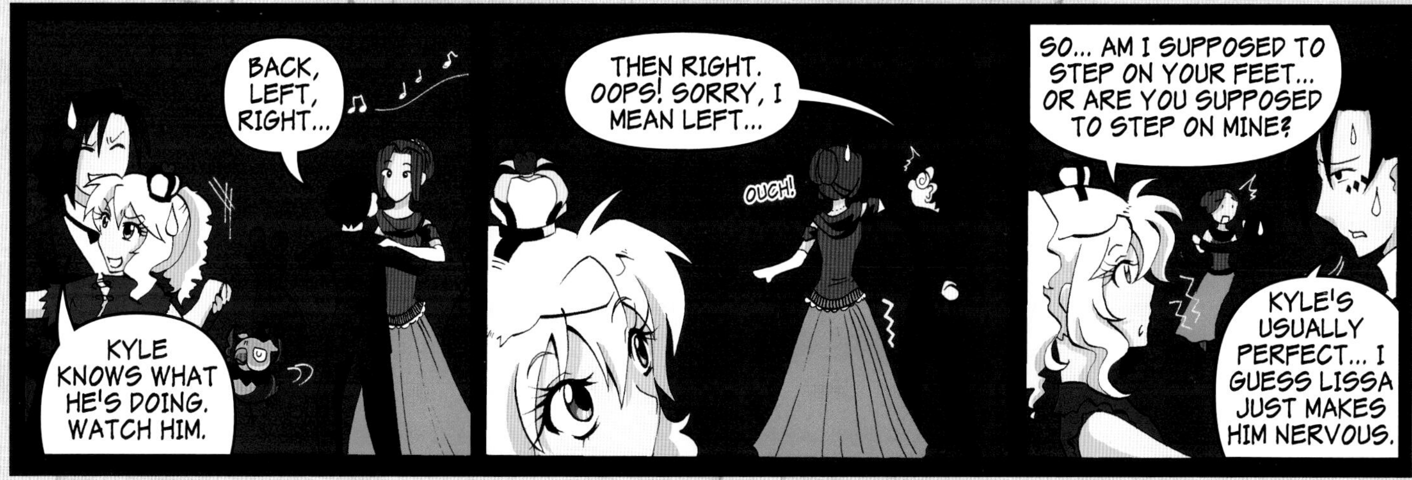
BACK, LEFT, RIGHT...
KYLE KNOWS WHAT HE'S DOING. WATCH HIM.
THEN RIGHT. OOPS! SORRY, I MEAN LEFT...
OUCH!
SO... AM I SUPPOSED TO STEP ON YOUR FEET... OR ARE YOU SUPPOSED TO STEP ON MINE?
KYLE'S USUALLY PERFECT... I GUESS LISSA JUST MAKES HIM NERVOUS.

Chaperone

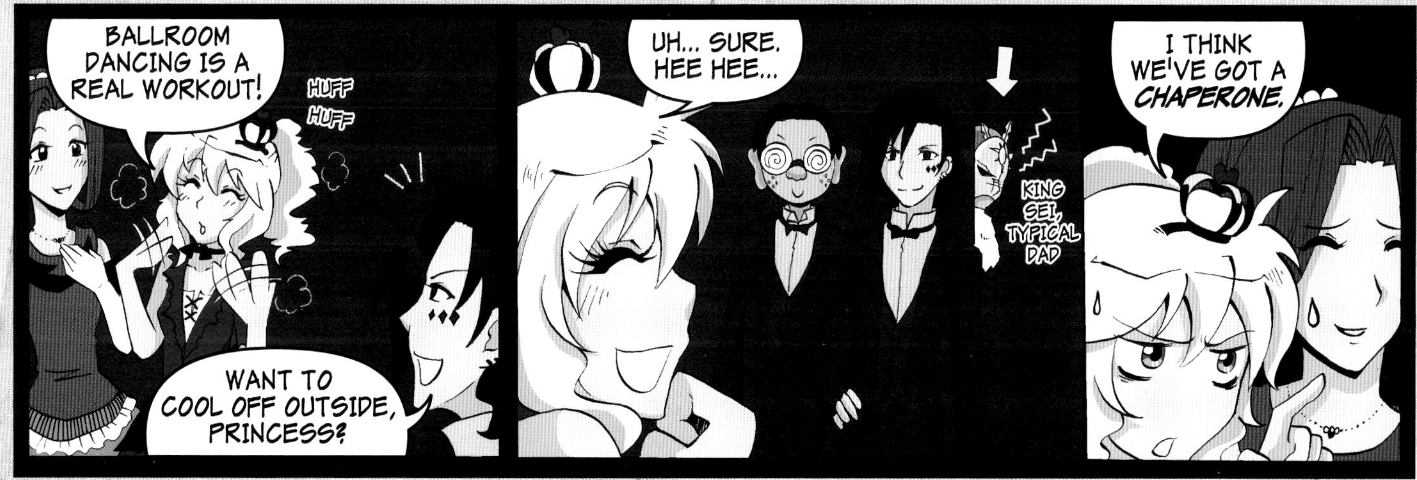
BALLROOM DANCING IS A REAL WORKOUT!
HUFF
HUFF
WANT TO COOL OFF OUTSIDE, PRINCESS?
UH... SURE. HEE HEE...
KING SEI, TYPICAL DAD
I THINK WE'VE GOT A *CHAPERONE.*

Full Moon

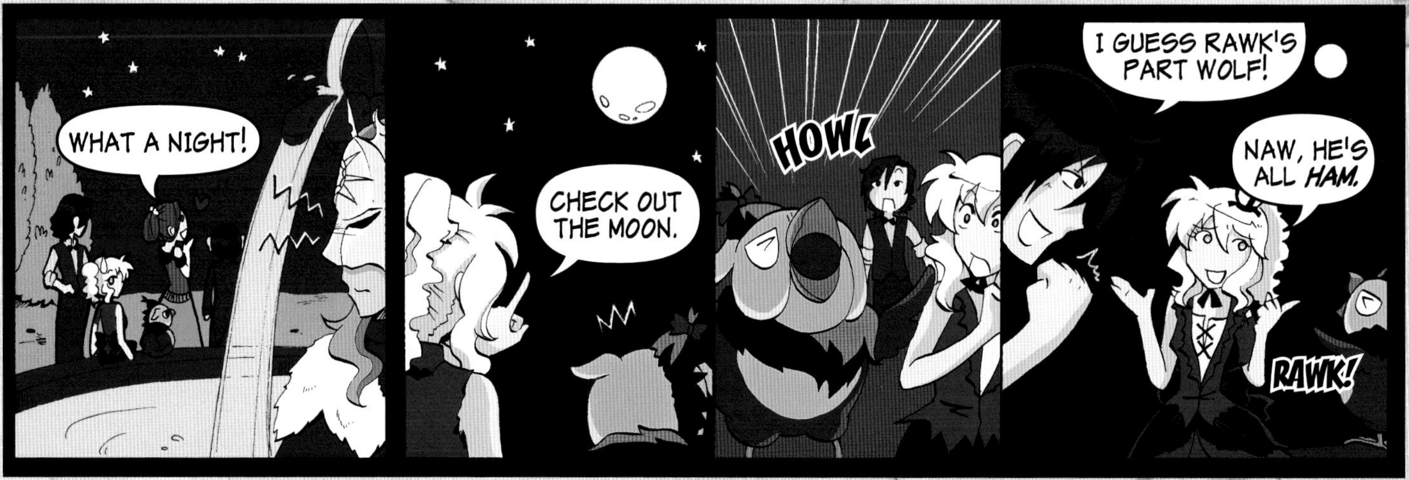

WHAT A NIGHT!
CHECK OUT THE MOON.
HOWL
I GUESS RAWK'S PART WOLF!
NAW, HE'S ALL *HAM.*
RAWK!

Trying Out For Size

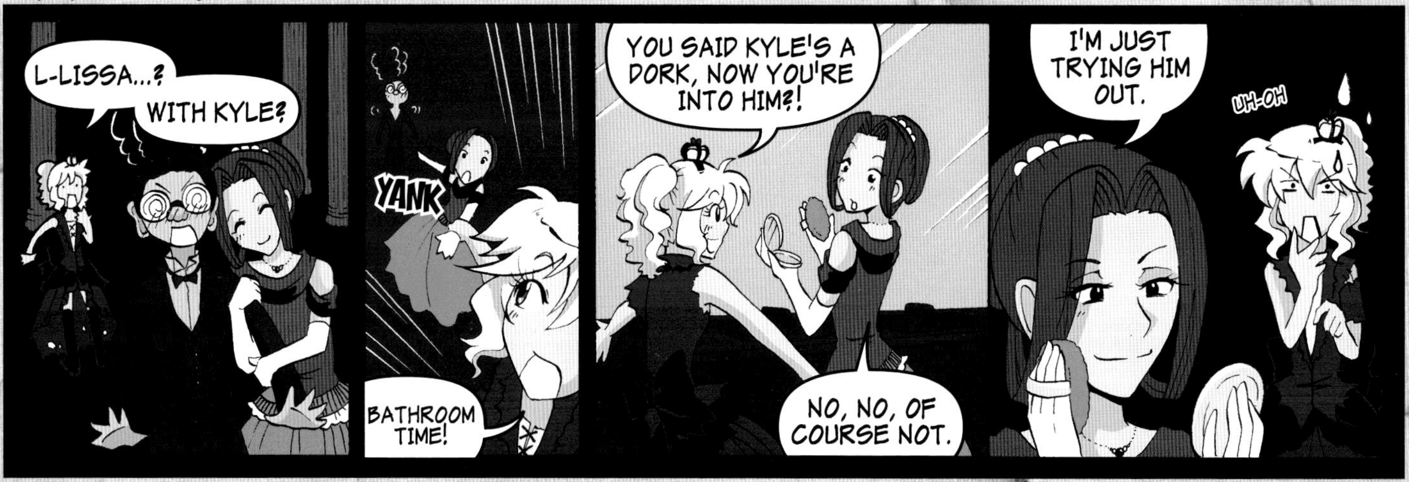

L-LISSA...?
WITH KYLE?
YANK
BATHROOM TIME!
YOU SAID KYLE'S A DORK, NOW YOU'RE INTO HIM?!
NO, NO, OF COURSE NOT.
I'M JUST TRYING HIM OUT.
UH-OH

dear d𝔄iry

Ai-Land is such a bizarre place. I wish I lived on Earth, the Other Side.

There, I wouldn't have to worry about these so-called traditions. I never wanted to be a debutante. It's just not me. But, to be honest, tonight wasn't so bad. The other girls were really cool--and even Daddy loosened up a bit and had a good time!

love forever

77

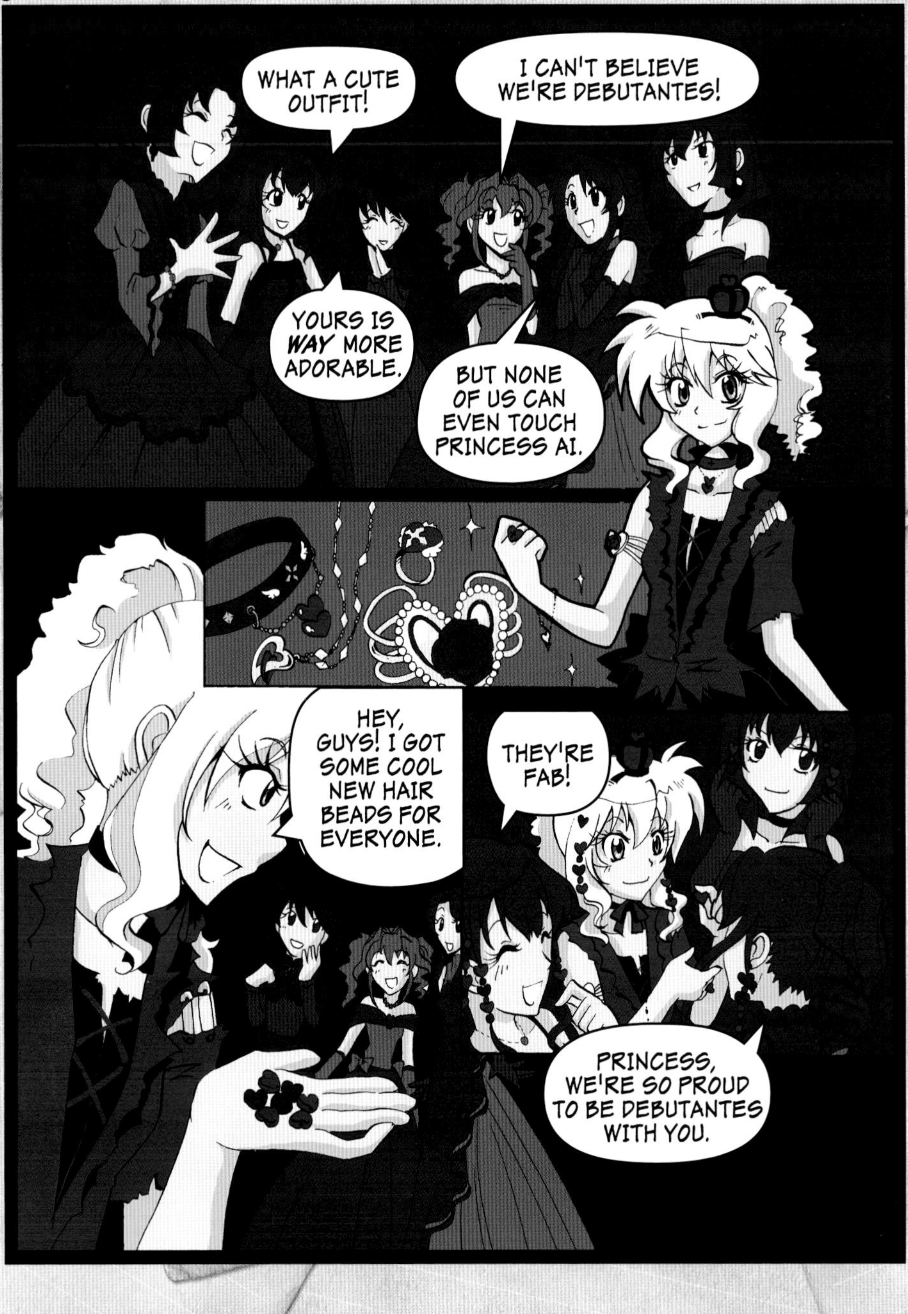
WHAT A CUTE OUTFIT!
I CAN'T BELIEVE WE'RE DEBUTANTES!
YOURS IS *WAY* MORE ADORABLE.
BUT NONE OF US CAN EVEN TOUCH PRINCESS AI.
HEY, GUYS! I GOT SOME COOL NEW HAIR BEADS FOR EVERYONE.
THEY'RE FAB!
PRINCESS, WE'RE SO PROUD TO BE DEBUTANTES WITH YOU.

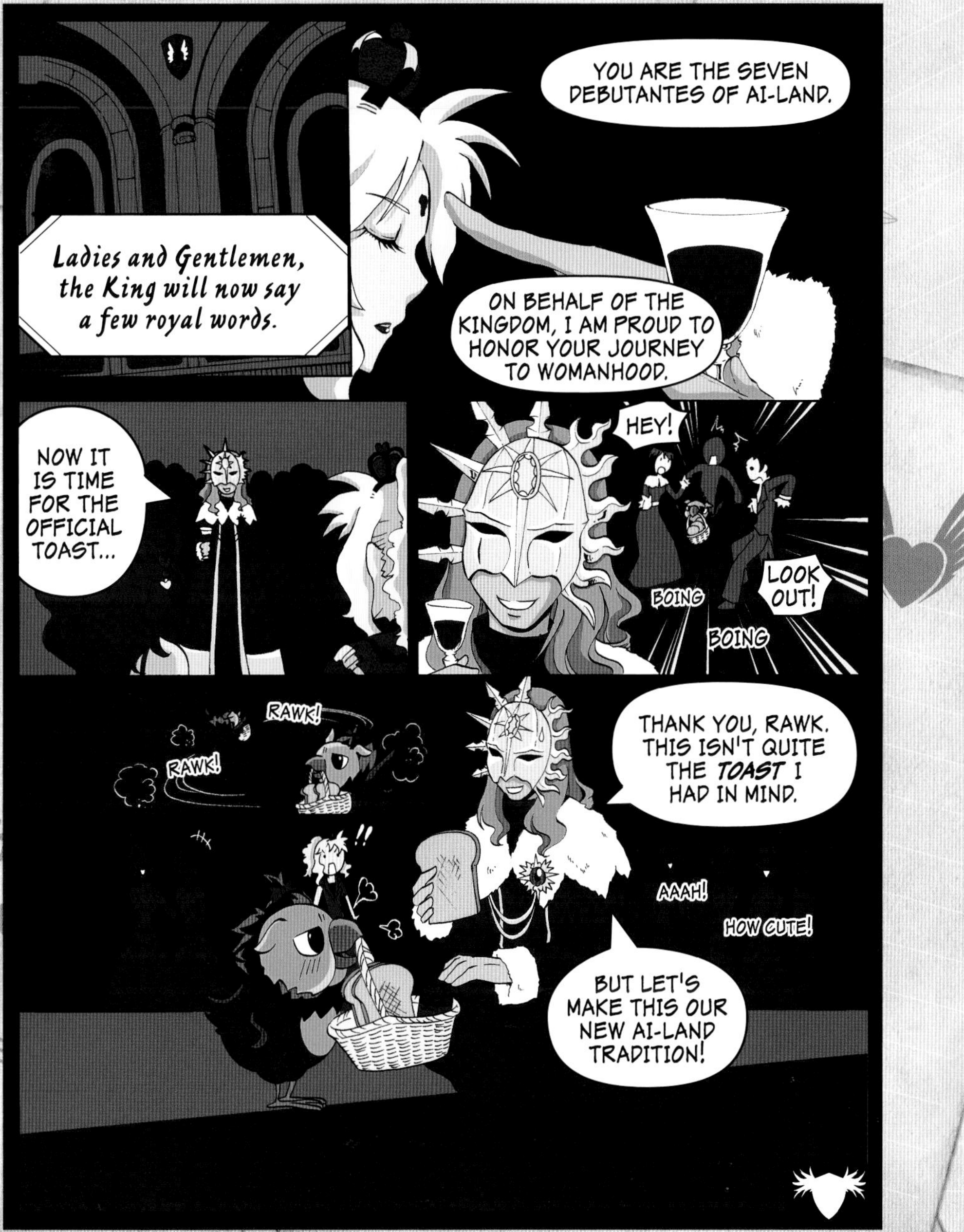
Ladies and Gentlemen, the King will now say a few royal words.
YOU ARE THE SEVEN DEBUTANTES OF AI-LAND.
ON BEHALF OF THE KINGDOM, I AM PROUD TO HONOR YOUR JOURNEY TO WOMANHOOD.
NOW IT IS TIME FOR THE OFFICIAL TOAST...
HEY!
LOOK OUT!
BOING
BOING
RAWK!
RAWK!
THANK YOU, RAWK. THIS ISN'T QUITE THE *TOAST* I HAD IN MIND.
AAAH!
HOW CUTE!
BUT LET'S MAKE THIS OUR NEW AI-LAND TRADITION!

Wrong About Everything

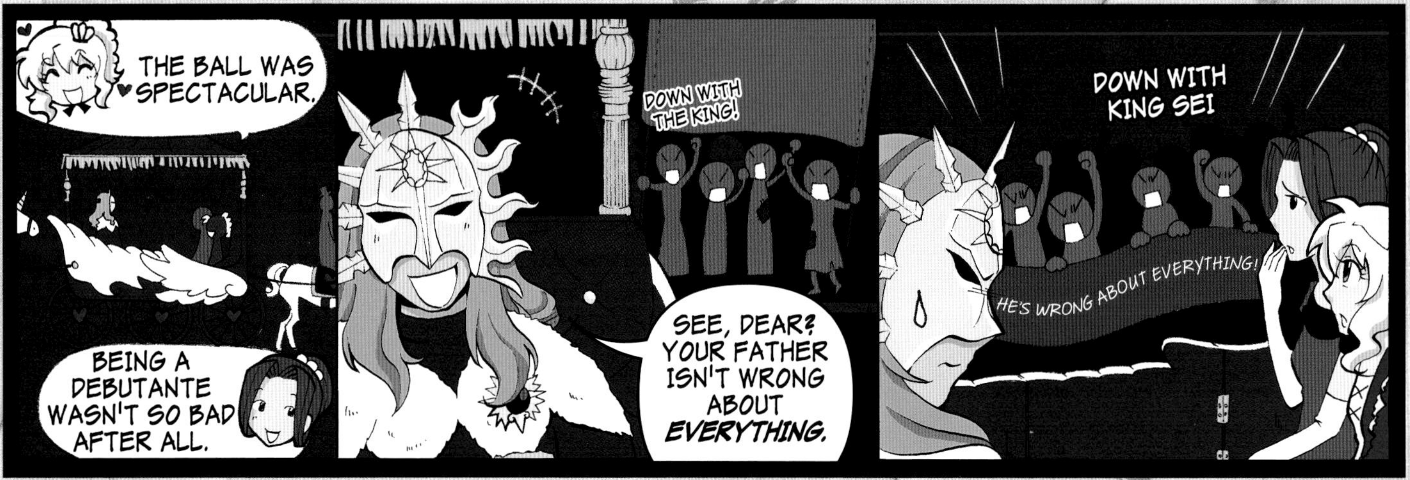
THE BALL WAS SPECTACULAR.
BEING A DEBUTANTE WASN'T SO BAD AFTER ALL.
DOWN WITH THE KING!
SEE, DEAR? YOUR FATHER ISN'T WRONG ABOUT EVERYTHING.
DOWN WITH KING SEI
HE'S WRONG ABOUT EVERYTHING!

Jealousy

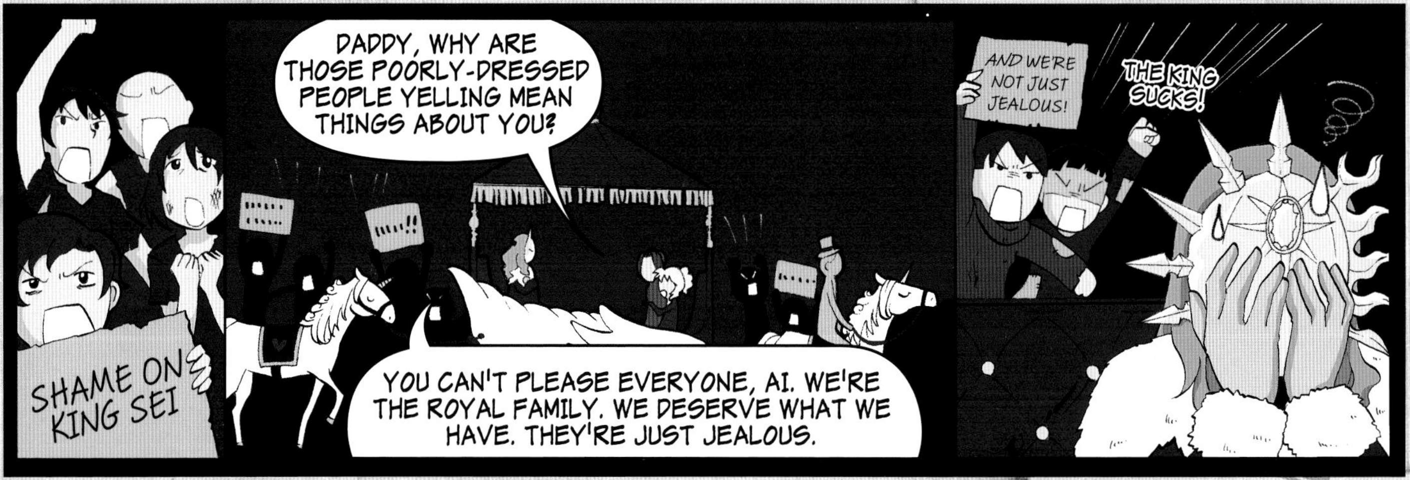
SHAME ON KING SEI
DADDY, WHY ARE THOSE POORLY-DRESSED PEOPLE YELLING MEAN THINGS ABOUT YOU?
YOU CAN'T PLEASE EVERYONE, AI. WE'RE THE ROYAL FAMILY. WE DESERVE WHAT WE HAVE. THEY'RE JUST JEALOUS.
AND WE'RE NOT JUST JEALOUS!
THE KING SUCKS!

Guilt Part 1

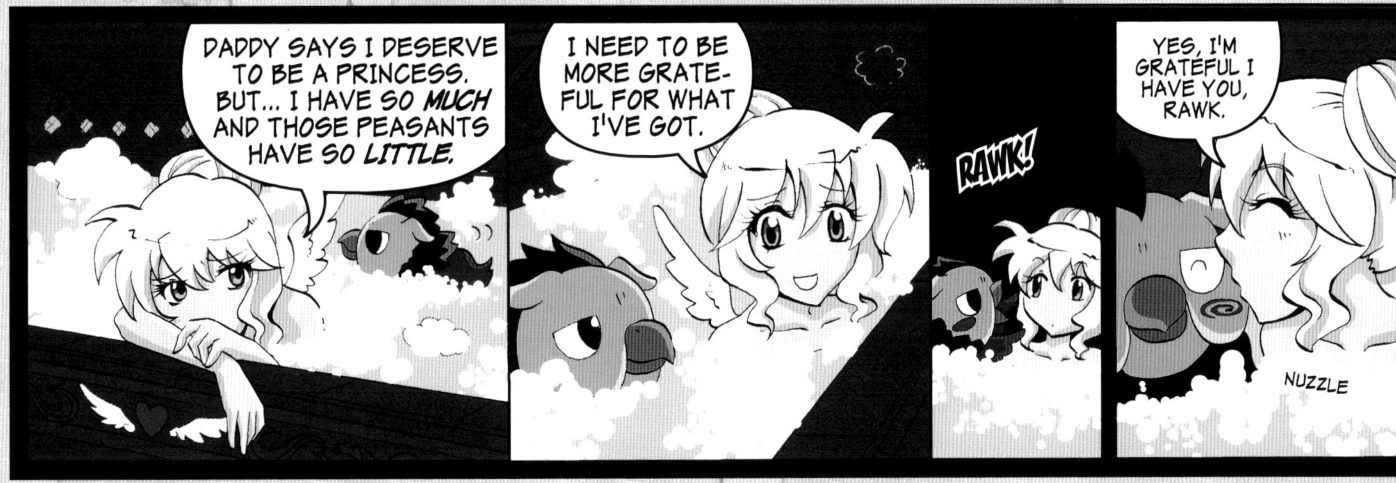
DADDY SAYS I DESERVE TO BE A PRINCESS. BUT... I HAVE SO *MUCH* AND THOSE PEASANTS HAVE SO *LITTLE.*
I NEED TO BE MORE GRATE-FUL FOR WHAT I'VE GOT.
RAWK!
YES, I'M GRATEFUL I HAVE YOU, RAWK.
NUZZLE

Change the World

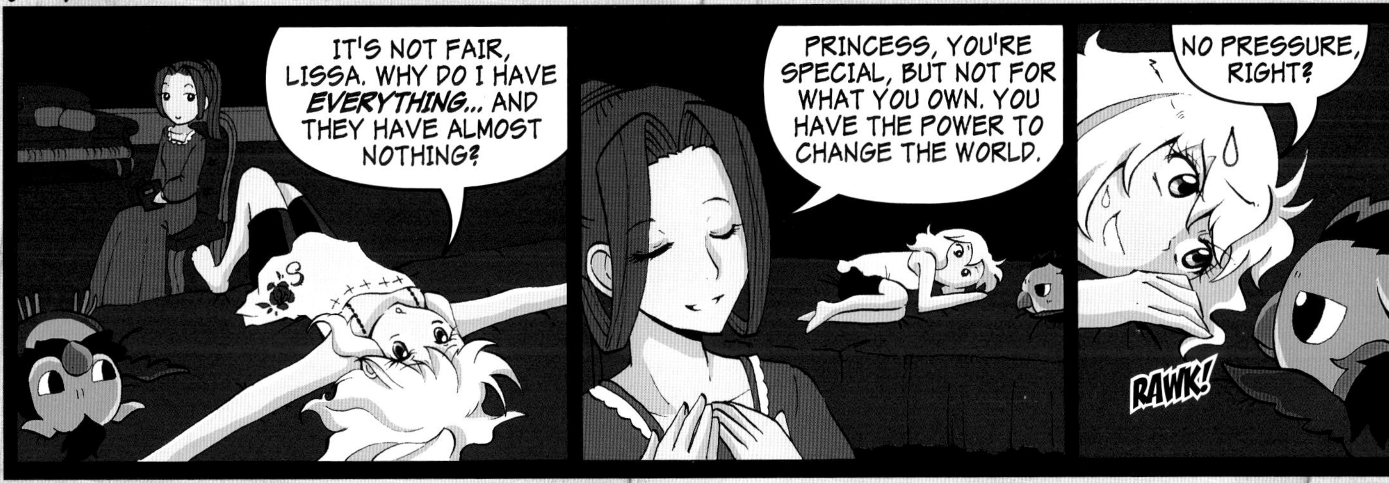
IT'S NOT FAIR, LISSA. WHY DO I HAVE *EVERYTHING...* AND THEY HAVE ALMOST NOTHING?
PRINCESS, YOU'RE SPECIAL, BUT NOT FOR WHAT YOU OWN. YOU HAVE THE POWER TO CHANGE THE WORLD.
NO PRESSURE, RIGHT?
RAWK!

Give Back

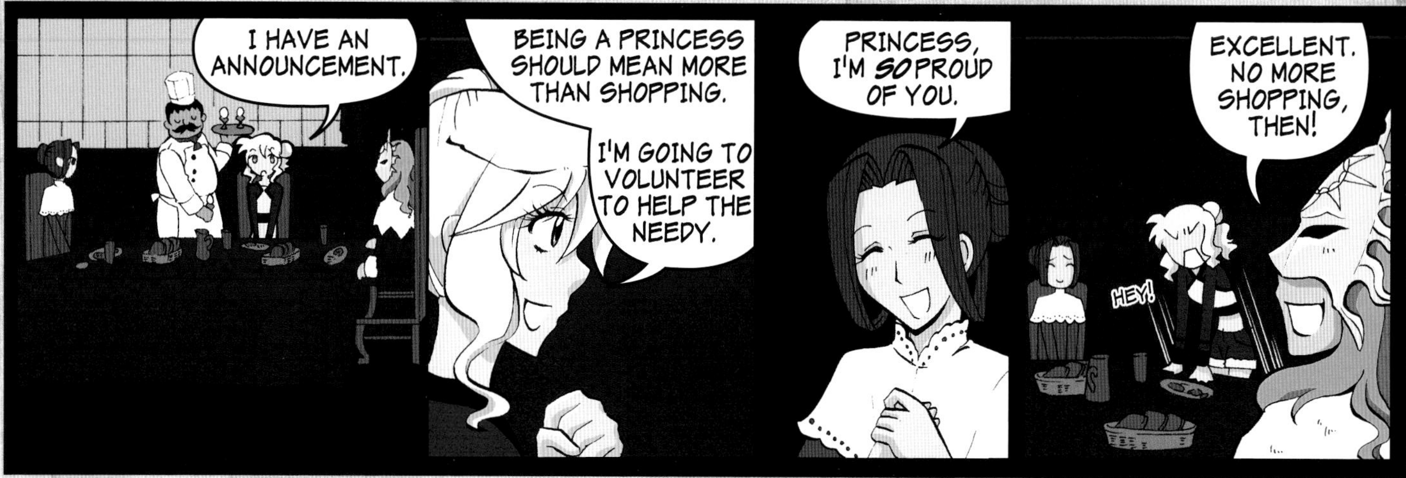

I HAVE AN ANNOUNCEMENT.
BEING A PRINCESS SHOULD MEAN MORE THAN SHOPPING.
I'M GOING TO VOLUNTEER TO HELP THE NEEDY.
PRINCESS, I'M *SO* PROUD OF YOU.
EXCELLENT. NO MORE SHOPPING, THEN!
HEY!

Volunteer

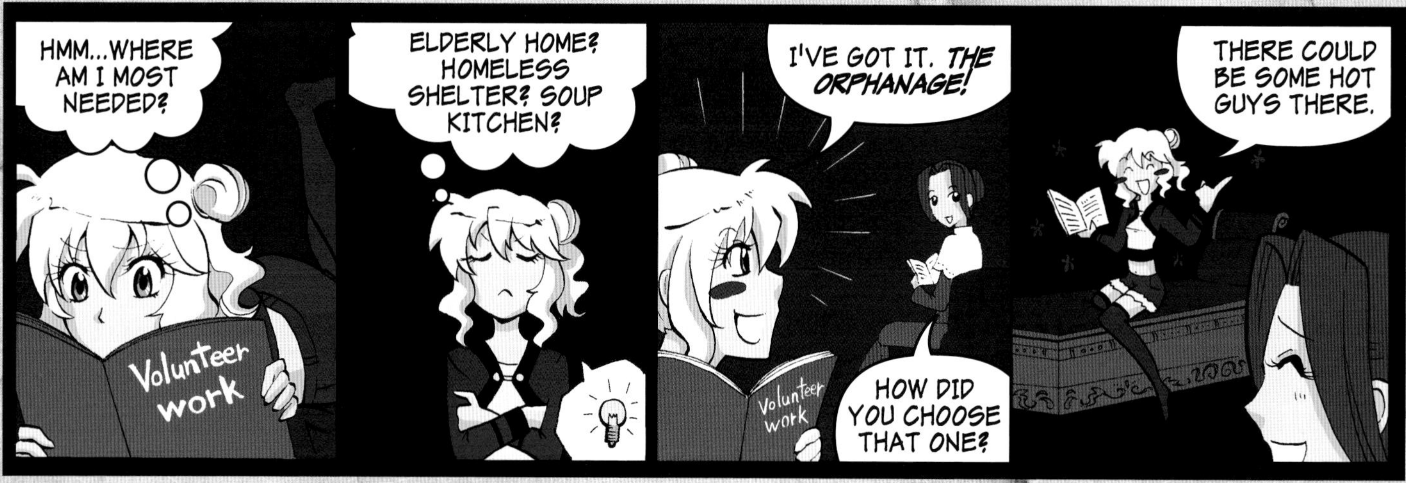

HMM...WHERE AM I MOST NEEDED?
Volunteer work
ELDERLY HOME? HOMELESS SHELTER? SOUP KITCHEN?
I'VE GOT IT. *THE ORPHANAGE!*
Volunteer work
HOW DID YOU CHOOSE THAT ONE?
THERE COULD BE SOME HOT GUYS THERE.

dear d*Ai*ry

I'm excited and nervous about today. It's my first time really venturing out into the "real world" of Ai-Land. As a volunteer at the orphanage, I'll get to give back to the community. Will they accept me? Will they hate me like they seem to hate Daddy? After all...I didn't ask to be born a princess. All I know is that I care about helping out. There's a voice inside of me that won't shut up--it says, "You're not who you think you are!" What if I was born an orphan? Life is fate. But we're all in this together, and I'm 13--old enough to do my share, even if Daddy doesn't like it!

love forever

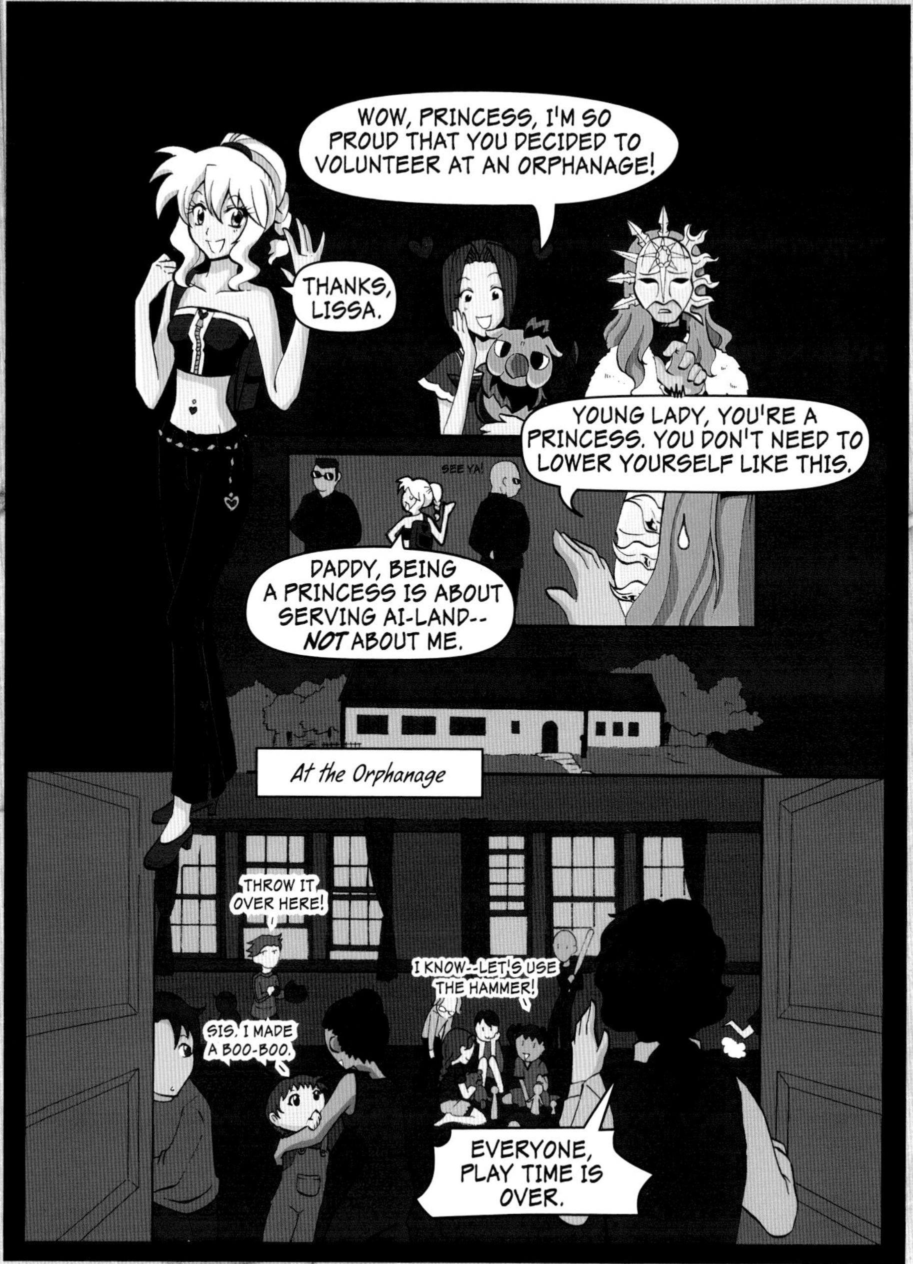
WOW, PRINCESS, I'M SO PROUD THAT YOU DECIDED TO VOLUNTEER AT AN ORPHANAGE!
THANKS, LISSA.
YOUNG LADY, YOU'RE A PRINCESS. YOU DON'T NEED TO LOWER YOURSELF LIKE THIS.
SEE YA!
DADDY, BEING A PRINCESS IS ABOUT SERVING AI-LAND--*NOT* ABOUT ME.
At the Orphanage
THROW IT OVER HERE!
I KNOW--LET'S USE THE HAMMER!
SIS, I MADE A BOO-BOO.
EVERYONE, PLAY TIME IS OVER.

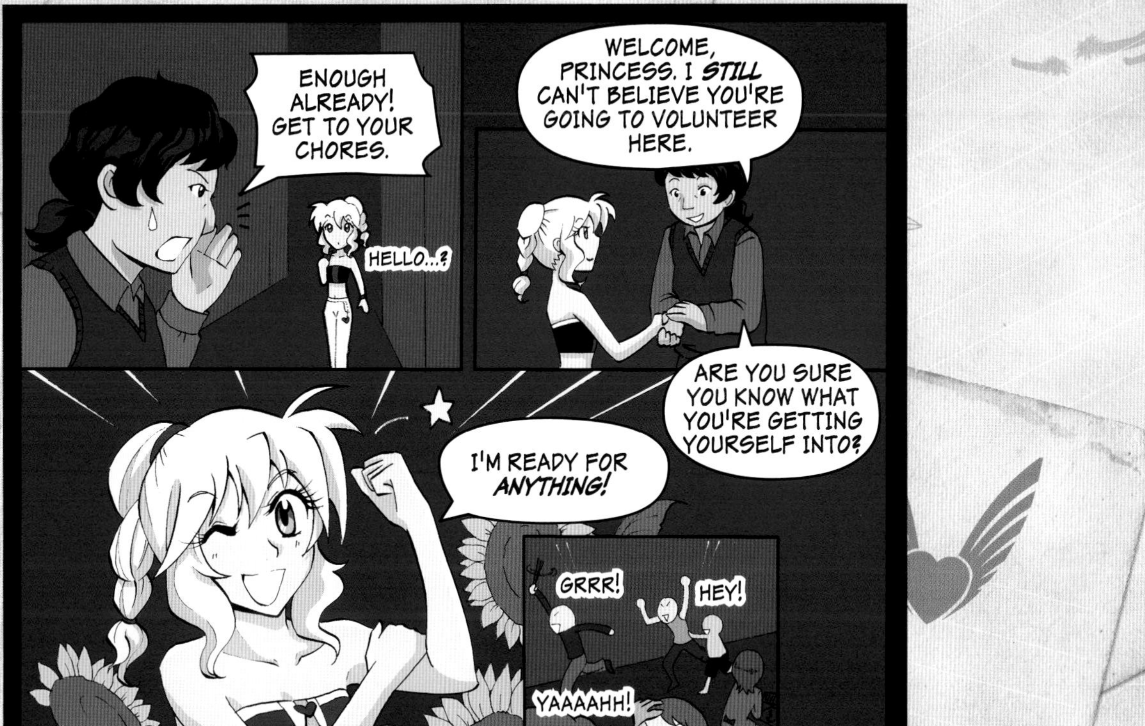
ENOUGH ALREADY! GET TO YOUR CHORES.
HELLO...?
WELCOME, PRINCESS. I *STILL* CAN'T BELIEVE YOU'RE GOING TO VOLUNTEER HERE.
ARE YOU SURE YOU KNOW WHAT YOU'RE GETTING YOURSELF INTO?
I'M READY FOR *ANYTHING!*
GRRR!
HEY!
YAAAAHH!
ANYTHING?
UH-OH.

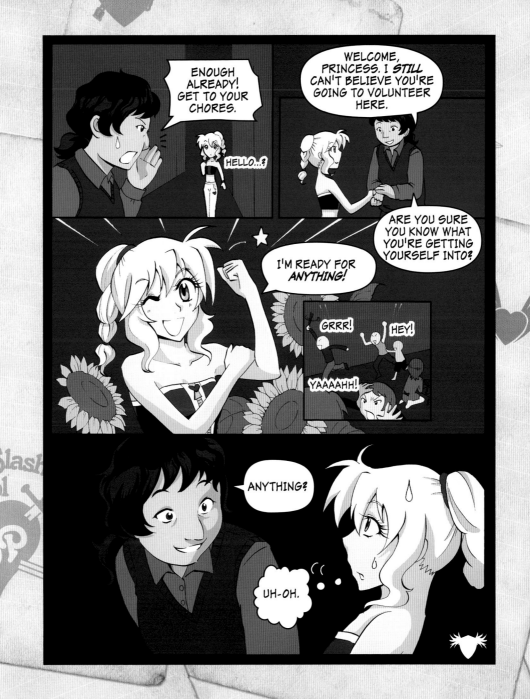

No Pool?

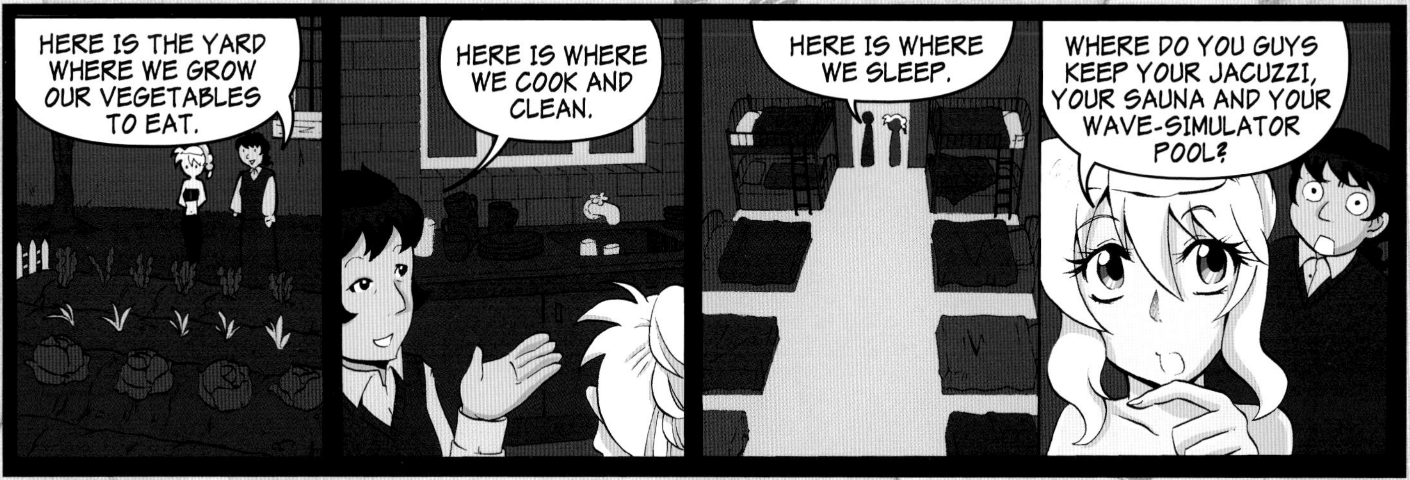
HERE IS THE YARD WHERE WE GROW OUR VEGETABLES TO EAT.
HERE IS WHERE WE COOK AND CLEAN.
HERE IS WHERE WE SLEEP.
WHERE DO YOU GUYS KEEP YOUR JACUZZI, YOUR SAUNA AND YOUR WAVE-SIMULATOR POOL?

Introductions

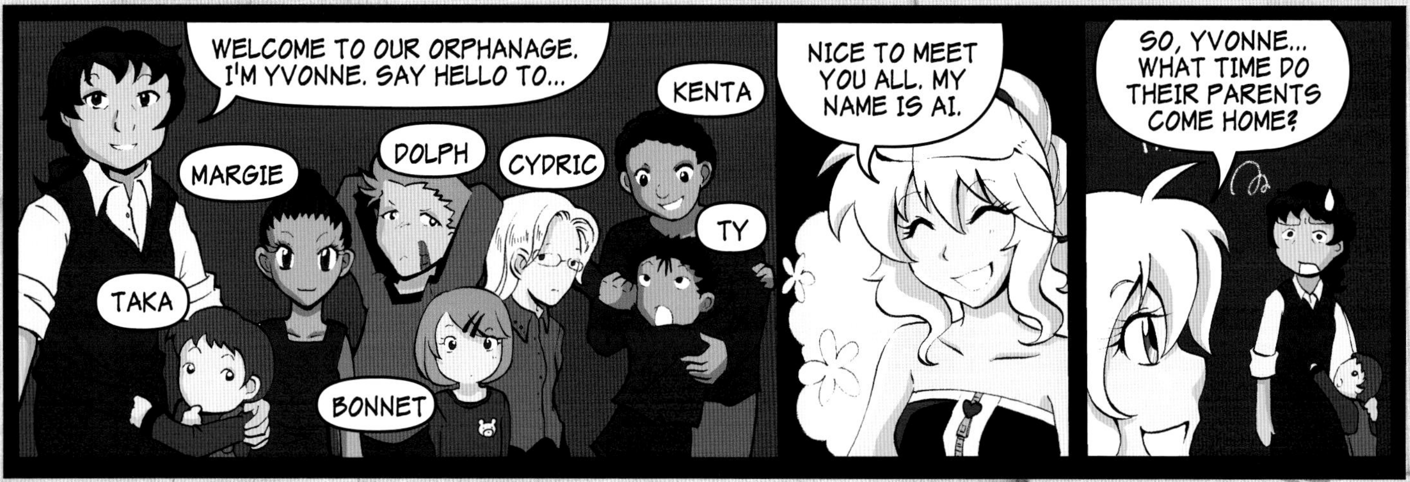
WELCOME TO OUR ORPHANAGE. I'M YVONNE. SAY HELLO TO...
MARGIE
DOLPH
CYDRIC
KENTA
TY
TAKA
BONNET
NICE TO MEET YOU ALL. MY NAME IS AI.
SO, YVONNE... WHAT TIME DO THEIR PARENTS COME HOME?

Each Has Their Story

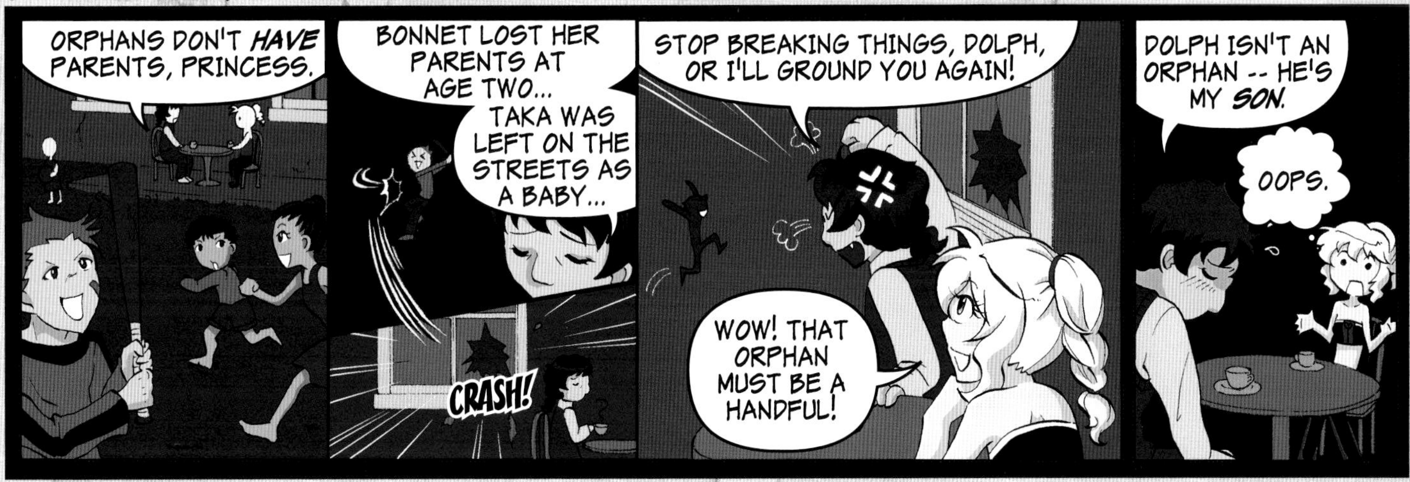
ORPHANS DON'T *HAVE* PARENTS, PRINCESS.
BONNET LOST HER PARENTS AT AGE TWO...
TAKA WAS LEFT ON THE STREETS AS A BABY...
CRASH!
STOP BREAKING THINGS, DOLPH, OR I'LL GROUND YOU AGAIN!
WOW! THAT ORPHAN MUST BE A HANDFUL!
DOLPH ISN'T AN ORPHAN -- HE'S MY ***SON***.
OOPS.

Veggies

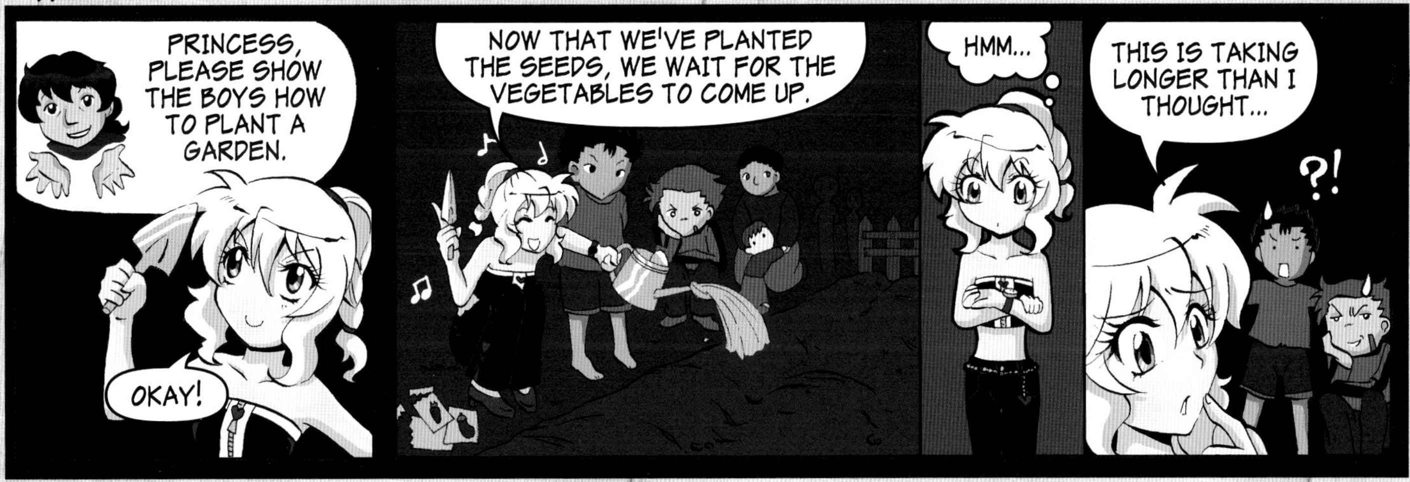
PRINCESS, PLEASE SHOW THE BOYS HOW TO PLANT A GARDEN.
OKAY!
NOW THAT WE'VE PLANTED THE SEEDS, WE WAIT FOR THE VEGETABLES TO COME UP.
HMM...
THIS IS TAKING LONGER THAN I THOUGHT...
?!

Clothes

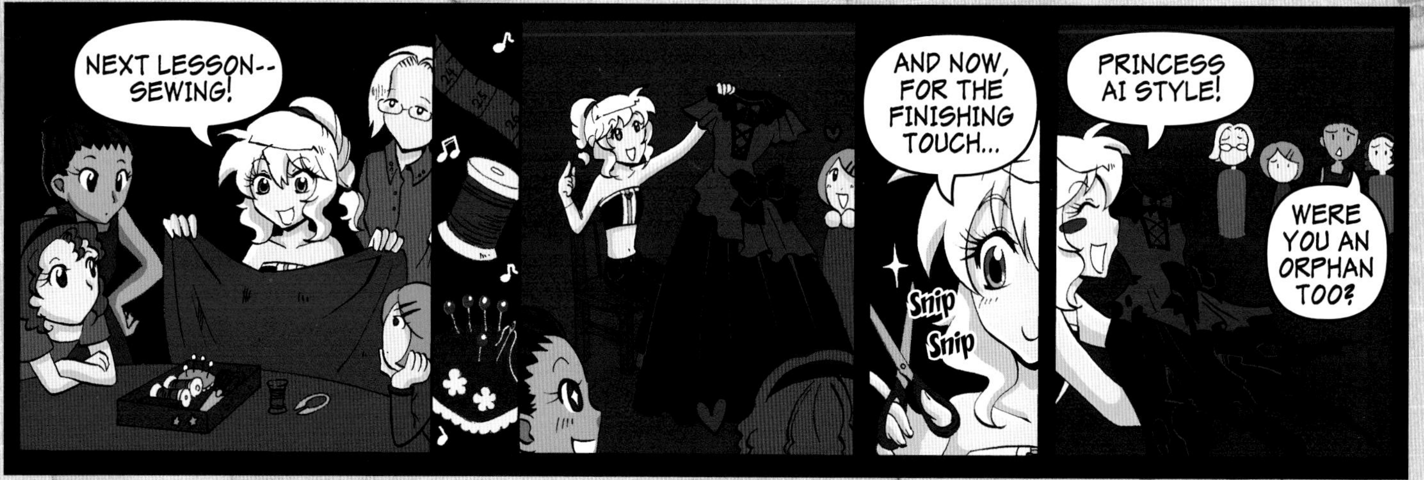
NEXT LESSON--SEWING!
AND NOW, FOR THE FINISHING TOUCH...
Snip
Snip
PRINCESS AI STYLE!
WERE YOU AN ORPHAN TOO?

Cooking

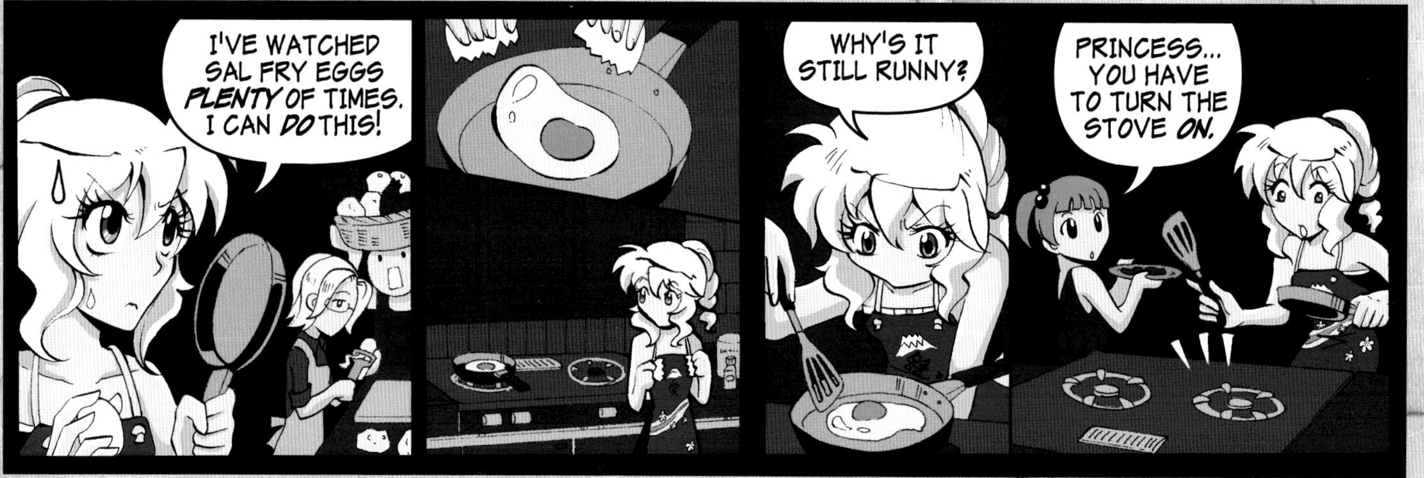
I'VE WATCHED SAL FRY EGGS *PLENTY* OF TIMES. I CAN *DO* THIS!
WHY'S IT STILL RUNNY?
PRINCESS... YOU HAVE TO TURN THE STOVE *ON.*

dear dAiry

Wow--what an amazing experience! Yvonne and the kids at the orphanage are so special-- I've never felt so appreciated, like someone truly needs me. It's not like that at the castle with Daddy and everyone. Sure, it's nice to be spoiled, but today I felt for the first time like I earned my dinner. Yard work, cooking, cleaning, sewing, teaching, babysitting--what a handful! Growing up without parents is very sad, but it makes me happy to see the orphans' love for each other.

love forever

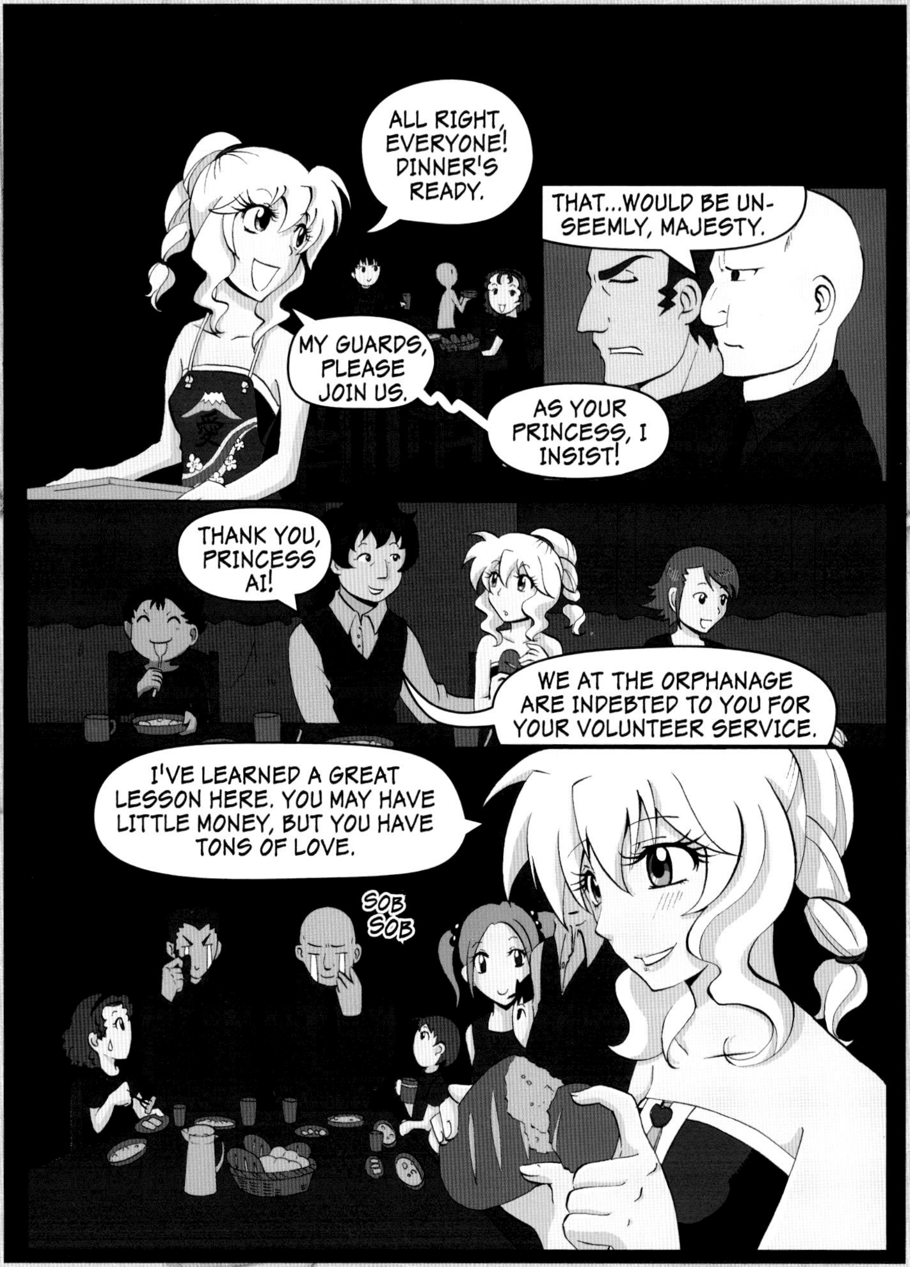
ALL RIGHT, EVERYONE! DINNER'S READY.
MY GUARDS, PLEASE JOIN US.
AS YOUR PRINCESS, I INSIST!
THAT...WOULD BE UN-SEEMLY, MAJESTY.
THANK YOU, PRINCESS AI!
WE AT THE ORPHANAGE ARE INDEBTED TO YOU FOR YOUR VOLUNTEER SERVICE.
I'VE LEARNED A GREAT LESSON HERE. YOU MAY HAVE LITTLE MONEY, BUT YOU HAVE TONS OF LOVE.
SOB SOB

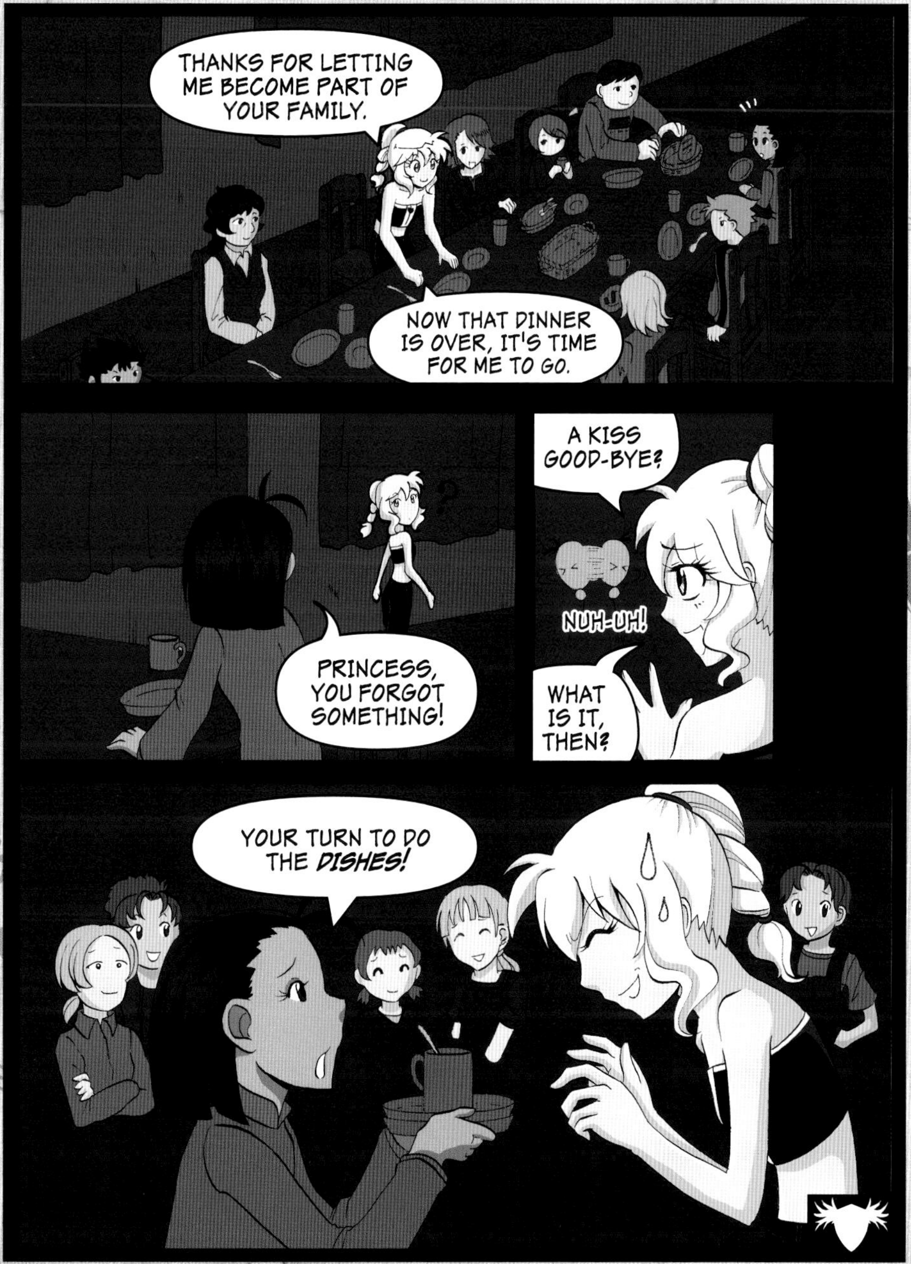
THANKS FOR LETTING ME BECOME PART OF YOUR FAMILY.
NOW THAT DINNER IS OVER, IT'S TIME FOR ME TO GO.
PRINCESS, YOU FORGOT SOMETHING!
A KISS GOOD-BYE?
NUH-UH!
WHAT IS IT, THEN?
YOUR TURN TO DO THE *DISHES!*

Kids Running Around

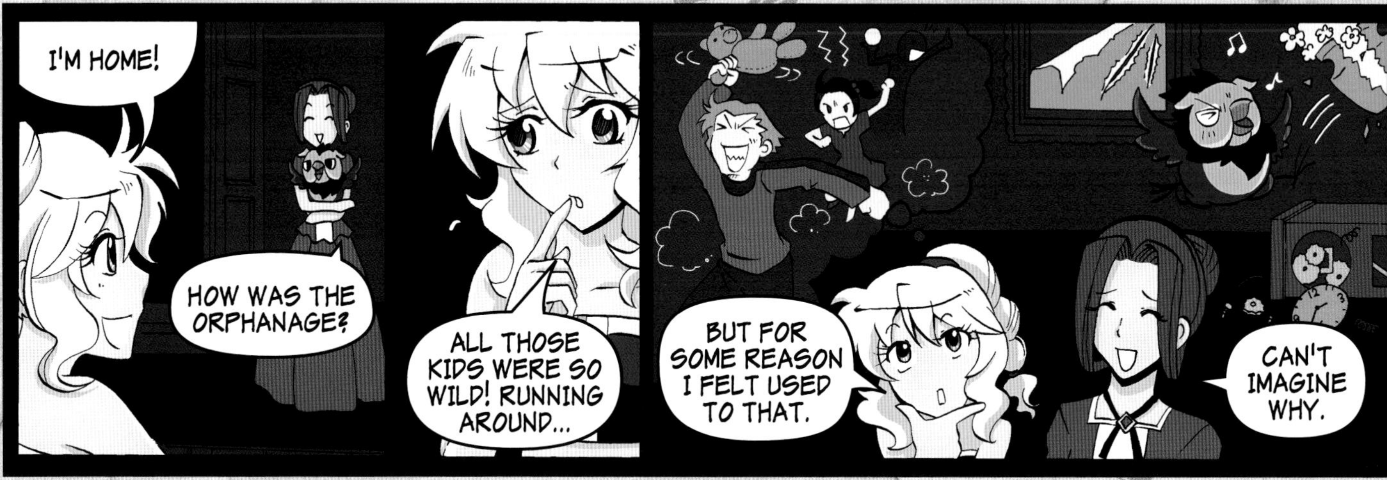
I'M HOME!
HOW WAS THE ORPHANAGE?
ALL THOSE KIDS WERE SO WILD! RUNNING AROUND...
BUT FOR SOME REASON I FELT USED TO THAT.
CAN'T IMAGINE WHY.

Hungry?

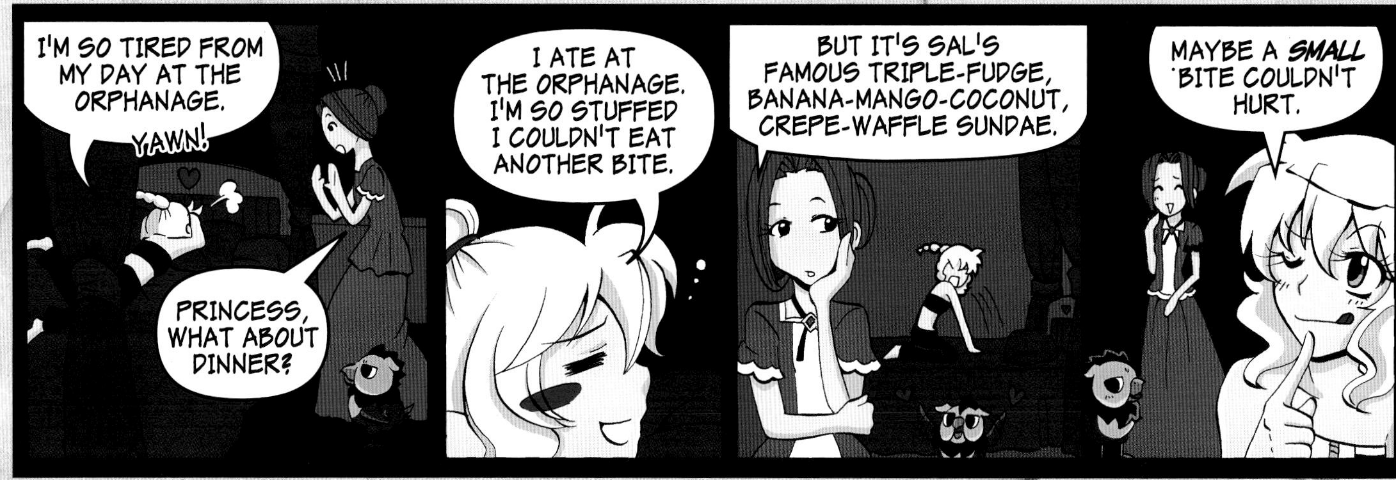
I'M SO TIRED FROM MY DAY AT THE ORPHANAGE.
YAWN!
PRINCESS, WHAT ABOUT DINNER?
I ATE AT THE ORPHANAGE. I'M SO STUFFED I COULDN'T EAT ANOTHER BITE.
BUT IT'S SAL'S FAMOUS TRIPLE-FUDGE, BANANA-MANGO-COCONUT, CREPE-WAFFLE SUNDAE.
MAYBE A SMALL BITE COULDN'T HURT.

Grease

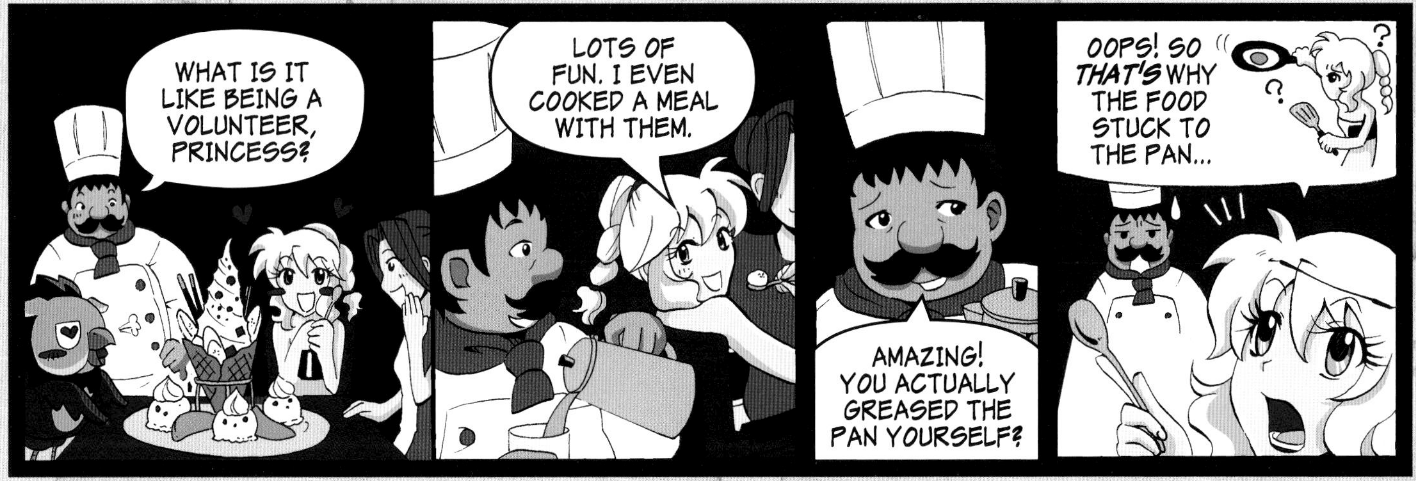
WHAT IS IT LIKE BEING A VOLUNTEER, PRINCESS?
LOTS OF FUN. I EVEN COOKED A MEAL WITH THEM.
AMAZING! YOU ACTUALLY GREASED THE PAN YOURSELF?
OOPS! SO *THAT'S* WHY THE FOOD STUCK TO THE PAN...

Lucky Friendships

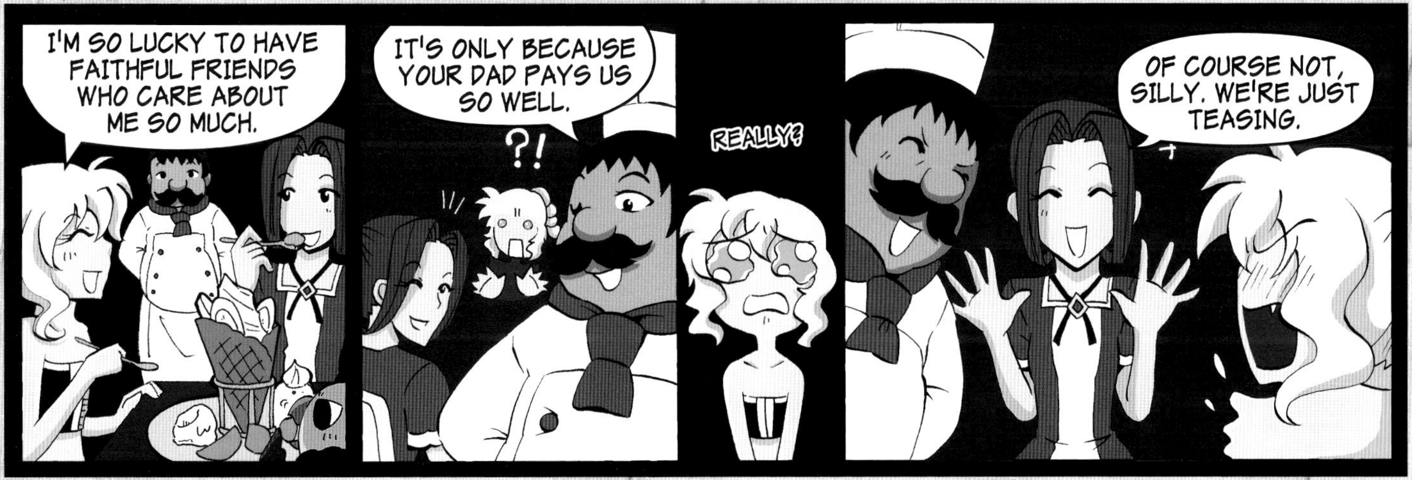
I'M SO LUCKY TO HAVE FAITHFUL FRIENDS WHO CARE ABOUT ME SO MUCH.
IT'S ONLY BECAUSE YOUR DAD PAYS US SO WELL.
?!
REALLY?
OF COURSE NOT, SILLY. WE'RE JUST TEASING.

No One Compares

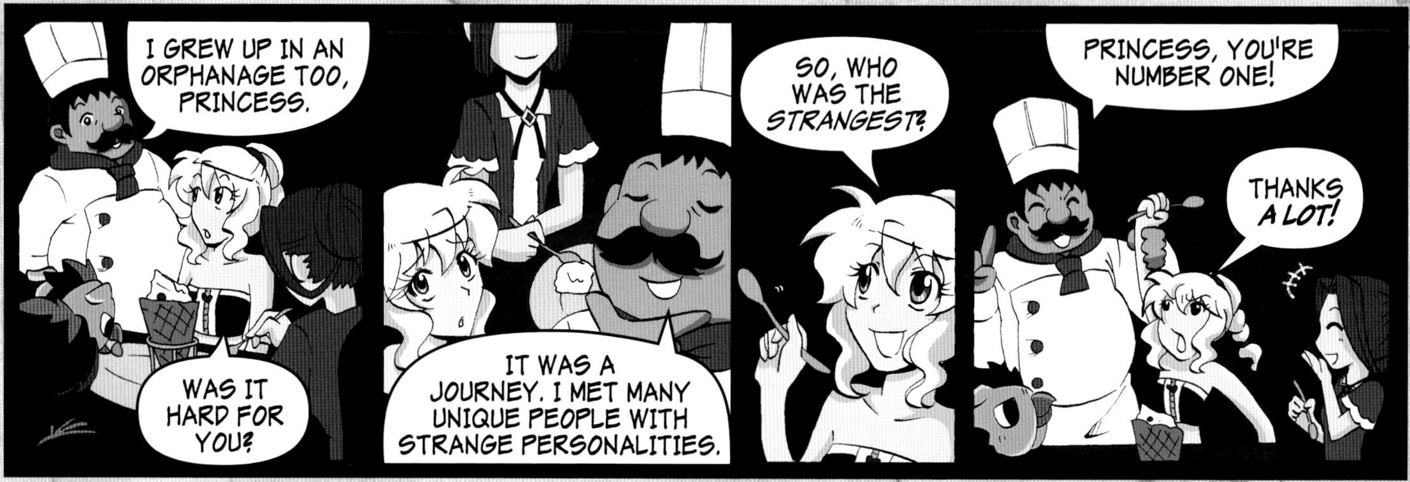

I GREW UP IN AN ORPHANAGE TOO, PRINCESS.
WAS IT HARD FOR YOU?
IT WAS A JOURNEY. I MET MANY UNIQUE PEOPLE WITH STRANGE PERSONALITIES.
SO, WHO WAS THE *STRANGEST*?
PRINCESS, YOU'RE NUMBER ONE!
THANKS *A LOT!*

Rawk & the Sundae

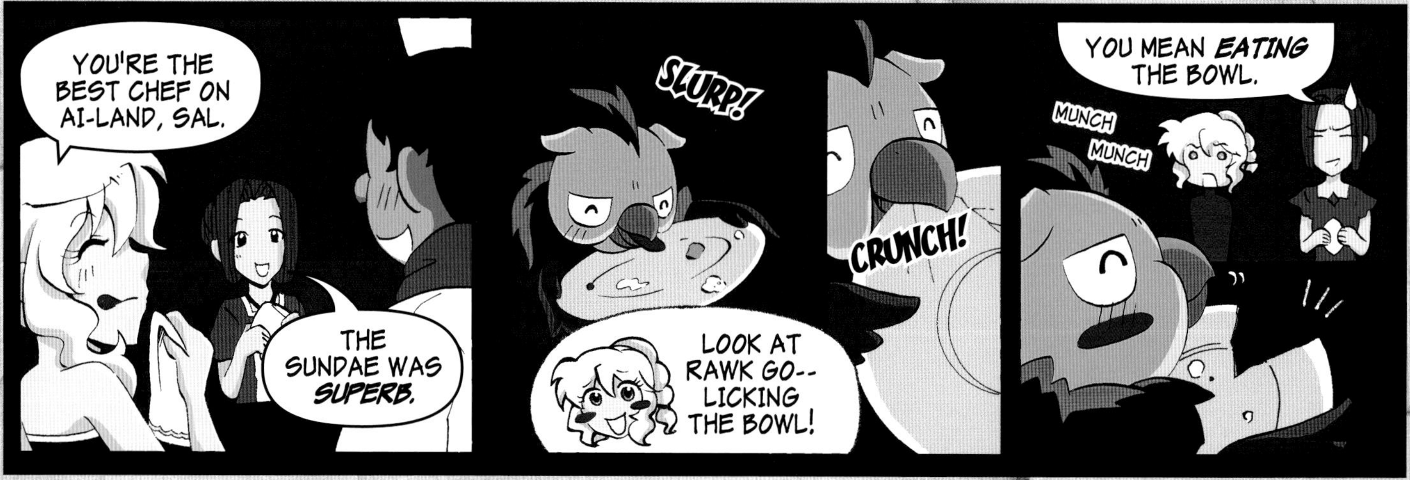

YOU'RE THE BEST CHEF ON AI-LAND, SAL.
THE SUNDAE WAS *SUPERB.*
SLURP!
LOOK AT RAWK GO-- LICKING THE BOWL!
CRUNCH!
YOU MEAN *EATING* THE BOWL.
MUNCH
MUNCH

dear d**Ai**ry

Okay, I admit it--most of the time, castle life drives me nuts, but every now and then, even I enjoy it. And Sal's one of those guys who knows how to make my tedious boredom just a tad more bearable. He's so lovable and cute! Oh yeah, Rawk, too! Daddy also makes me laugh sometimes, even if he doesn't know it. And Lissa's so adorable. You know what? With people I love around me, maybe life's not that bad after all.

love forever

Ai

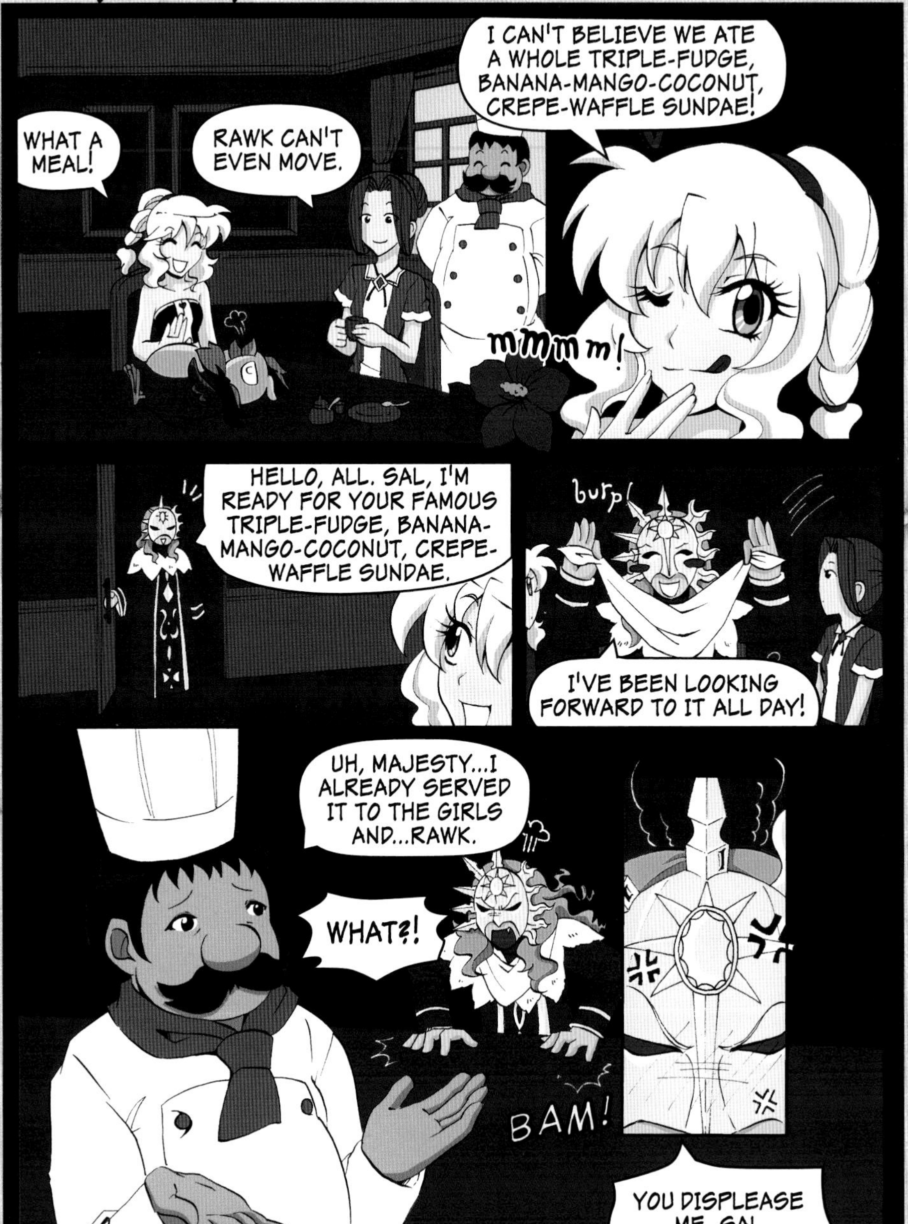
WHAT A MEAL!
RAWK CAN'T EVEN MOVE.
I CAN'T BELIEVE WE ATE A WHOLE TRIPLE-FUDGE, BANANA-MANGO-COCONUT, CREPE-WAFFLE SUNDAE!
MMMMM!
HELLO, ALL. SAL, I'M READY FOR YOUR FAMOUS TRIPLE-FUDGE, BANANA-MANGO-COCONUT, CREPE-WAFFLE SUNDAE.
burp!
I'VE BEEN LOOKING FORWARD TO IT ALL DAY!
UH, MAJESTY...I ALREADY SERVED IT TO THE GIRLS AND...RAWK.
WHAT?!
BAM!
YOU DISPLEASE ME, SAL.

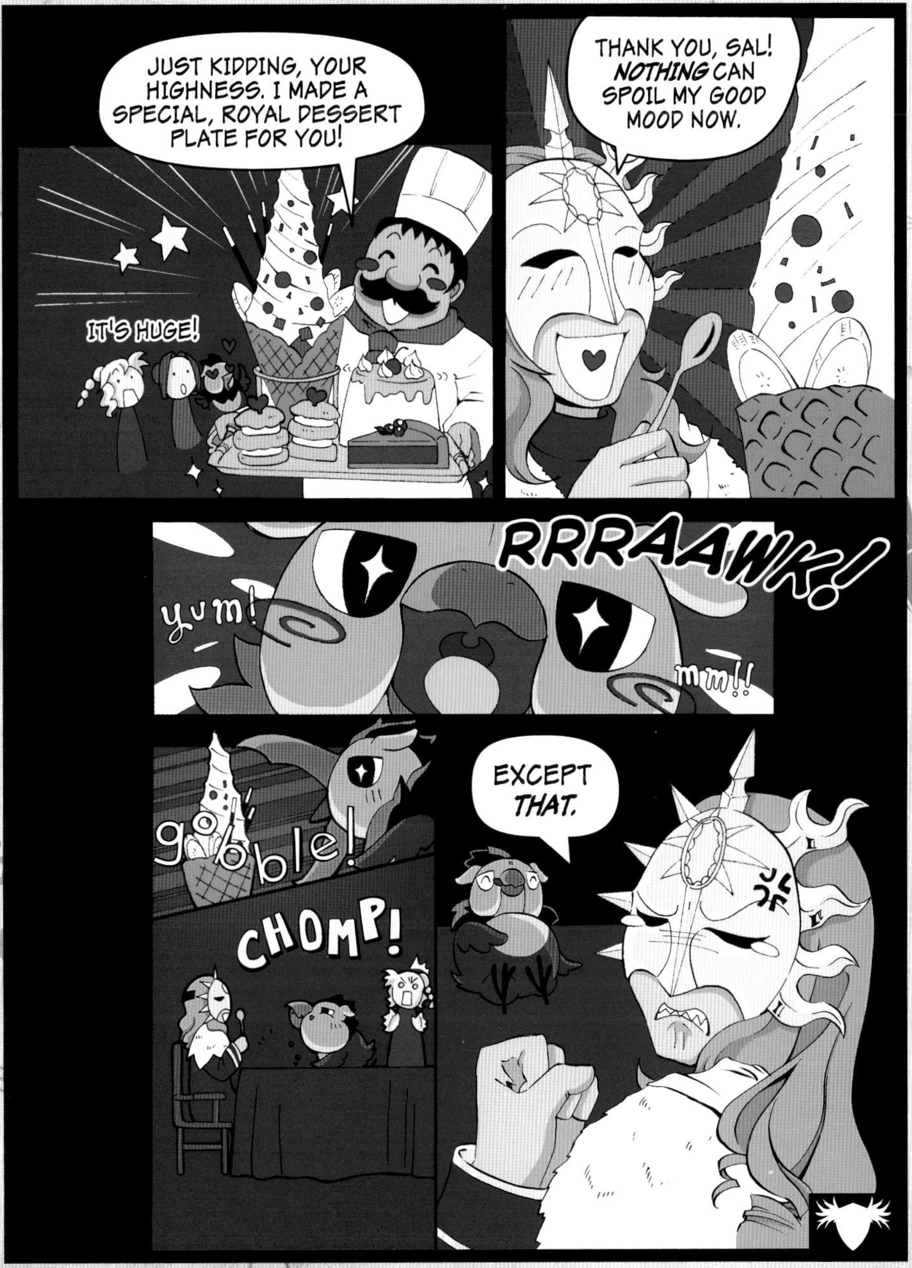
JUST KIDDING, YOUR HIGHNESS. I MADE A SPECIAL, ROYAL DESSERT PLATE FOR YOU!
IT'S HUGE!
THANK YOU, SAL! *NOTHING* CAN SPOIL MY GOOD MOOD NOW.
yum!
RRRAAWK!
mm!!
gobble!
CHOMP!
EXCEPT *THAT.*

Fall

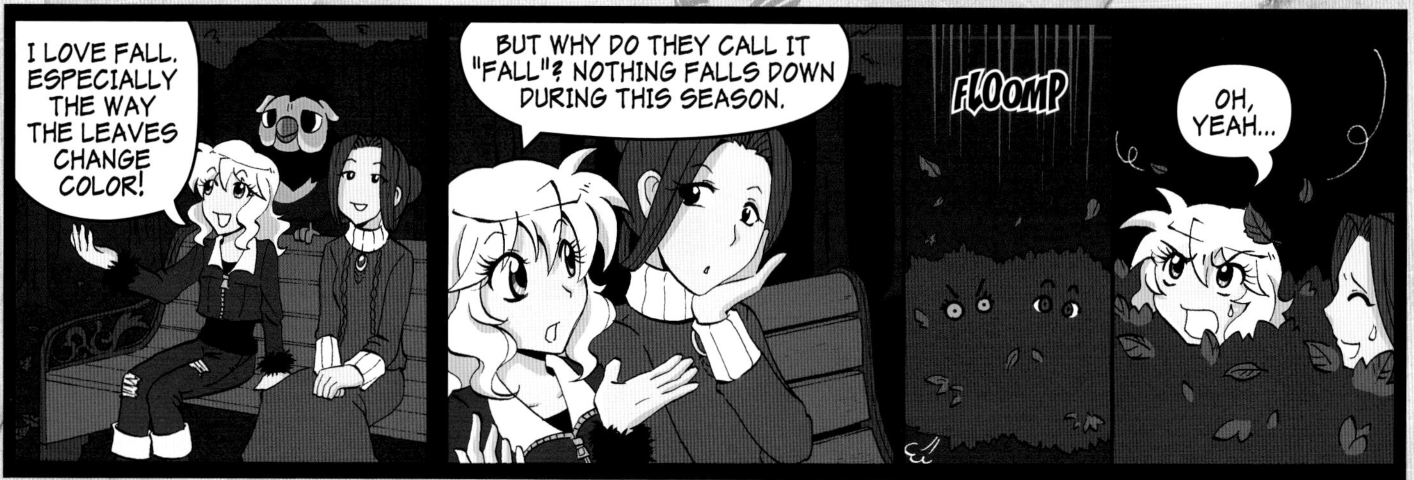
I LOVE FALL. ESPECIALLY THE WAY THE LEAVES CHANGE COLOR!
BUT WHY DO THEY CALL IT "FALL"? NOTHING FALLS DOWN DURING THIS SEASON.
FLOOMP
OH, YEAH...

Show-Off

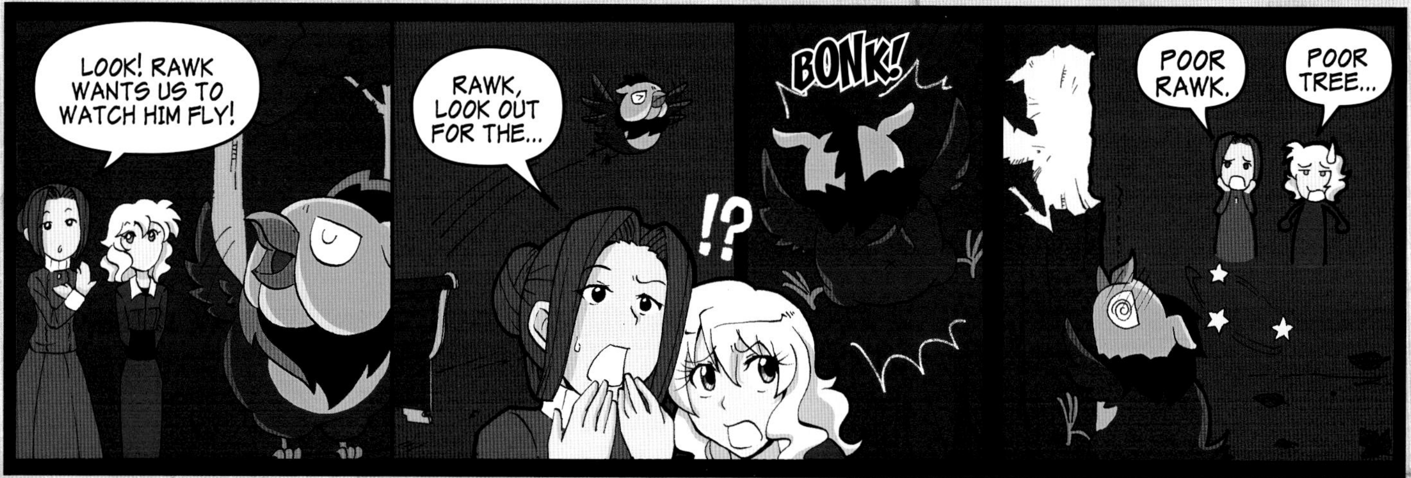
LOOK! RAWK WANTS US TO WATCH HIM FLY!
RAWK, LOOK OUT FOR THE...
!?
BONK!
POOR RAWK.
POOR TREE...

Scary Squirrel

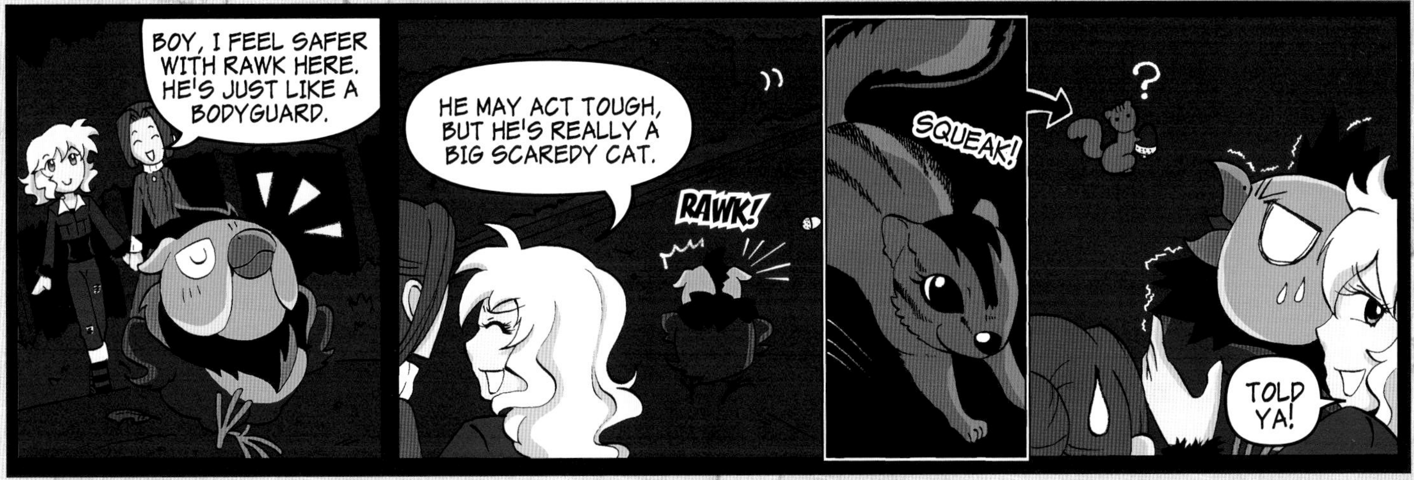
BOY, I FEEL SAFER WITH RAWK HERE. HE'S JUST LIKE A BODYGUARD.
HE MAY ACT TOUGH, BUT HE'S REALLY A BIG SCAREDY CAT.
RAWK!
SQUEAK!
?
TOLD YA!

Axe to Grind

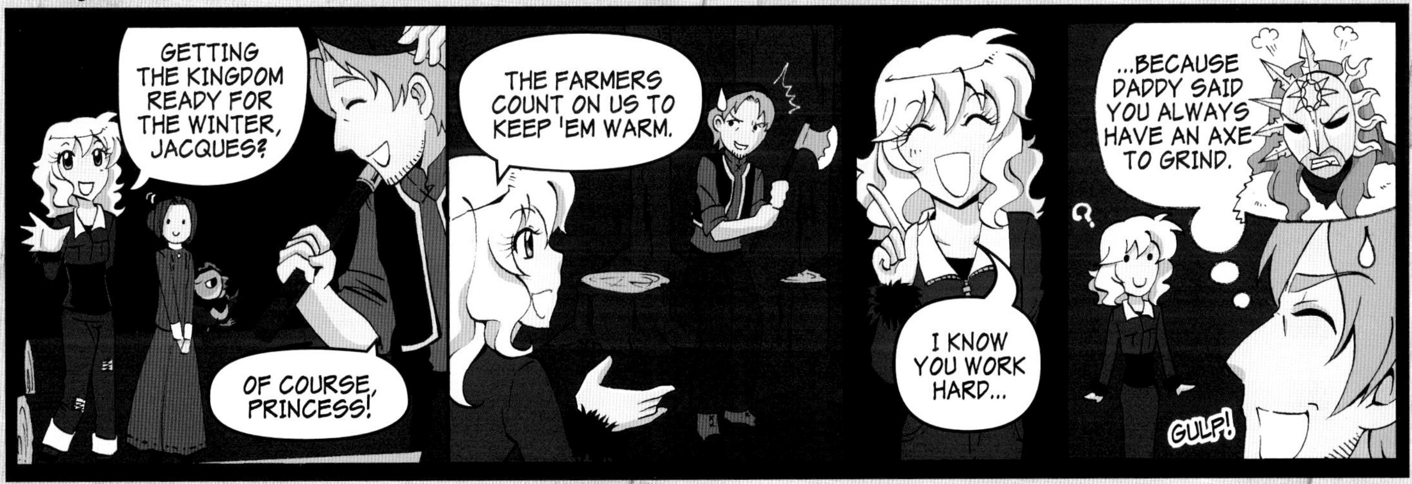
GETTING THE KINGDOM READY FOR THE WINTER, JACQUES?
OF COURSE, PRINCESS!
THE FARMERS COUNT ON US TO KEEP 'EM WARM.
I KNOW YOU WORK HARD...
...BECAUSE DADDY SAID YOU ALWAYS HAVE AN AXE TO GRIND.
?
GULP!

Mushrooms

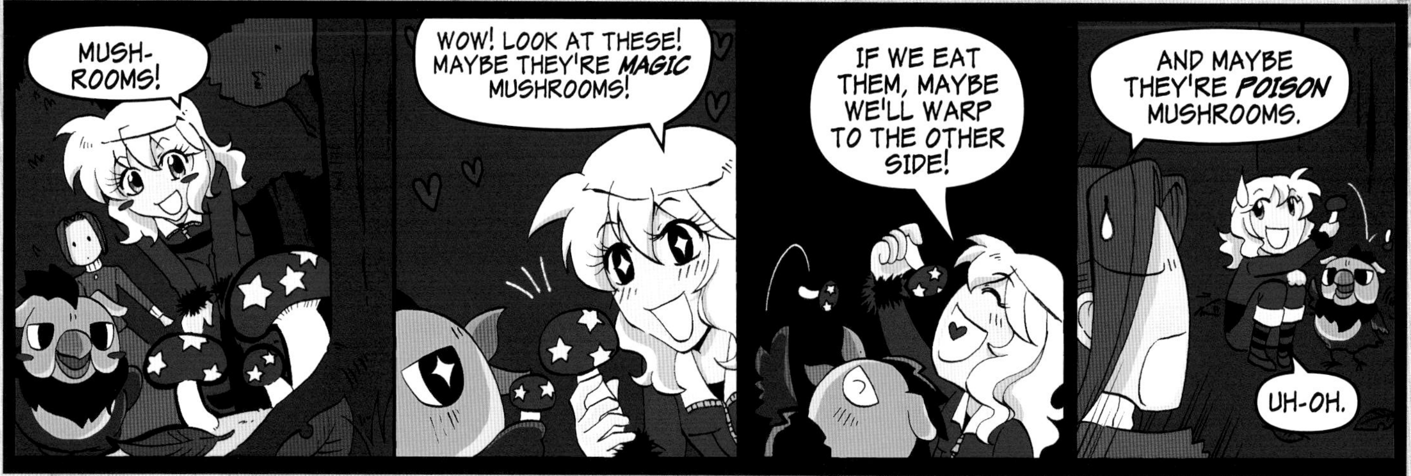
MUSH-ROOMS!
WOW! LOOK AT THESE! MAYBE THEY'RE MAGIC MUSHROOMS!
IF WE EAT THEM, MAYBE WE'LL WARP TO THE OTHER SIDE!
AND MAYBE THEY'RE POISON MUSHROOMS.
UH-OH.

Turtleneck

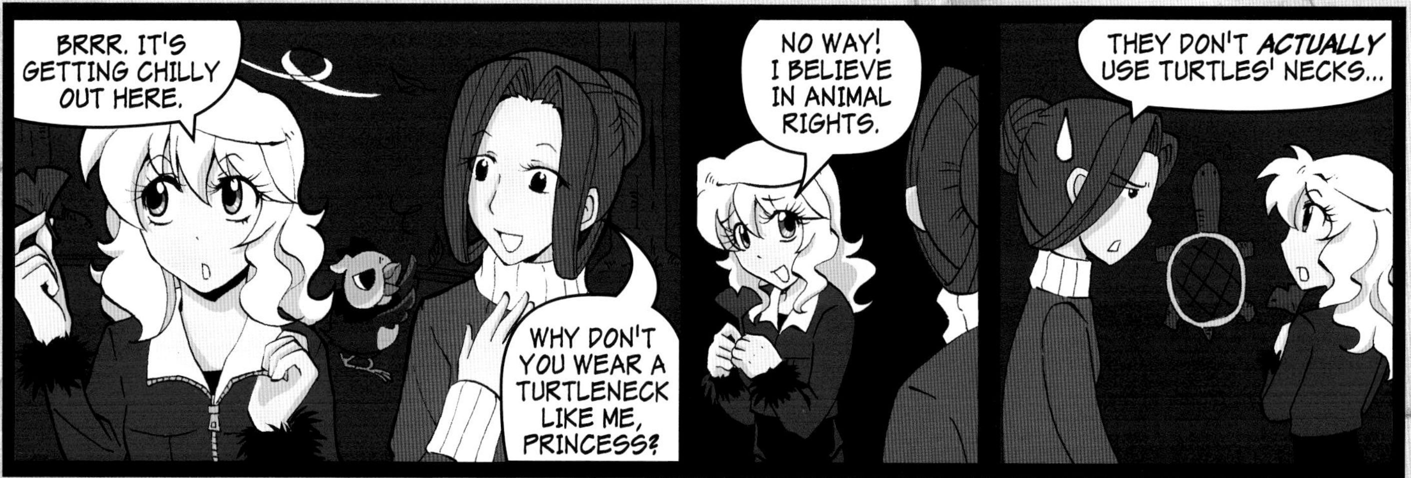
BRRR. IT'S GETTING CHILLY OUT HERE.
WHY DON'T YOU WEAR A TURTLENECK LIKE ME, PRINCESS?
NO WAY! I BELIEVE IN ANIMAL RIGHTS.
THEY DON'T ACTUALLY USE TURTLES' NECKS...

dear d**Ai**ry

There's something about autumn--the brisk air on my face, the brown, red and orange leaves on the trees and ground-- something in the air feels both sad and exciting. It's a nice time to get outside and go for a walk. Summer's over, which of course is a bummer, but maybe this next year, something exciting will finally happen. Even though castle life can be sooo boring, Lissa and I always scheme up some sort of trouble.

love forever

 **Ai**

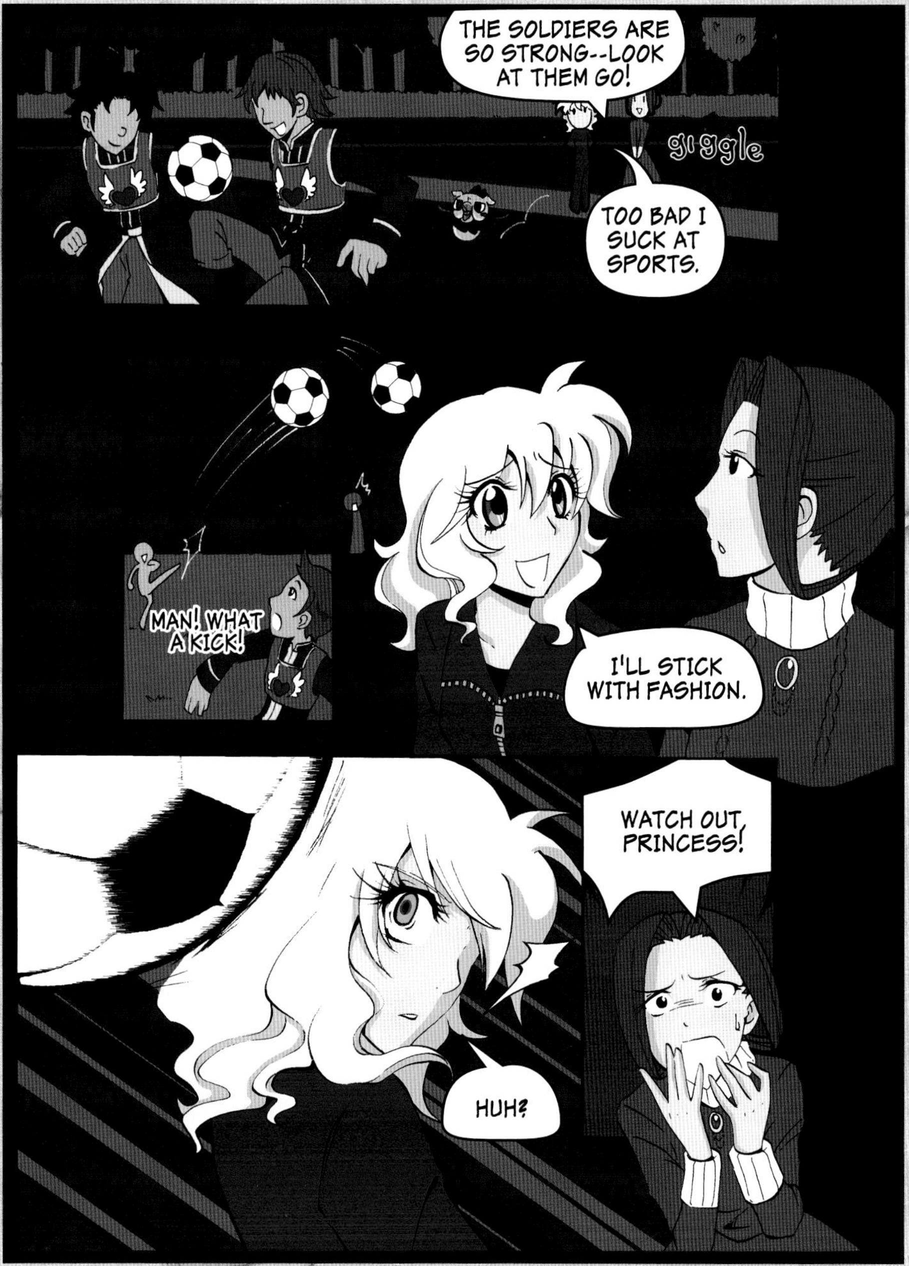
THE SOLDIERS ARE SO STRONG--LOOK AT THEM GO!
giggle
TOO BAD I SUCK AT SPORTS.
MAN! WHAT A KICK!
I'LL STICK WITH FASHION.
HUH?
WATCH OUT, PRINCESS!

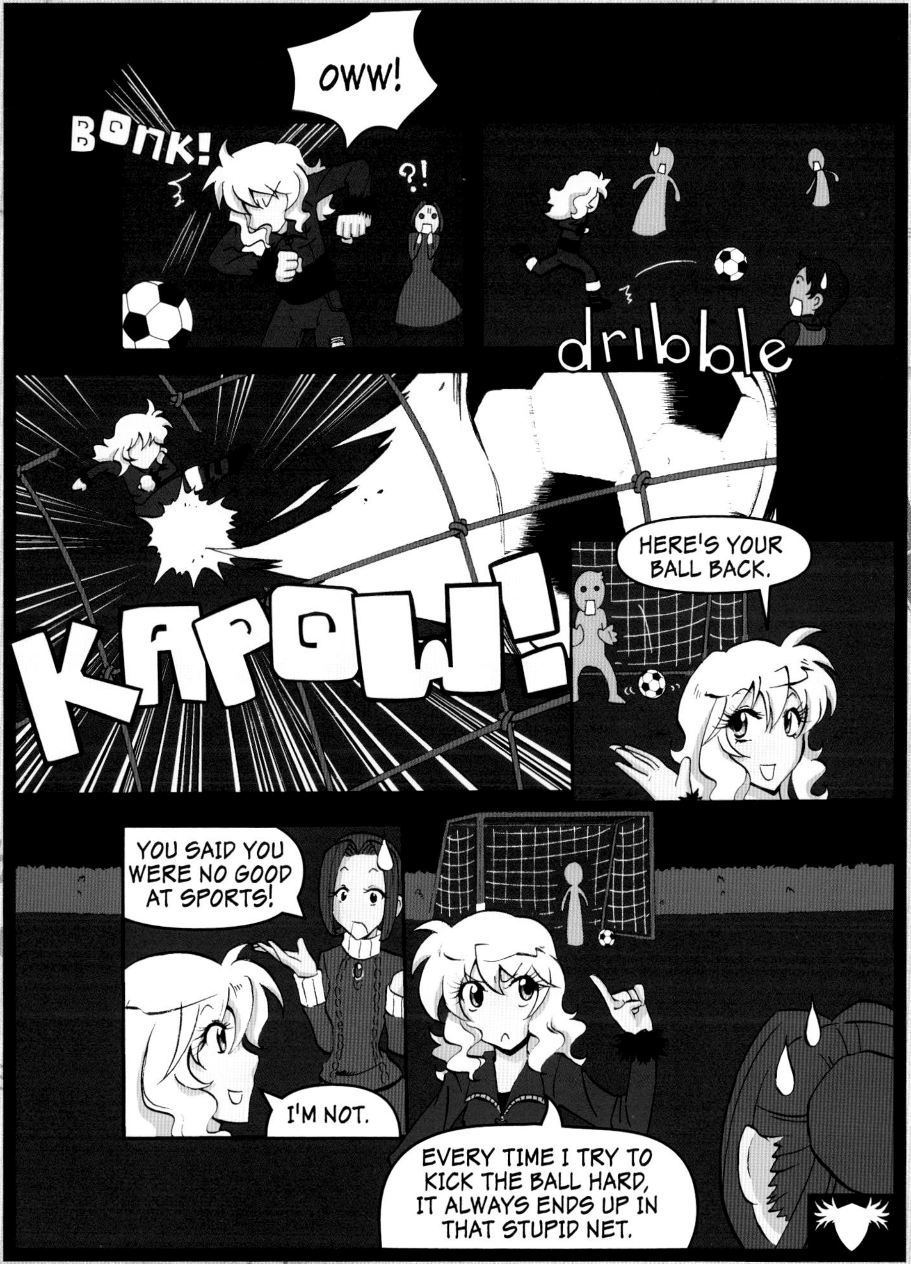
BONK!
OWW!
?!
dribble
KAPOW!
HERE'S YOUR BALL BACK.
YOU SAID YOU WERE NO GOOD AT SPORTS!
I'M NOT.
EVERY TIME I TRY TO KICK THE BALL HARD, IT ALWAYS ENDS UP IN THAT STUPID NET.

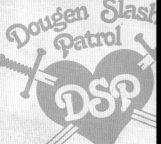

Cut my Dress

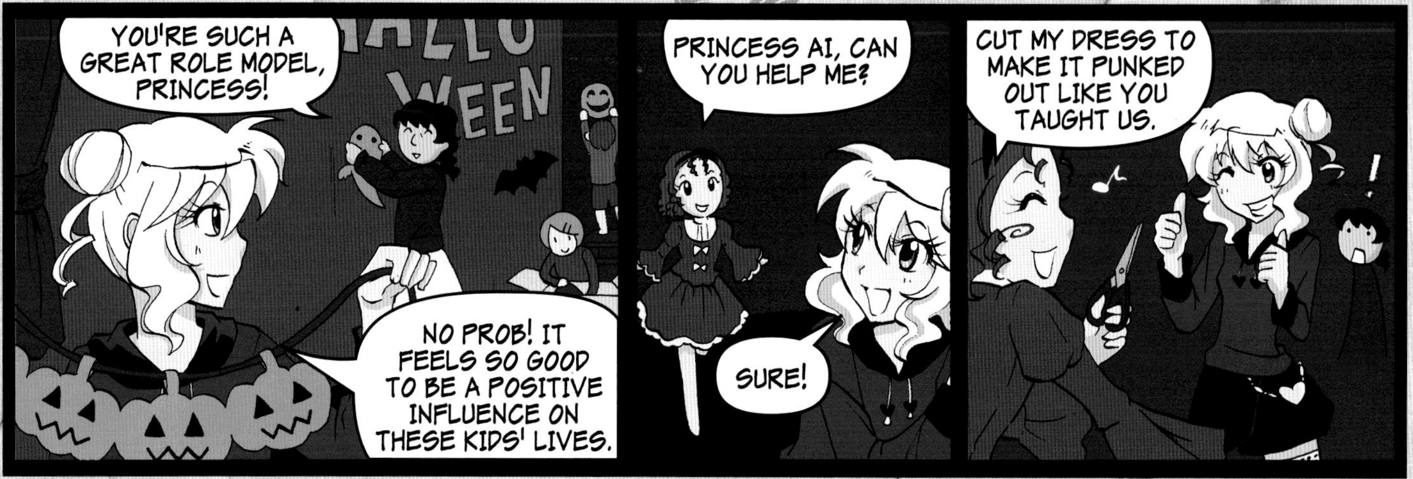
YOU'RE SUCH A GREAT ROLE MODEL, PRINCESS!
NO PROB! IT FEELS SO GOOD TO BE A POSITIVE INFLUENCE ON THESE KIDS' LIVES.
PRINCESS AI, CAN YOU HELP ME?
SURE!
CUT MY DRESS TO MAKE IT PUNKED OUT LIKE YOU TAUGHT US.

Hello-ween

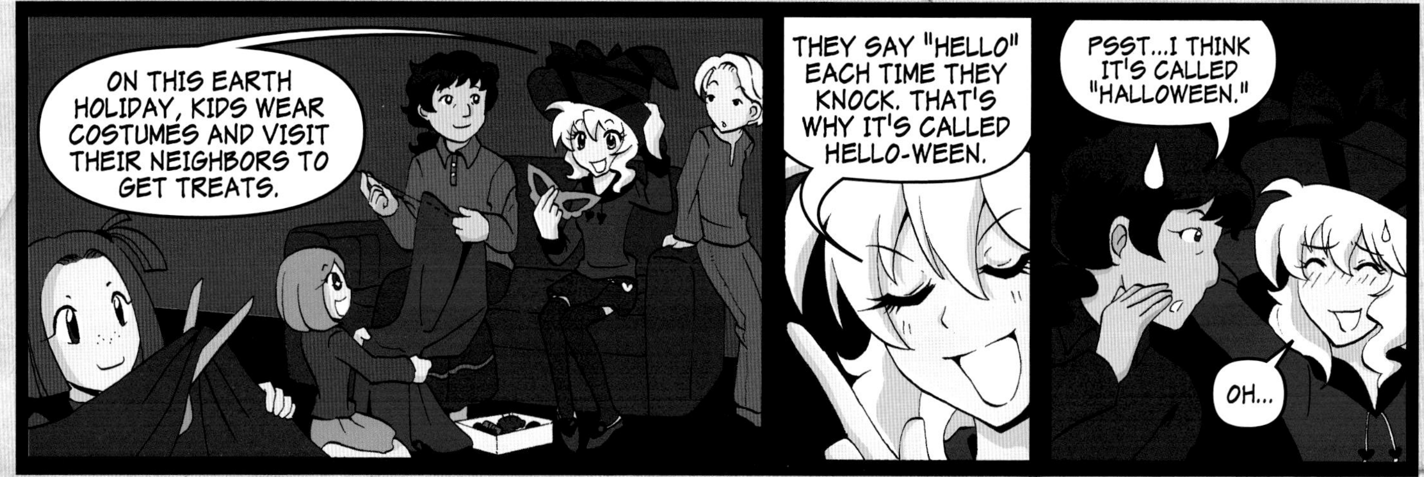
ON THIS EARTH HOLIDAY, KIDS WEAR COSTUMES AND VISIT THEIR NEIGHBORS TO GET TREATS.
THEY SAY "HELLO" EACH TIME THEY KNOCK. THAT'S WHY IT'S CALLED HELLO-WEEN.
PSST...I THINK IT'S CALLED "HALLOWEEN."
OH...

Pumpkins

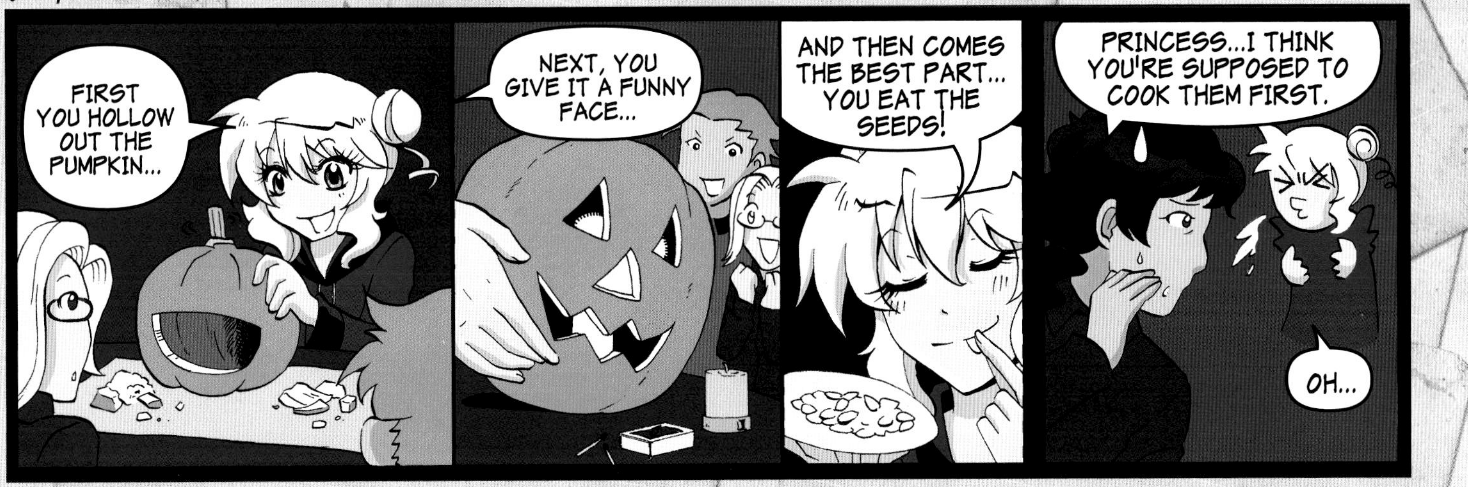
FIRST YOU HOLLOW OUT THE PUMPKIN...
NEXT, YOU GIVE IT A FUNNY FACE...
AND THEN COMES THE BEST PART... YOU EAT THE SEEDS!
PRINCESS...I THINK YOU'RE SUPPOSED TO COOK THEM FIRST.
OH...

Thick or Thin

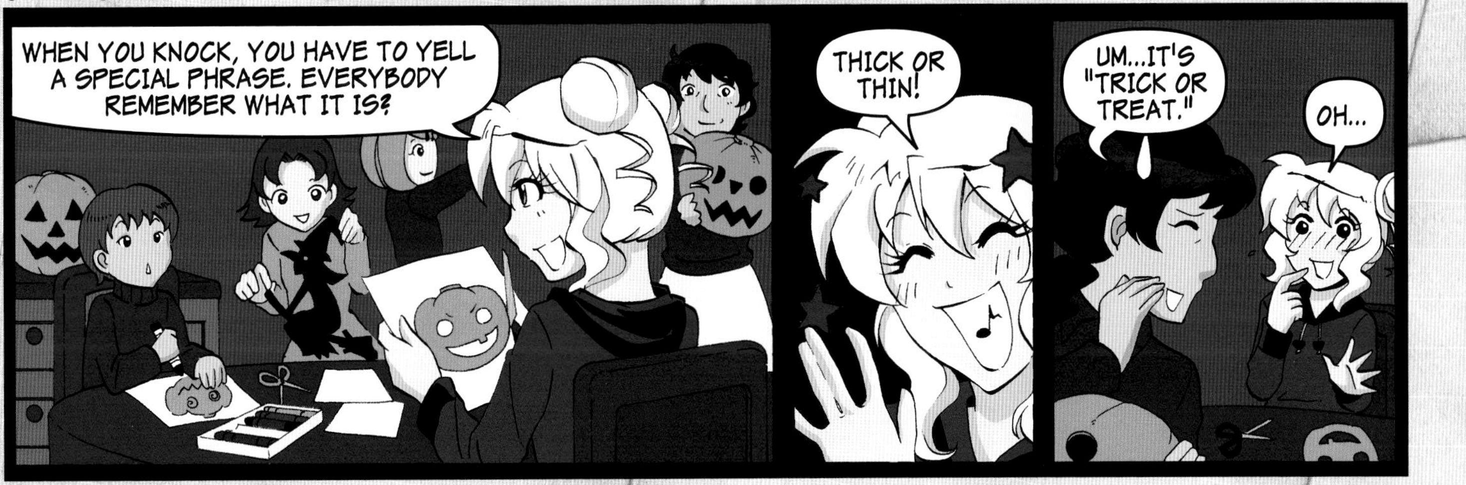
WHEN YOU KNOCK, YOU HAVE TO YELL A SPECIAL PHRASE. EVERYBODY REMEMBER WHAT IT IS?
THICK OR THIN!
UM...IT'S "TRICK OR TREAT."
OH...

Outfits

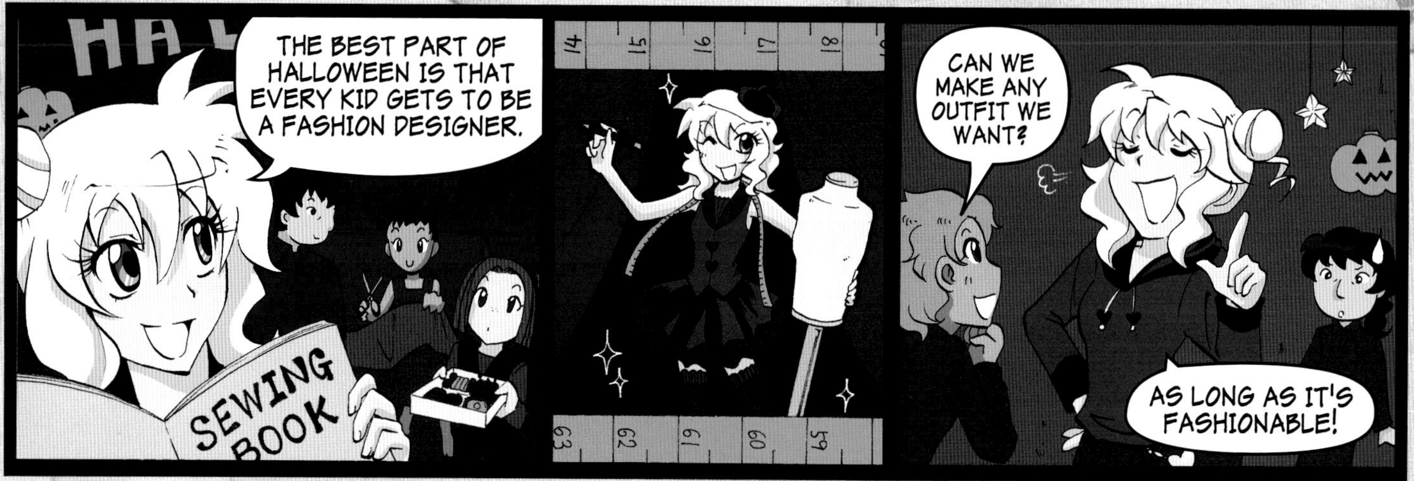
THE BEST PART OF HALLOWEEN IS THAT EVERY KID GETS TO BE A FASHION DESIGNER.
SEWING BOOK
CAN WE MAKE ANY OUTFIT WE WANT?
AS LONG AS IT'S FASHIONABLE!

Costumes

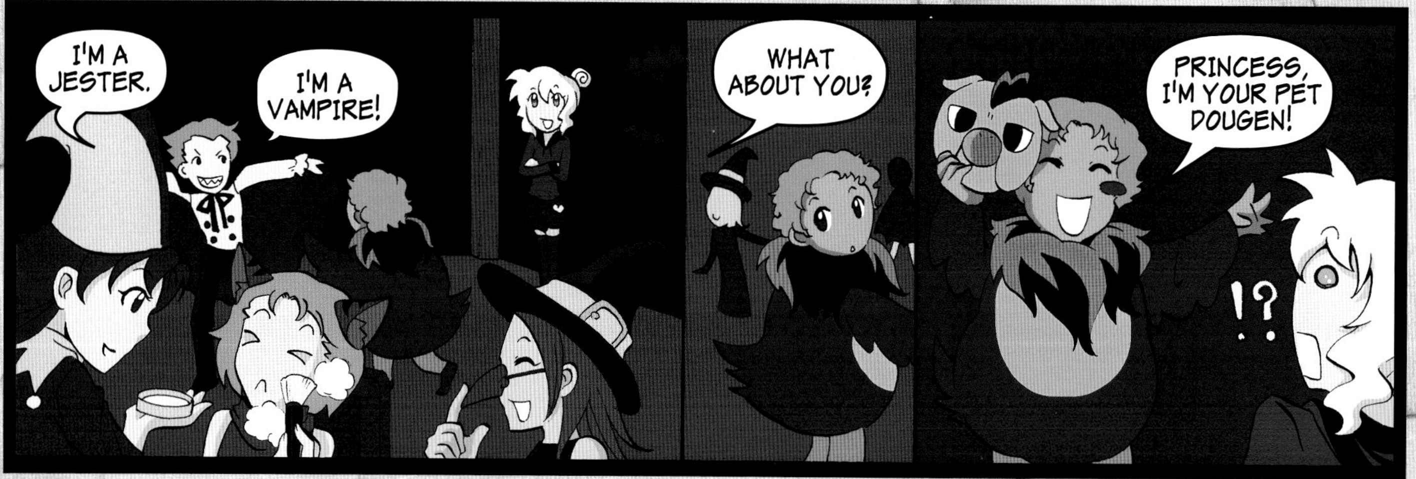
I'M A JESTER.
I'M A VAMPIRE!
WHAT ABOUT YOU?
PRINCESS, I'M YOUR PET DOUGEN!
!?

dear dAiry

There's something about the Other Side--the place they call Earth--that seems so amazing. I keep thinking about it. It's my dream to visit one day. Here on Ai-Land, my life feels like it's controlled entirely by Daddy. That's why volunteering at the orphanage was so important to me. Somewhere, somehow, I feel that I can make a difference. Maybe bringing a little bit of Earth to Ai-Land can be my first step.

love forever

Ai

Dougen Slash Patrol DSP

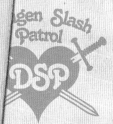

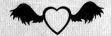

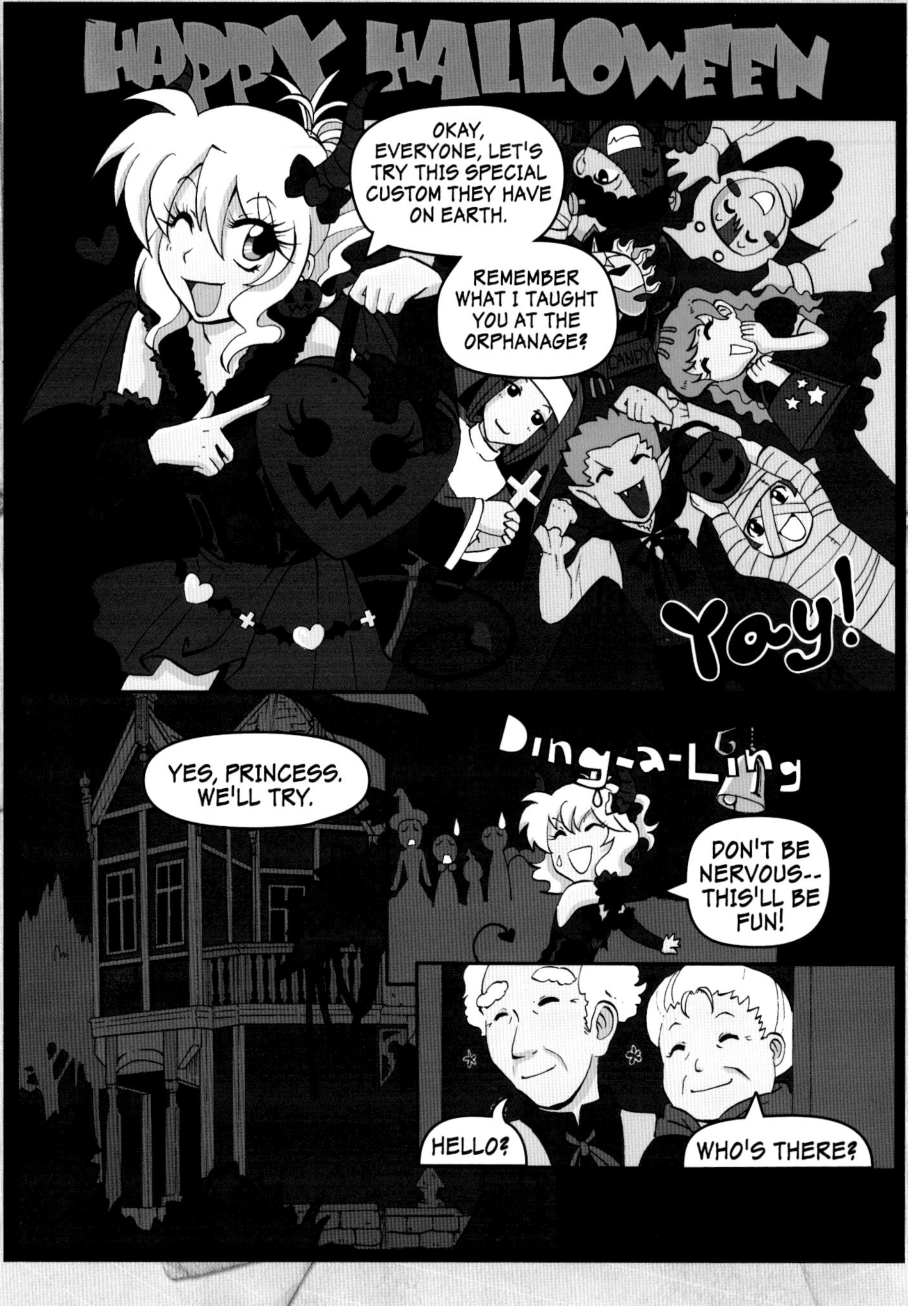
HAPPY HALLOWEEN
OKAY, EVERYONE, LET'S TRY THIS SPECIAL CUSTOM THEY HAVE ON EARTH.
REMEMBER WHAT I TAUGHT YOU AT THE ORPHANAGE?
CANDY
YAY!
YES, PRINCESS. WE'LL TRY.
Ding-a-Ling
DON'T BE NERVOUS-- THIS'LL BE FUN!
HELLO?
WHO'S THERE?

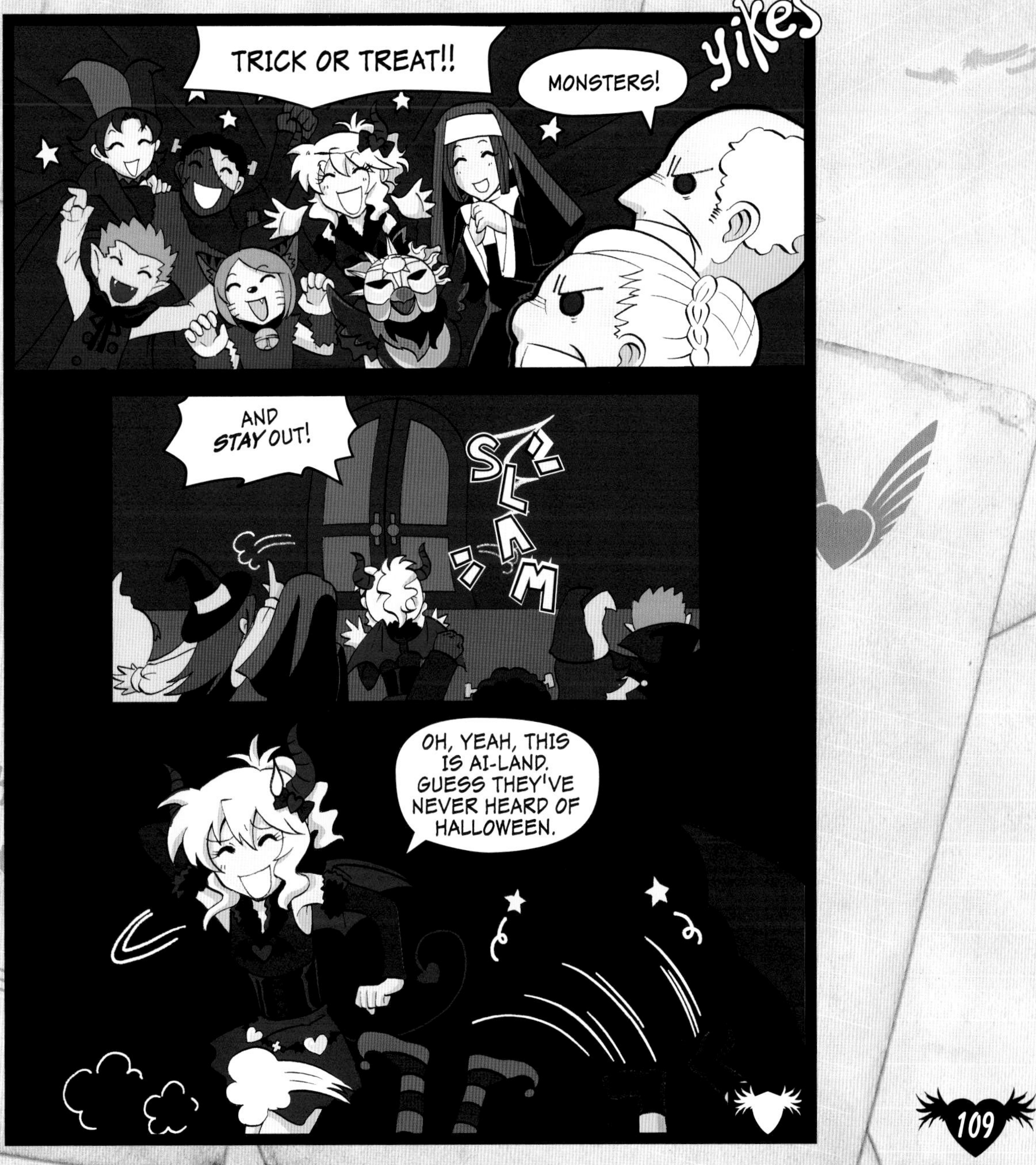
TRICK OR TREAT!!
MONSTERS!
yikes
AND STAY OUT!
SLAM
OH, YEAH, THIS IS AI-LAND. GUESS THEY'VE NEVER HEARD OF HALLOWEEN.

Aches and Pains

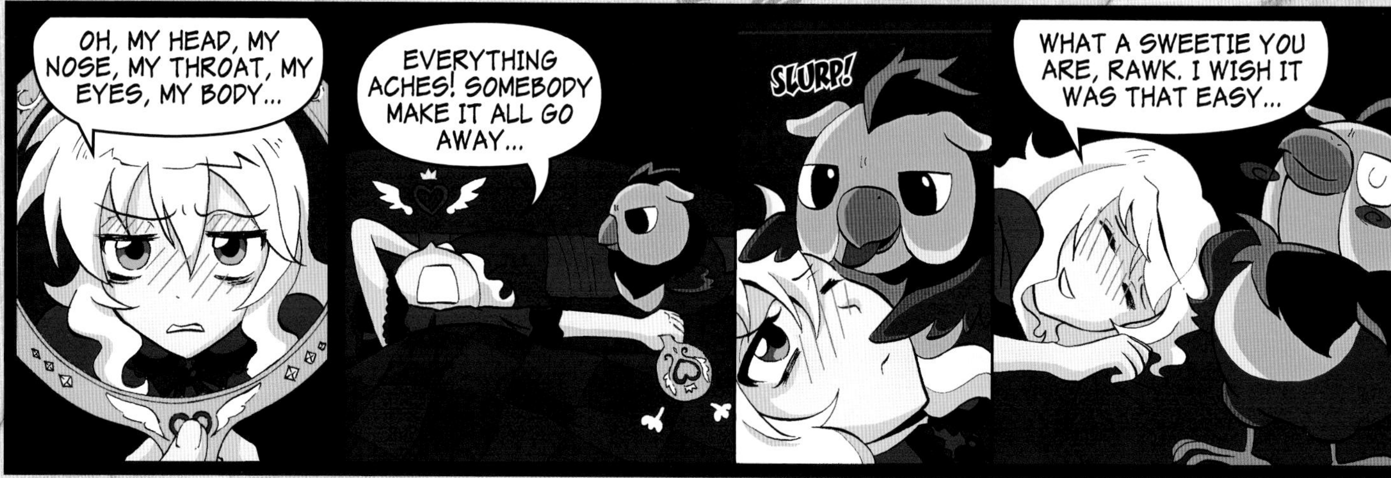
OH, MY HEAD, MY NOSE, MY THROAT, MY EYES, MY BODY...
EVERYTHING ACHES! SOMEBODY MAKE IT ALL GO AWAY...
SLURP!
WHAT A SWEETIE YOU ARE, RAWK. I WISH IT WAS THAT EASY...

Buzzzzzz

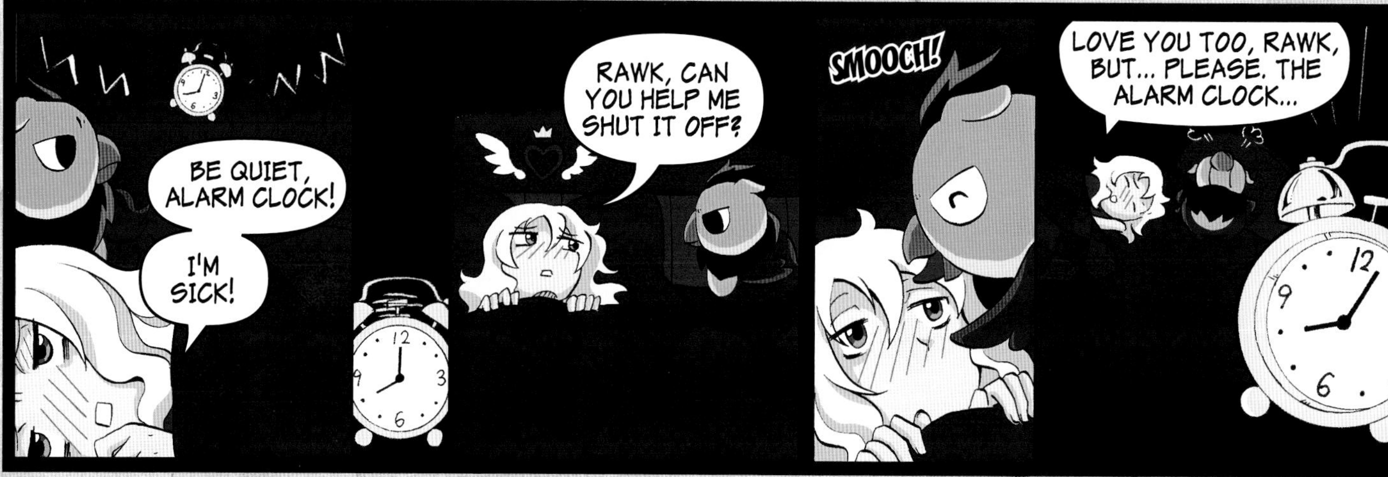
BE QUIET, ALARM CLOCK!
I'M SICK!
RAWK, CAN YOU HELP ME SHUT IT OFF?
SMOOCH!
LOVE YOU TOO, RAWK, BUT... PLEASE. THE ALARM CLOCK...

Dying Cows

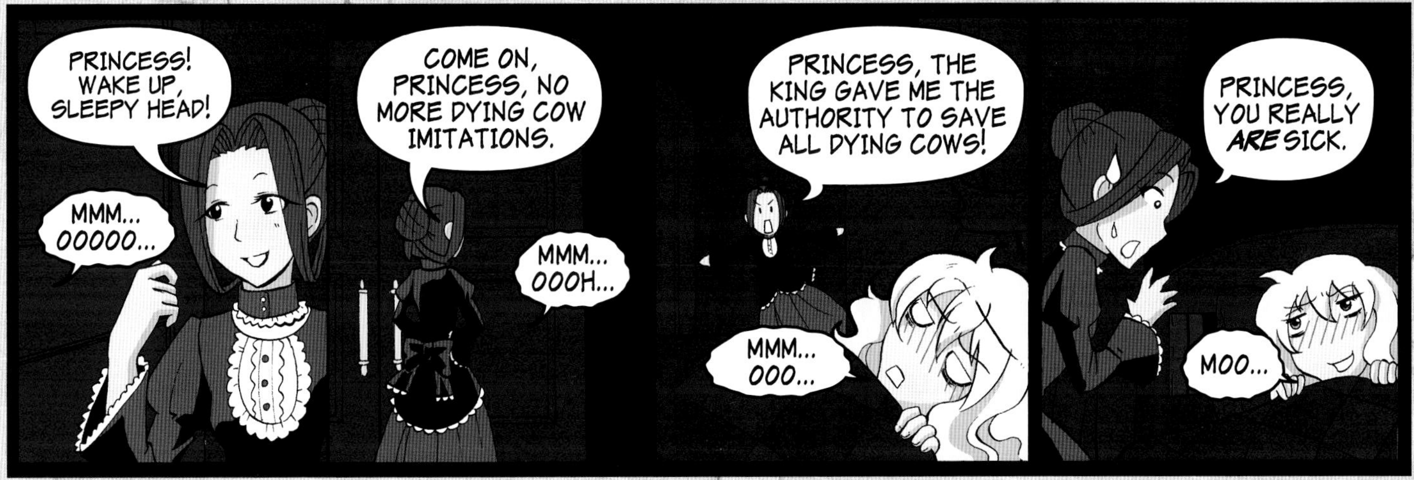
PRINCESS! WAKE UP, SLEEPY HEAD!
MMM... OOOOO...
COME ON, PRINCESS, NO MORE DYING COW IMITATIONS.
MMM... OOOH...
PRINCESS, THE KING GAVE ME THE AUTHORITY TO SAVE ALL DYING COWS!
MMM... OOO...
PRINCESS, YOU REALLY ARE SICK.
MOO...

Really Sick

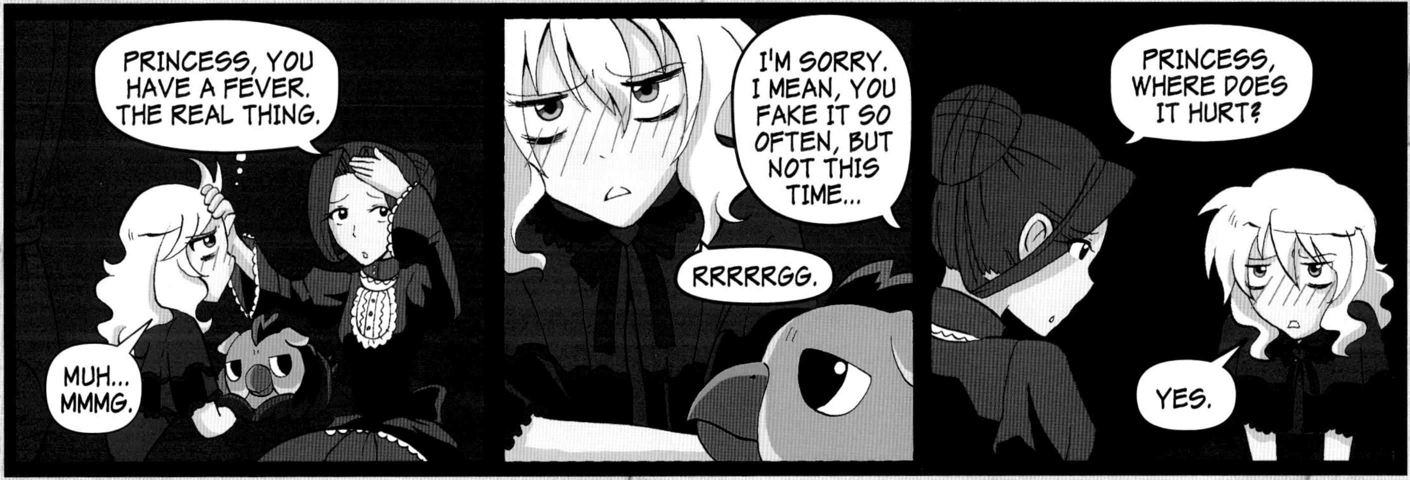
PRINCESS, YOU HAVE A FEVER. THE REAL THING.
MUH... MMMG.
I'M SORRY. I MEAN, YOU FAKE IT SO OFTEN, BUT NOT THIS TIME...
RRRRRGG.
PRINCESS, WHERE DOES IT HURT?
YES.

Say Ahhh

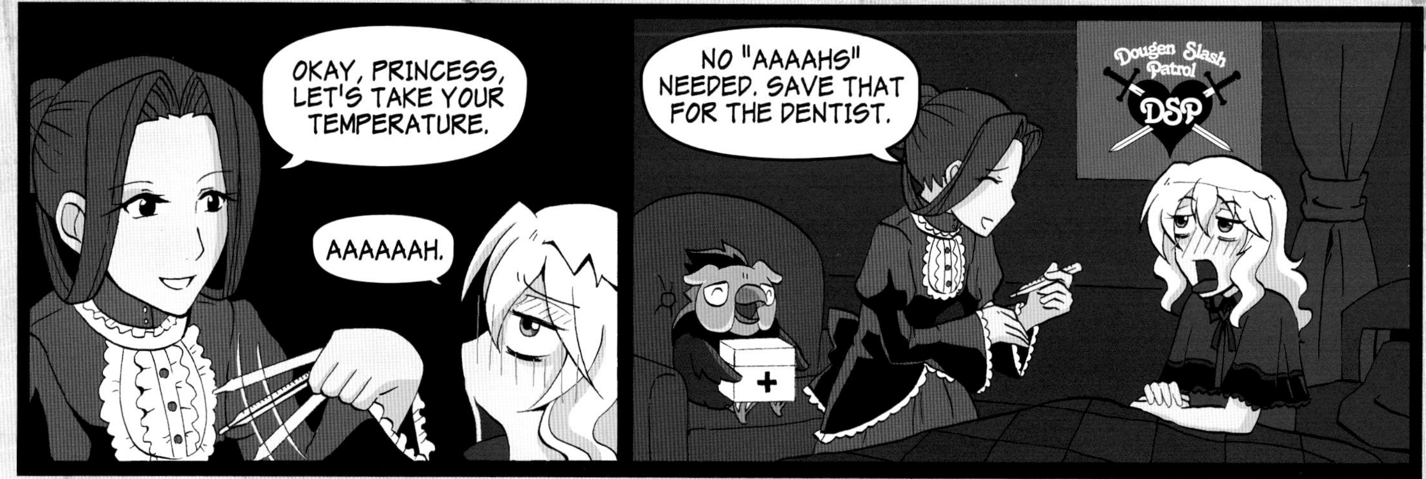

OKAY, PRINCESS, LET'S TAKE YOUR TEMPERATURE.
AAAAAAH.
NO "AAAAHS" NEEDED. SAVE THAT FOR THE DENTIST.
Dougen Slash Patrol
DSP

Stuck in Bed

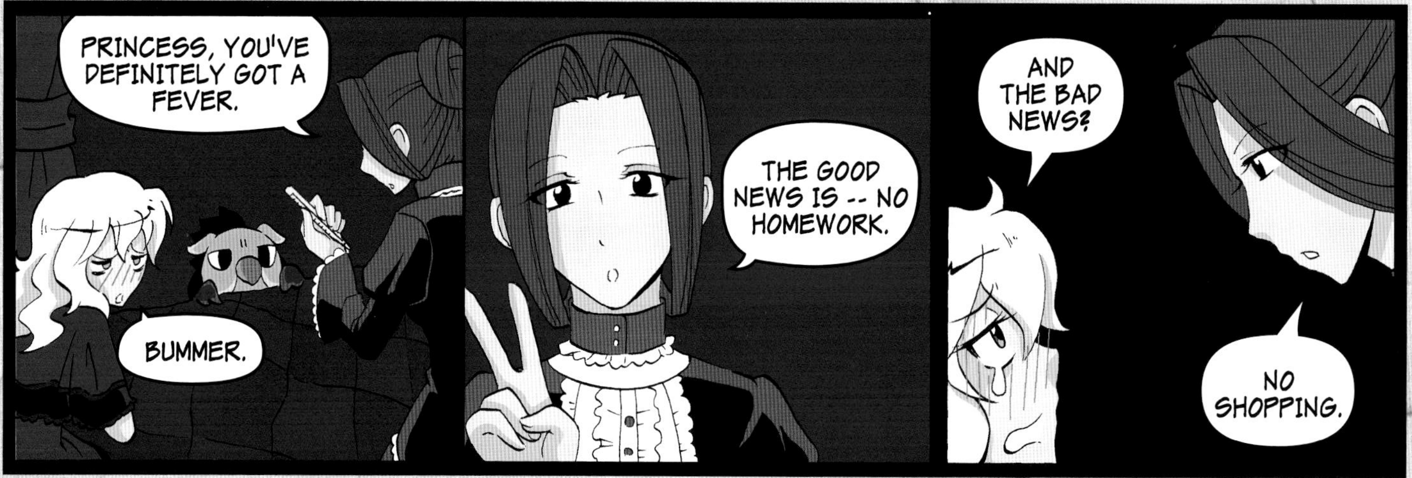

PRINCESS, YOU'VE DEFINITELY GOT A FEVER.
BUMMER.
THE GOOD NEWS IS -- NO HOMEWORK.
AND THE BAD NEWS?
NO SHOPPING.

dear dAiry

It's one thing to wish you were sick to get a peaceful day at home--but it's a totally different story when you're actually sick. Basically, being sick sucks. My head, my throat, my eyes, my entire body--everything that moves aches. Even so, I can't let Daddy know--he's way too extreme. He'll end up sealing me away from germs for life.

love forever

Ai

Dougen Slash Patrol

DSP

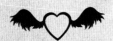

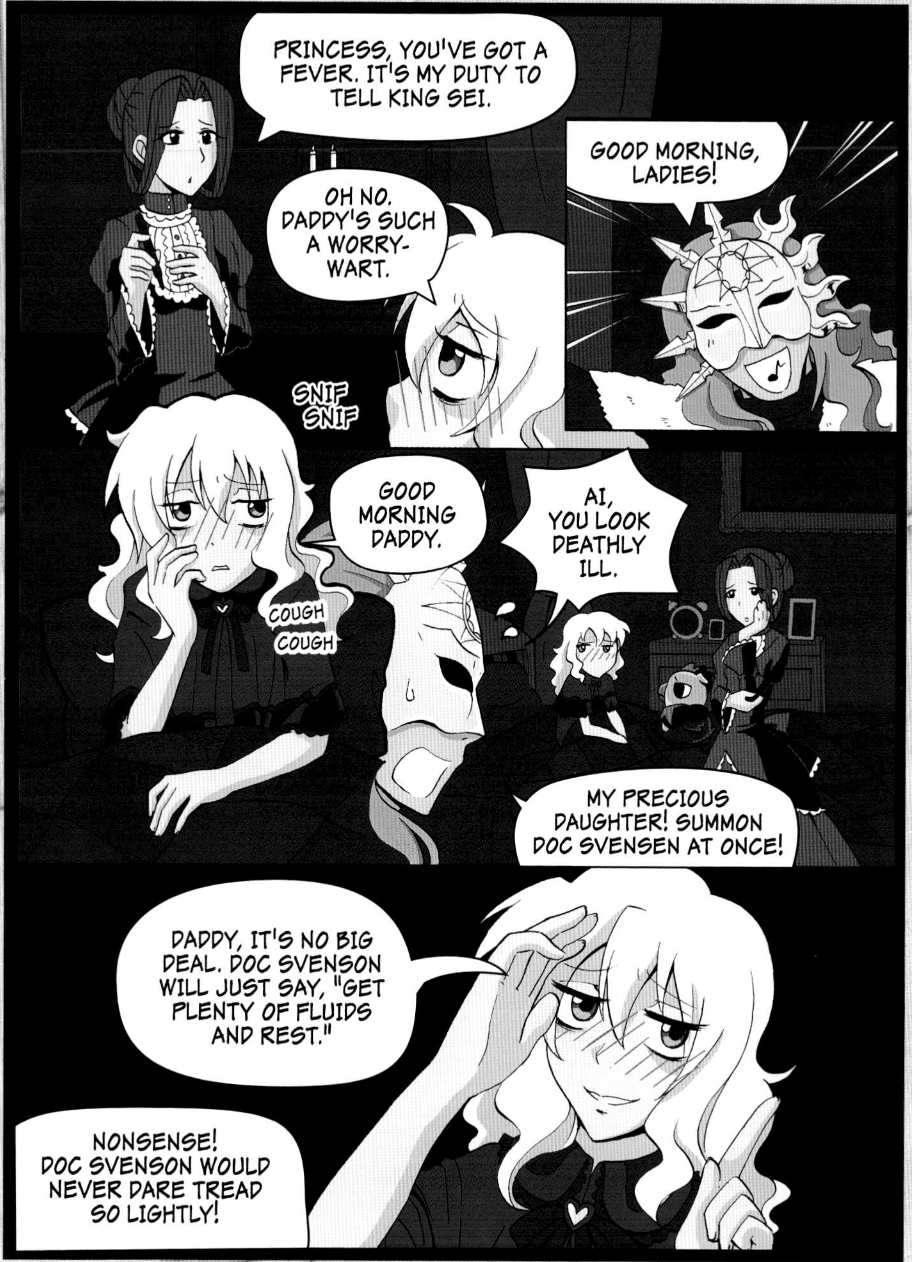
PRINCESS, YOU'VE GOT A FEVER. IT'S MY DUTY TO TELL KING SEI.
OH NO. DADDY'S SUCH A WORRY-WART.
SNIF SNIF
GOOD MORNING, LADIES!
GOOD MORNING DADDY.
COUGH COUGH
AI, YOU LOOK DEATHLY ILL.
MY PRECIOUS DAUGHTER! SUMMON DOC SVENSEN AT ONCE!
DADDY, IT'S NO BIG DEAL. DOC SVENSON WILL JUST SAY, "GET PLENTY OF FLUIDS AND REST."
NONSENSE! DOC SVENSON WOULD NEVER DARE TREAD SO LIGHTLY!

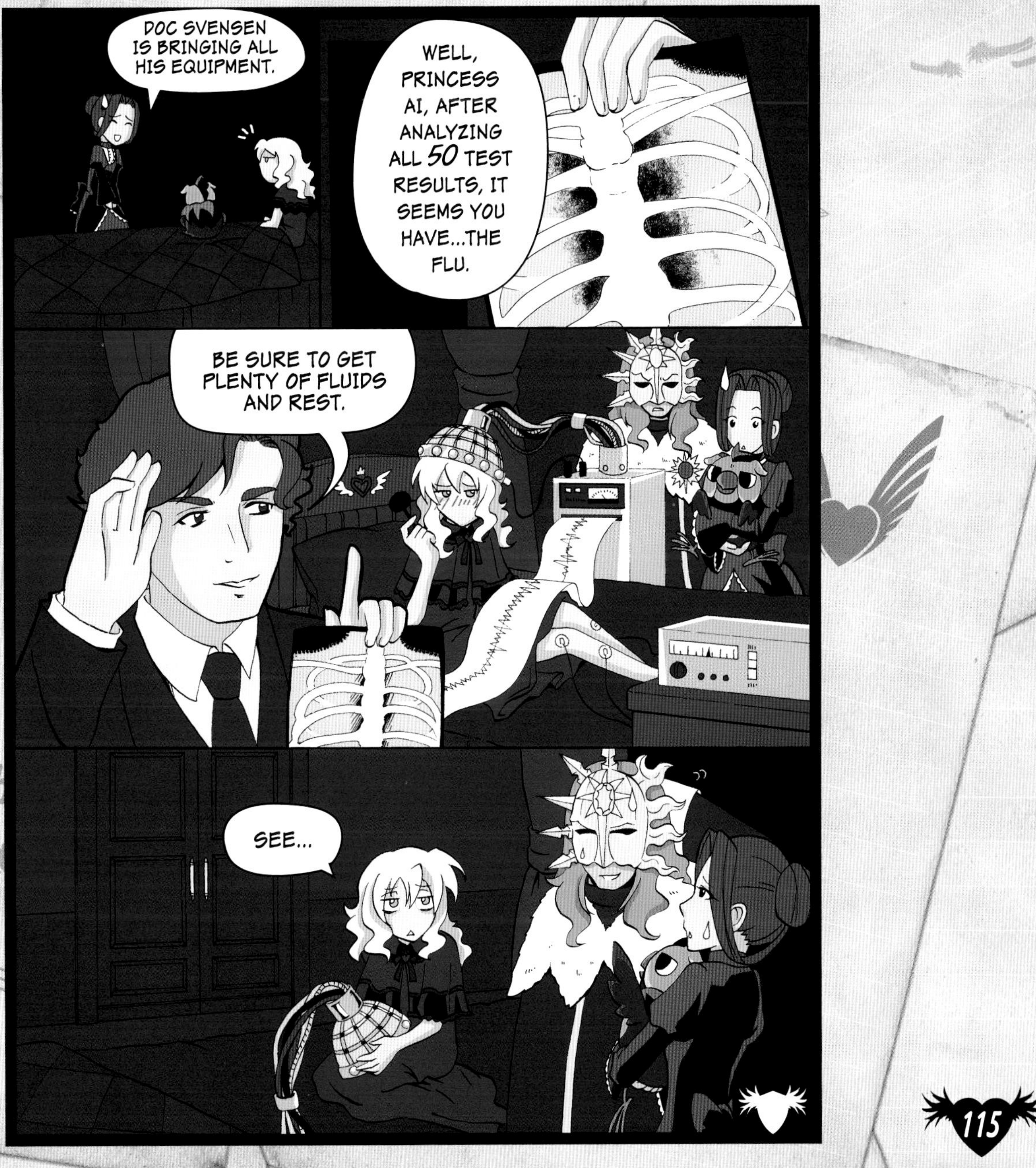
DOC SVENSEN IS BRINGING ALL HIS EQUIPMENT.
WELL, PRINCESS AI, AFTER ANALYZING ALL 50 TEST RESULTS, IT SEEMS YOU HAVE...THE FLU.
BE SURE TO GET PLENTY OF FLUIDS AND REST.
SEE...

Chicken Soup

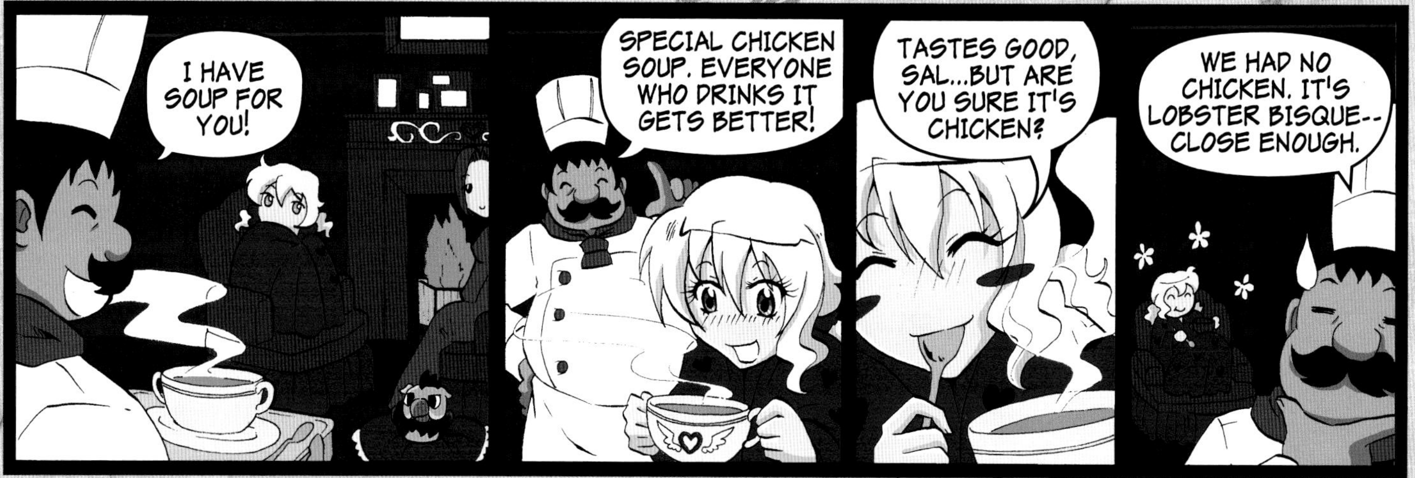
I HAVE SOUP FOR YOU!
SPECIAL CHICKEN SOUP. EVERYONE WHO DRINKS IT GETS BETTER!
TASTES GOOD, SAL...BUT ARE YOU SURE IT'S CHICKEN?
WE HAD NO CHICKEN. IT'S LOBSTER BISQUE--CLOSE ENOUGH.

Shot of Whiskey

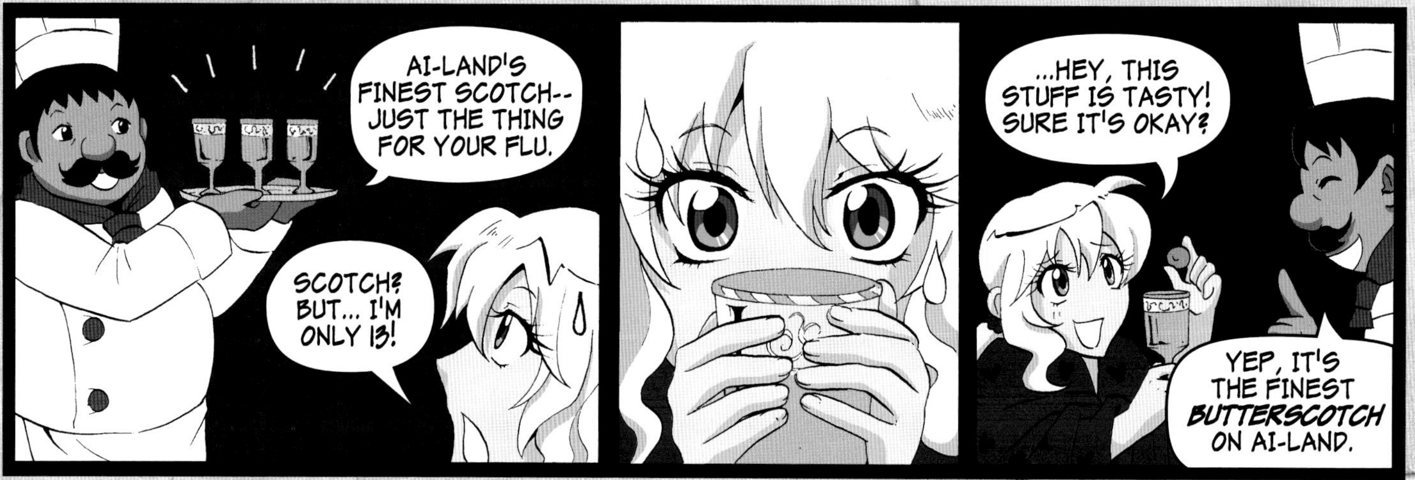
AI-LAND'S FINEST SCOTCH--JUST THE THING FOR YOUR FLU.
SCOTCH? BUT... I'M ONLY 13!
...HEY, THIS STUFF IS TASTY! SURE IT'S OKAY?
YEP, IT'S THE FINEST ***BUTTERSCOTCH*** ON AI-LAND.

Gargle

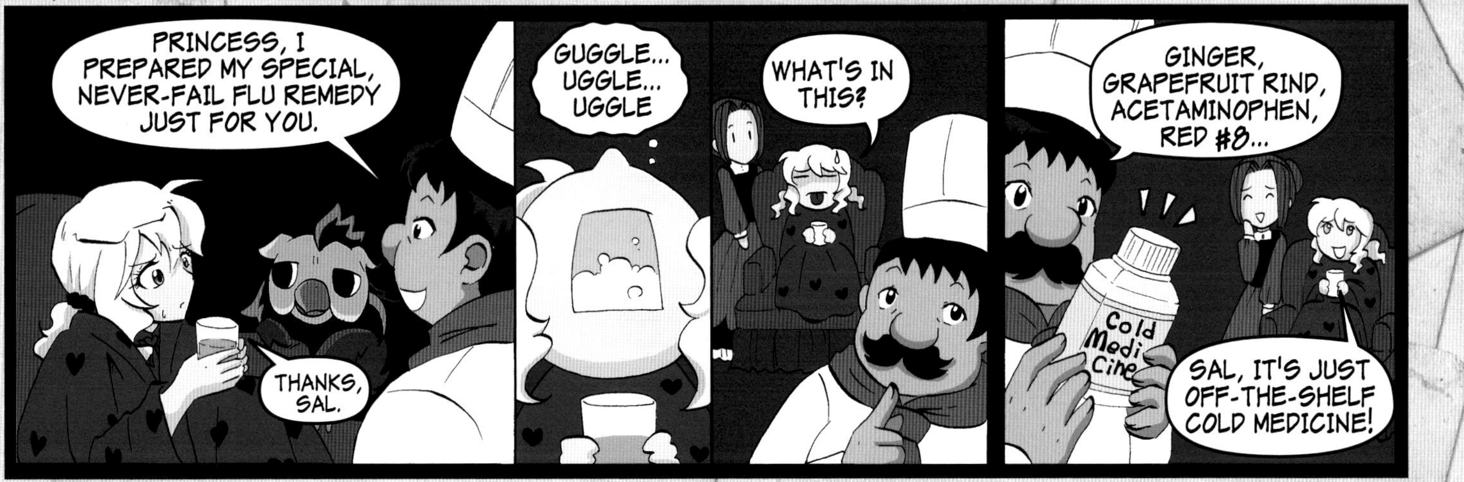
PRINCESS, I PREPARED MY SPECIAL, NEVER-FAIL FLU REMEDY JUST FOR YOU.
THANKS, SAL.
GUGGLE... UGGLE... UGGLE
WHAT'S IN THIS?
GINGER, GRAPEFRUIT RIND, ACETAMINOPHEN, RED #8...
Cold Medicine
SAL, IT'S JUST OFF-THE-SHELF COLD MEDICINE!

Vitamins

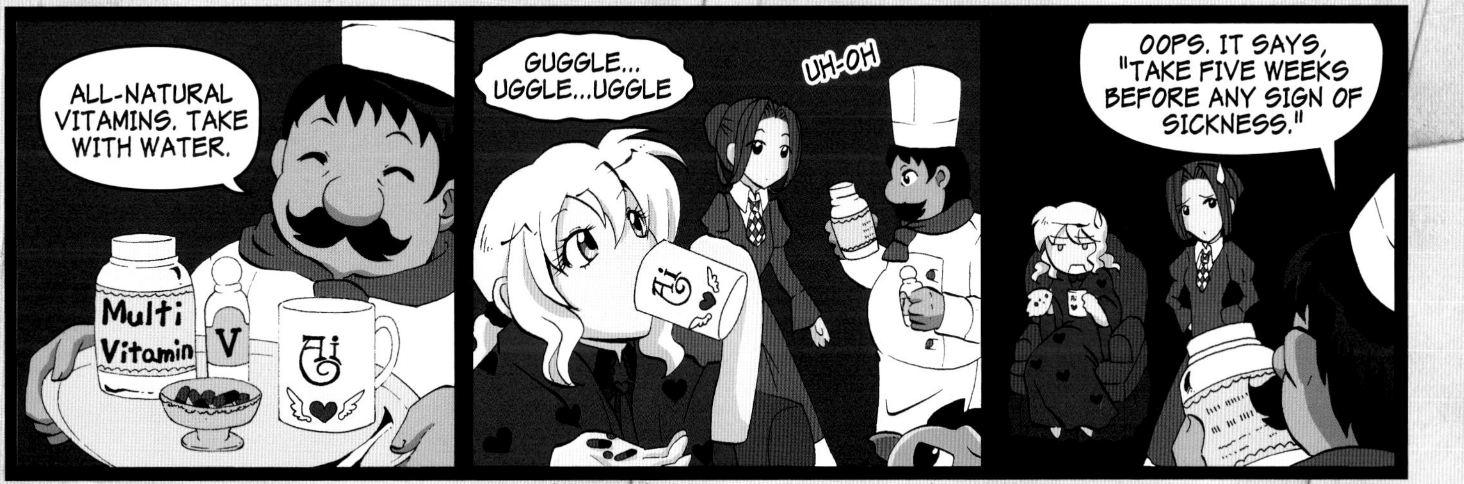
ALL-NATURAL VITAMINS. TAKE WITH WATER.
Multi Vitamin
V
GUGGLE... UGGLE...UGGLE
UH-OH
OOPS. IT SAYS, "TAKE FIVE WEEKS BEFORE ANY SIGN OF SICKNESS."

Jello & Ice Cream

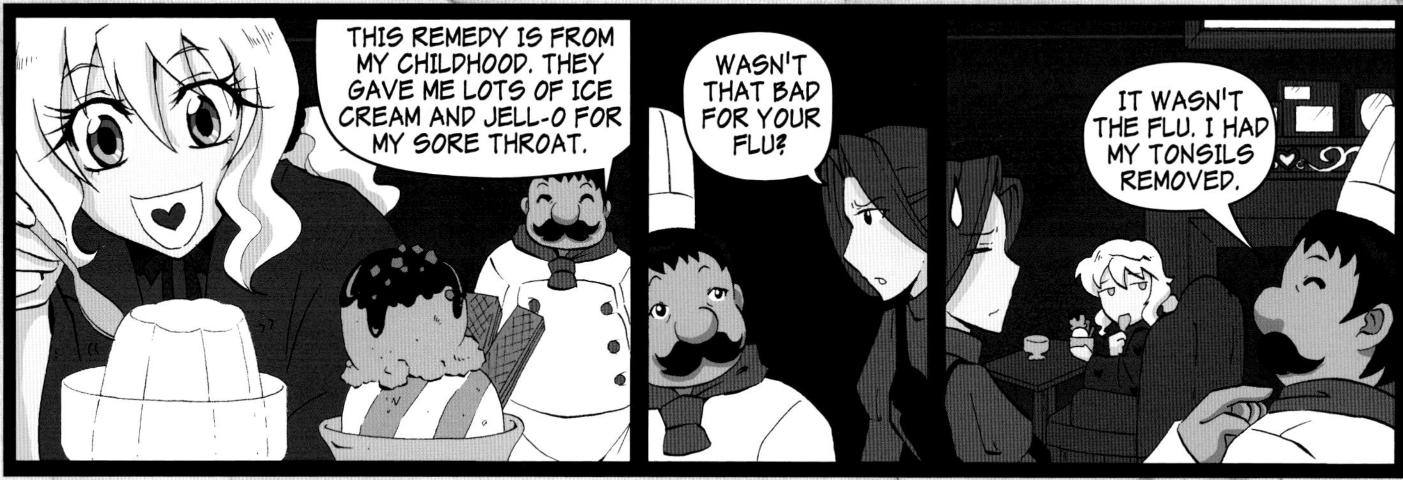
THIS REMEDY IS FROM MY CHILDHOOD. THEY GAVE ME LOTS OF ICE CREAM AND JELL-O FOR MY SORE THROAT.
WASN'T THAT BAD FOR YOUR FLU?
IT WASN'T THE FLU. I HAD MY TONSILS REMOVED.

Sweet and Sour

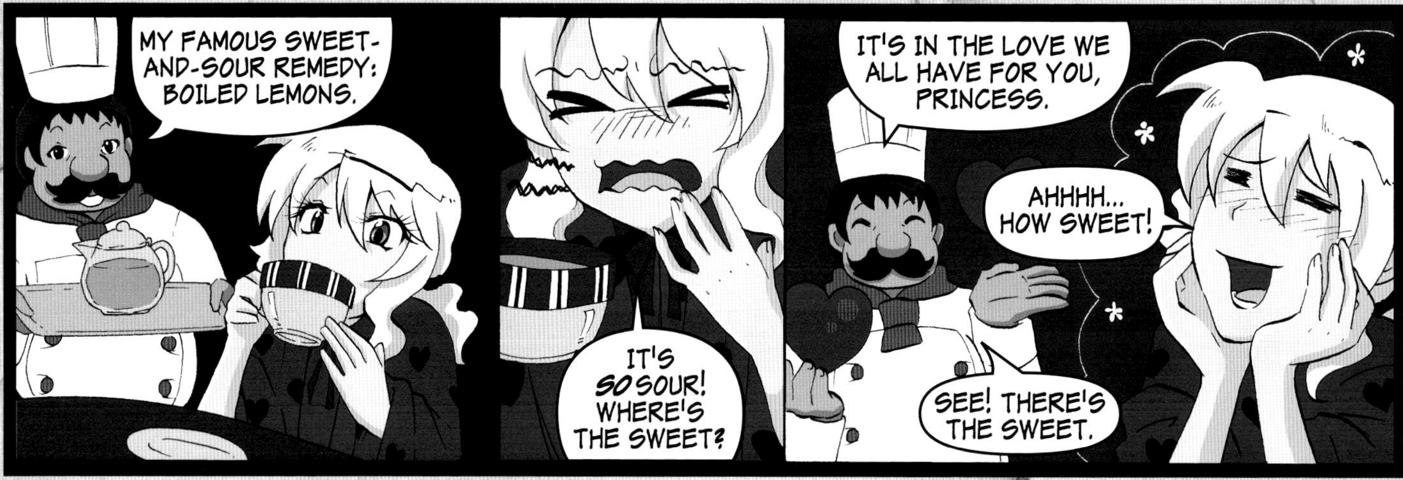
MY FAMOUS SWEET-AND-SOUR REMEDY: BOILED LEMONS.
IT'S SO SOUR! WHERE'S THE SWEET?
IT'S IN THE LOVE WE ALL HAVE FOR YOU, PRINCESS.
AHHHH... HOW SWEET!
SEE! THERE'S THE SWEET.

dear d**Ai**ry

Even though being sick was a week of aches, pains and general misery, there's one thing that made it bearable--my friends and family. I didn't quite appreciate how much they really do care for me. I'm so lucky. I just hope that one day they'll somehow learn how much I care for <u>them</u>.

love forever

Ai

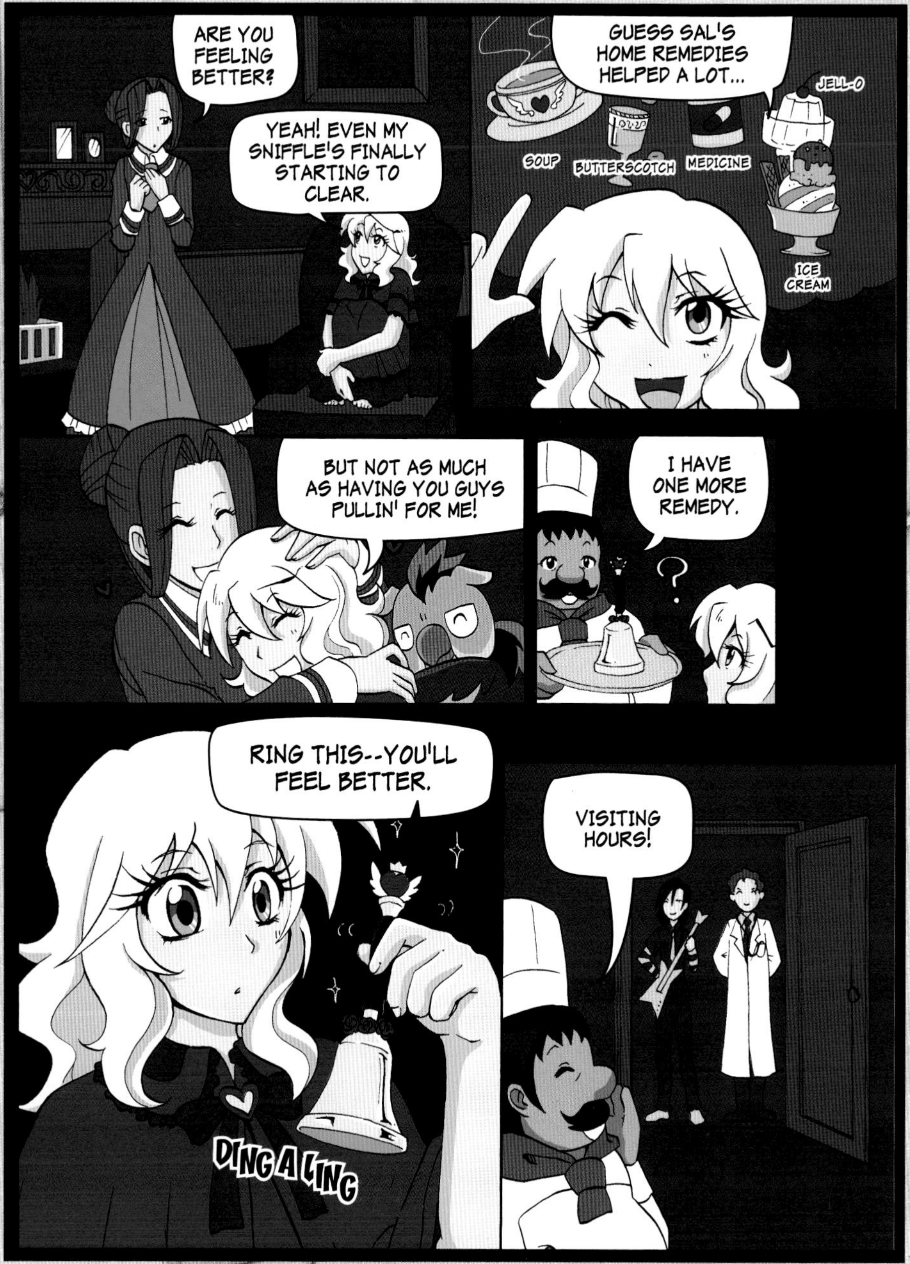
ARE YOU FEELING BETTER?
YEAH! EVEN MY SNIFFLE'S FINALLY STARTING TO CLEAR.
GUESS SAL'S HOME REMEDIES HELPED A LOT...
SOUP
BUTTERSCOTCH
MEDICINE
JELL-O
ICE CREAM
BUT NOT AS MUCH AS HAVING YOU GUYS PULLIN' FOR ME!
I HAVE ONE MORE REMEDY.
RING THIS--YOU'LL FEEL BETTER.
DING A LING
VISITING HOURS!

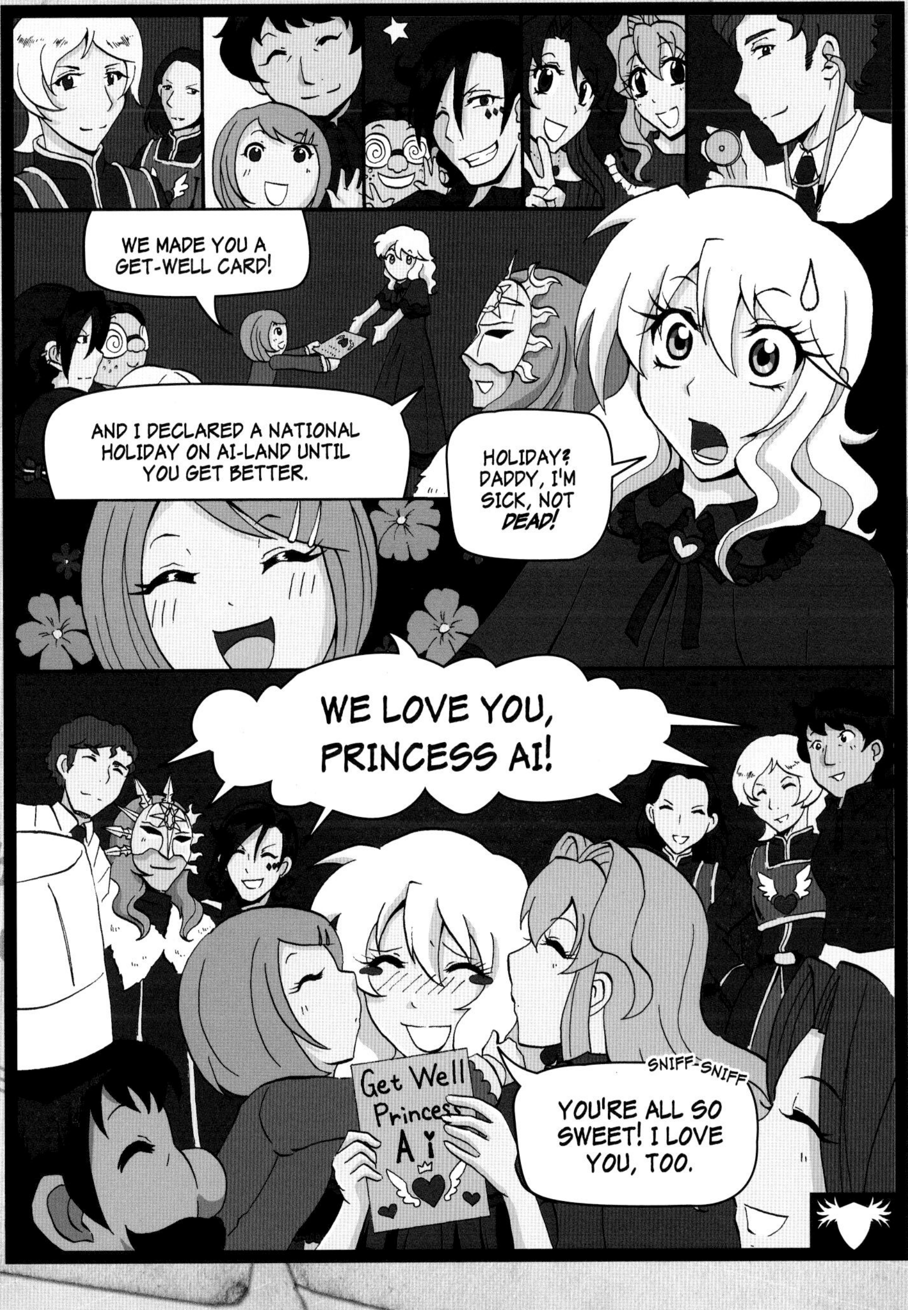
WE MADE YOU A GET-WELL CARD!
AND I DECLARED A NATIONAL HOLIDAY ON AI-LAND UNTIL YOU GET BETTER.
HOLIDAY? DADDY, I'M SICK, NOT *DEAD!*
WE LOVE YOU, PRINCESS AI!
Get Well Princess Ai
SNIFF-SNIFF
YOU'RE ALL SO SWEET! I LOVE YOU, TOO.

Diet

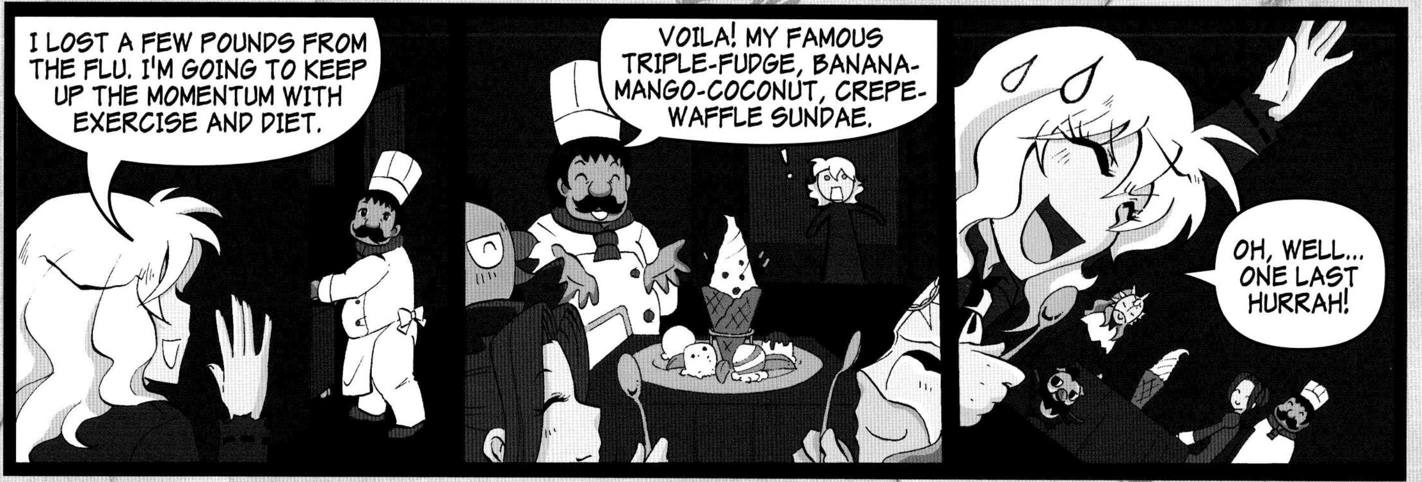
I LOST A FEW POUNDS FROM THE FLU. I'M GOING TO KEEP UP THE MOMENTUM WITH EXERCISE AND DIET.
VOILA! MY FAMOUS TRIPLE-FUDGE, BANANA-MANGO-COCONUT, CREPE-WAFFLE SUNDAE.
OH, WELL... ONE LAST HURRAH!

Rain, Rain

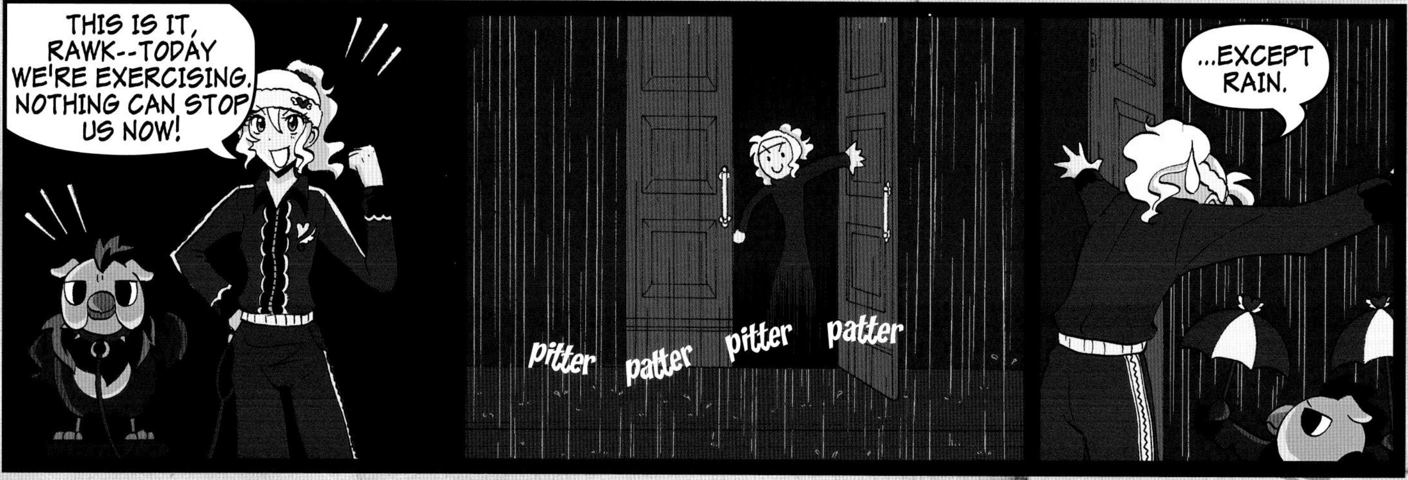
THIS IS IT, RAWK--TODAY WE'RE EXERCISING. NOTHING CAN STOP US NOW!
pitter patter pitter patter
...EXCEPT RAIN.

Lunchtime

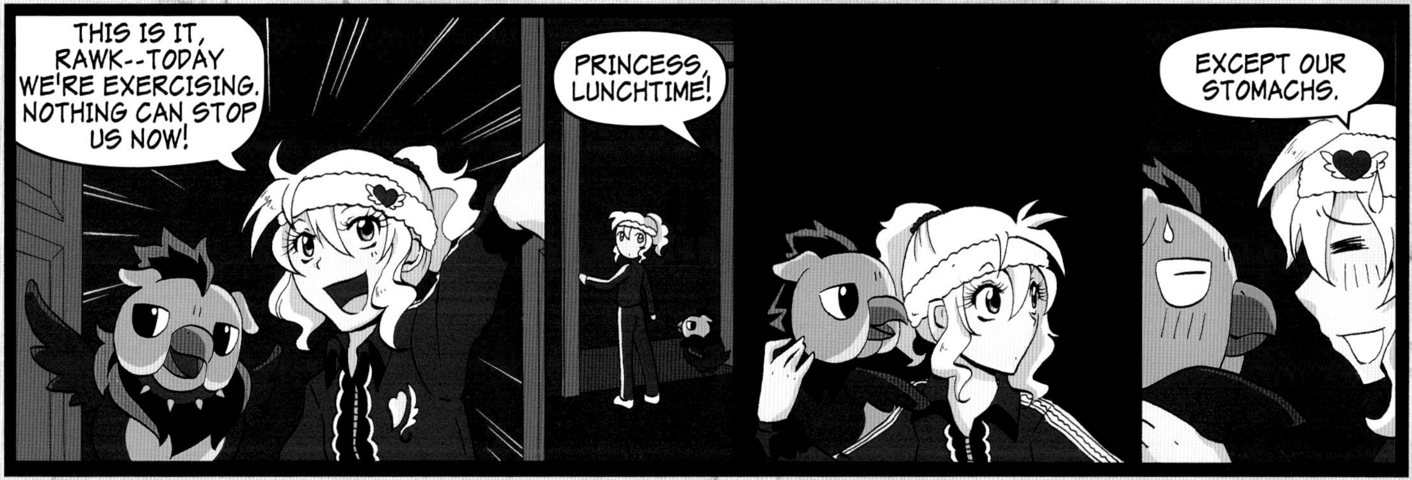

THIS IS IT, RAWK--TODAY WE'RE EXERCISING. NOTHING CAN STOP US NOW!
PRINCESS, LUNCHTIME!
EXCEPT OUR STOMACHS.

Jammin'

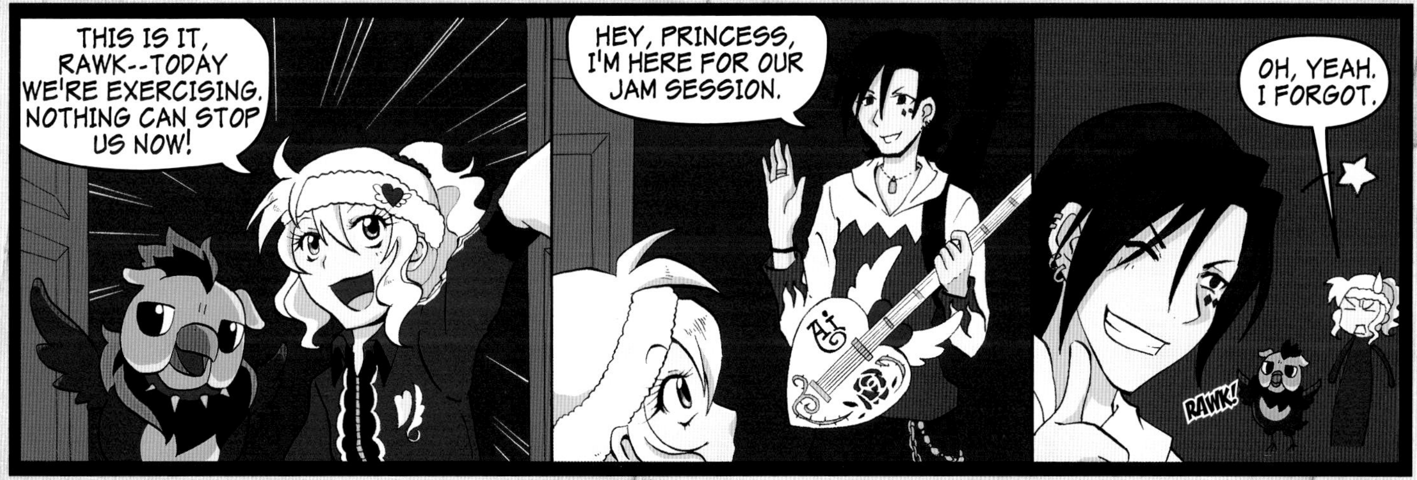

THIS IS IT, RAWK--TODAY WE'RE EXERCISING. NOTHING CAN STOP US NOW!
HEY, PRINCESS, I'M HERE FOR OUR JAM SESSION.
OH, YEAH. I FORGOT.
RAWK!

Day for Shopping

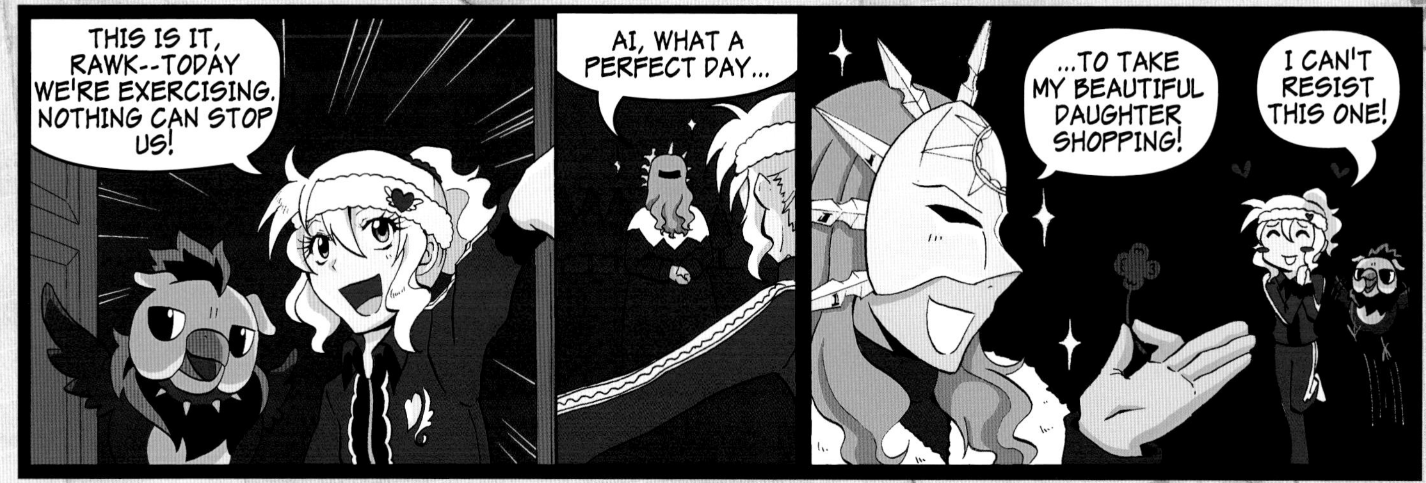
THIS IS IT, RAWK--TODAY WE'RE EXERCISING. NOTHING CAN STOP US!
AI, WHAT A PERFECT DAY...
...TO TAKE MY BEAUTIFUL DAUGHTER SHOPPING!
I CAN'T RESIST THIS ONE!

Eclipse

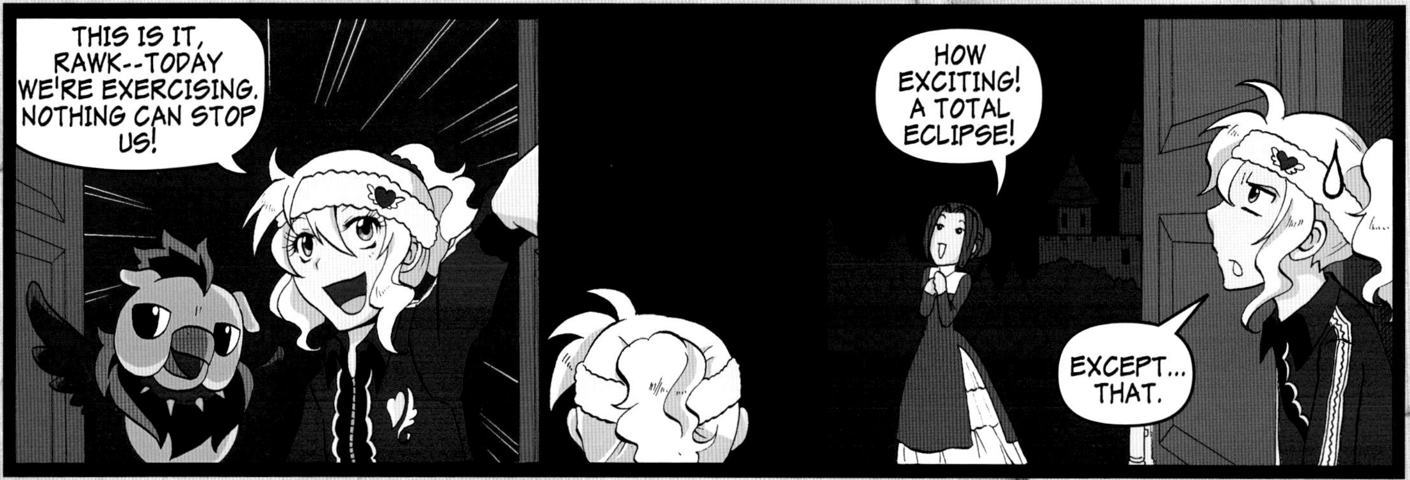
THIS IS IT, RAWK--TODAY WE'RE EXERCISING. NOTHING CAN STOP US!
HOW EXCITING! A TOTAL ECLIPSE!
EXCEPT... THAT.

dear d**Ai**ry

I've been putting off exercise day after day. That's it--I'm finally gonna go to it! The key to getting motivated is wearing the right outfit. With stylish sweats and fresh kicks, I'm ready to lose some extra poundage! And doesn't little Rawk look simply adorable?

love forever

Ai

 125

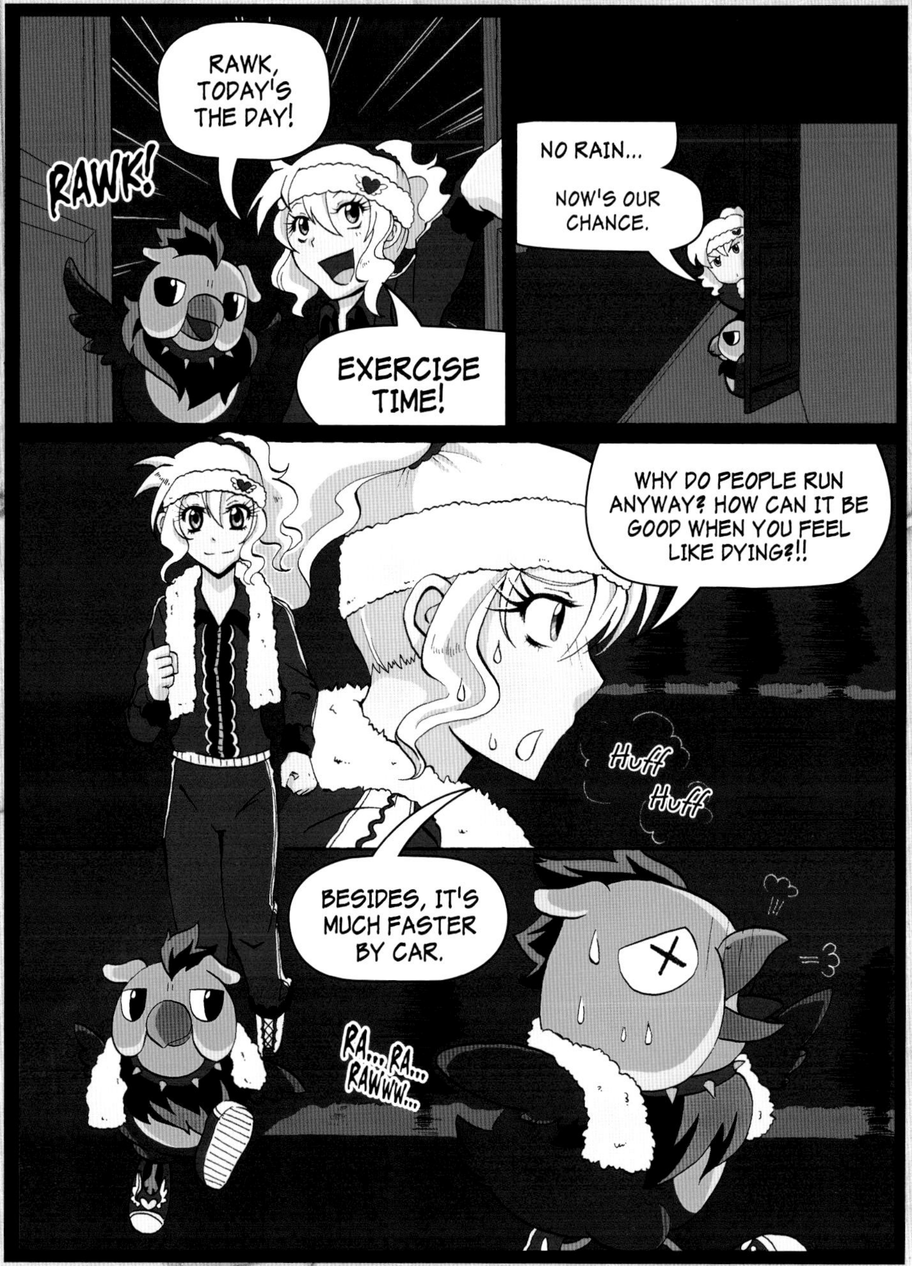
RAWK, TODAY'S THE DAY!
RAWK!
EXERCISE TIME!
NO RAIN...
NOW'S OUR CHANCE.
WHY DO PEOPLE RUN ANYWAY? HOW CAN IT BE GOOD WHEN YOU FEEL LIKE DYING?!!
Huff
Huff
BESIDES, IT'S MUCH FASTER BY CAR.
RA... RA... RAWWW...

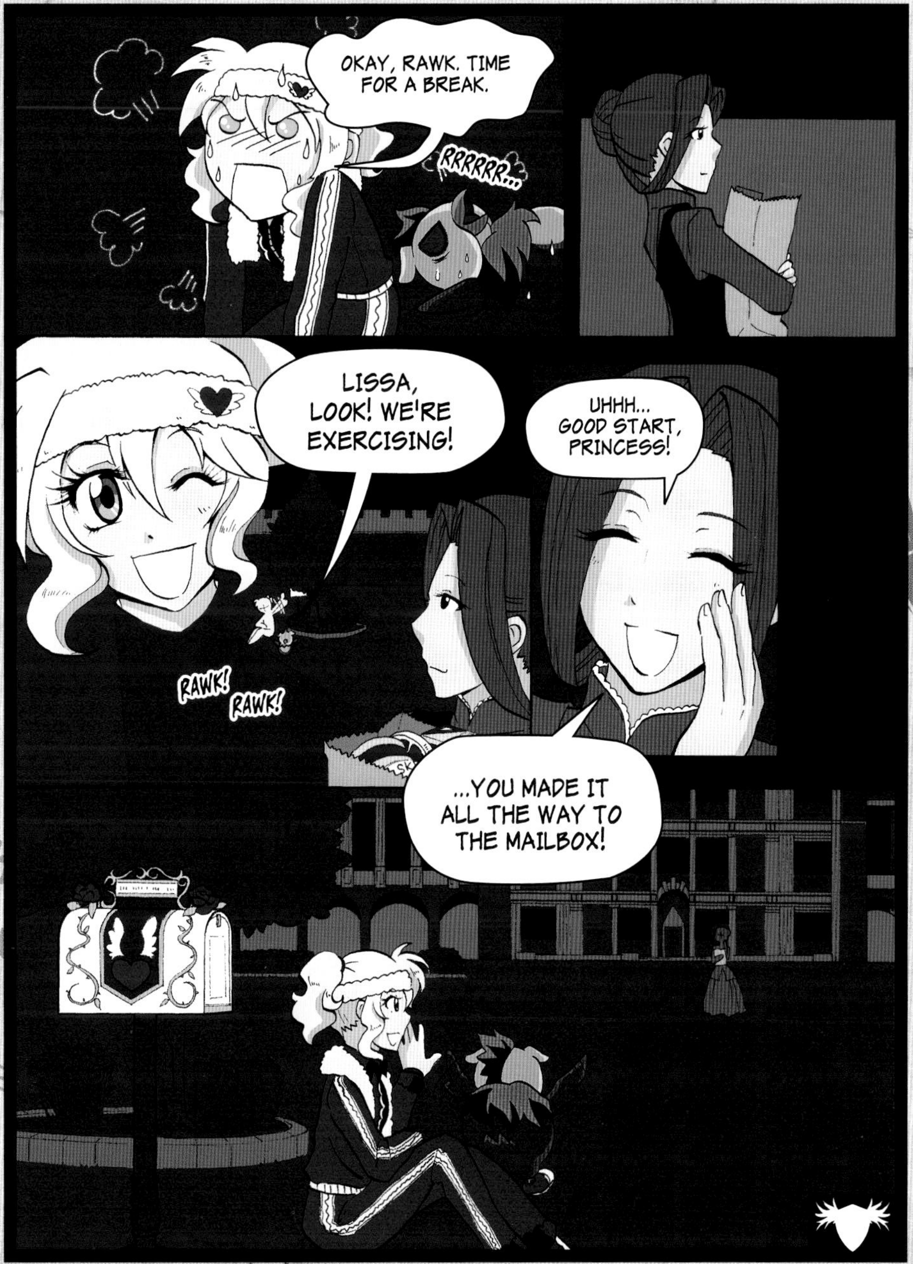
OKAY, RAWK. TIME FOR A BREAK.
RRRRRR...
LISSA, LOOK! WE'RE EXERCISING!
RAWK! RAWK!
UHHH... GOOD START, PRINCESS!
...YOU MADE IT ALL THE WAY TO THE MAILBOX!

Die It

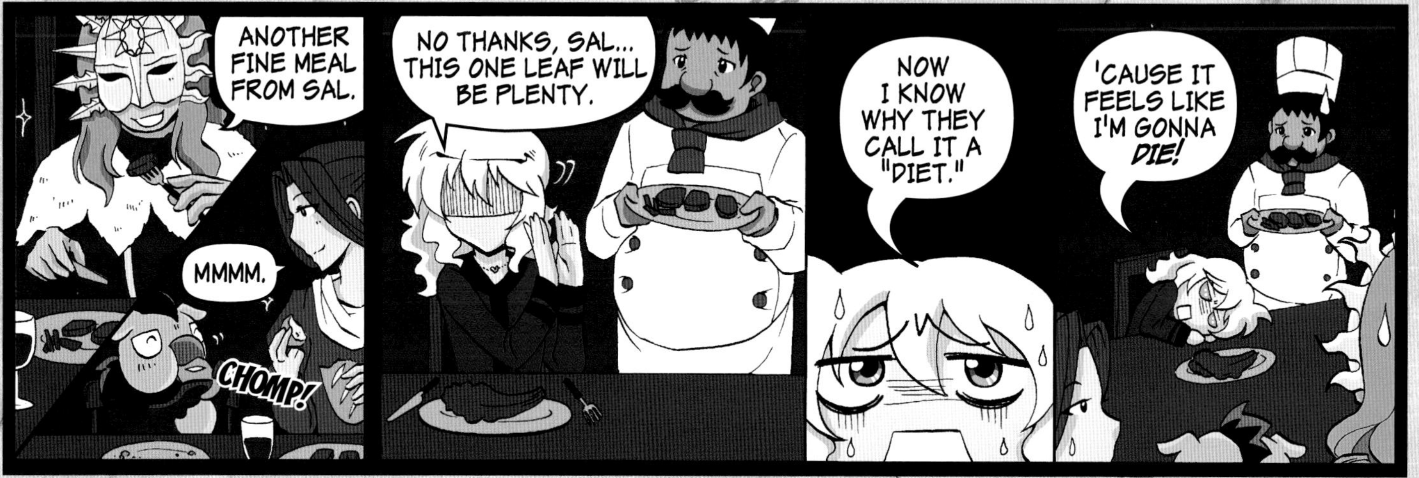
ANOTHER FINE MEAL FROM SAL.
MMMM.
CHOMP!
NO THANKS, SAL... THIS ONE LEAF WILL BE PLENTY.
NOW I KNOW WHY THEY CALL IT A "DIET."
'CAUSE IT FEELS LIKE I'M GONNA *DIE!*

Carbs

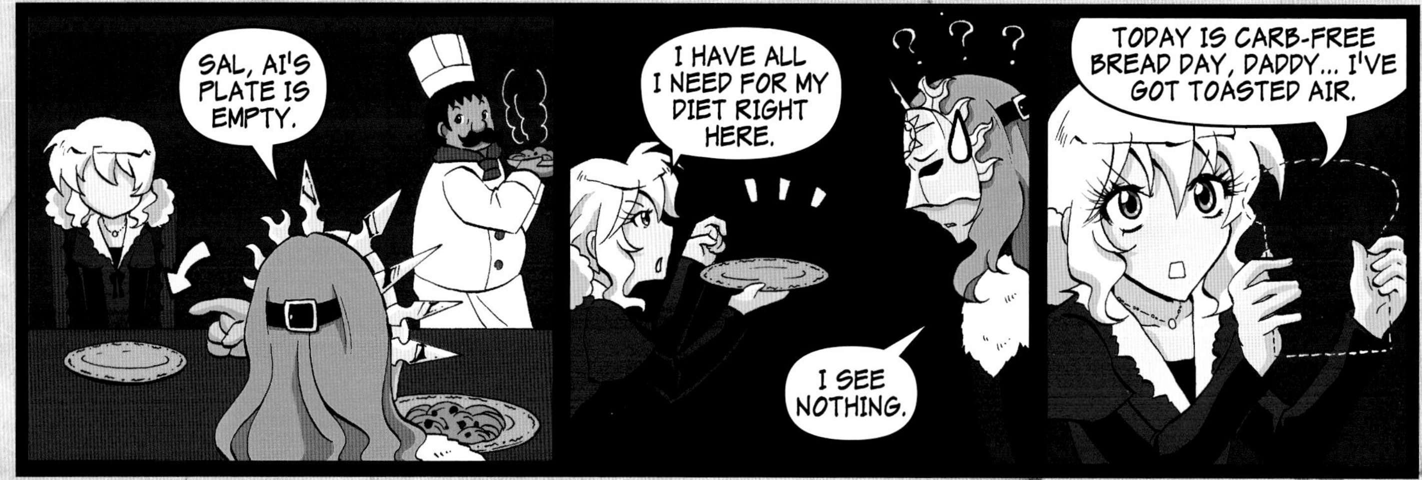
SAL, AI'S PLATE IS EMPTY.
I HAVE ALL I NEED FOR MY DIET RIGHT HERE.
? ? ?
I SEE NOTHING.
TODAY IS CARB-FREE BREAD DAY, DADDY... I'VE GOT TOASTED AIR.

Veggie Steak

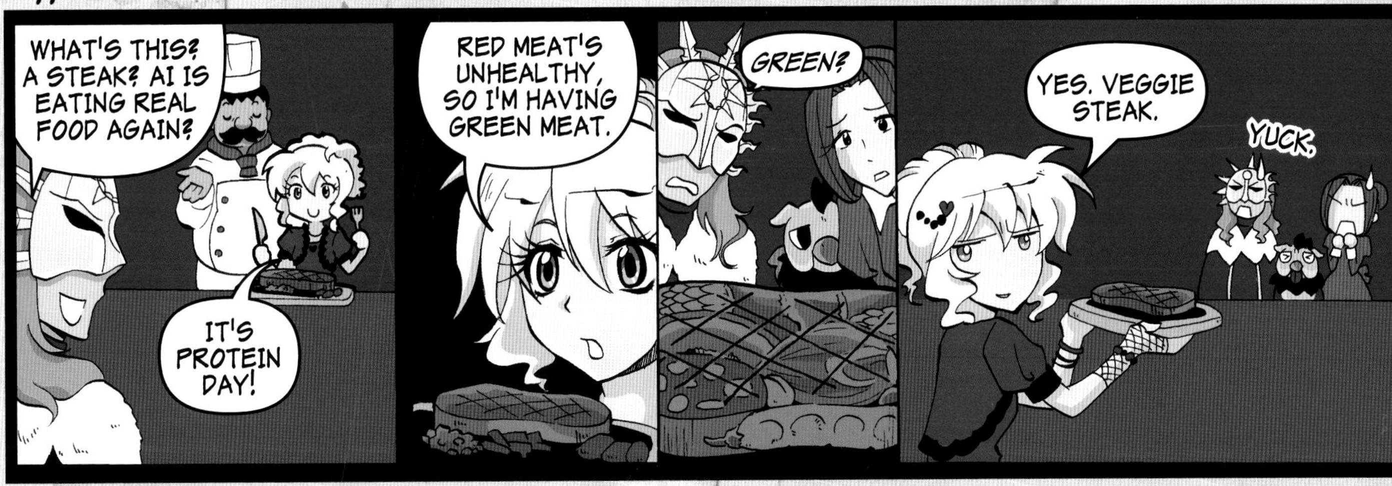
WHAT'S THIS? A STEAK? AI IS EATING REAL FOOD AGAIN?
IT'S PROTEIN DAY!
RED MEAT'S UNHEALTHY, SO I'M HAVING GREEN MEAT.
GREEN?
YES. VEGGIE STEAK.
YUCK.

I See Cream

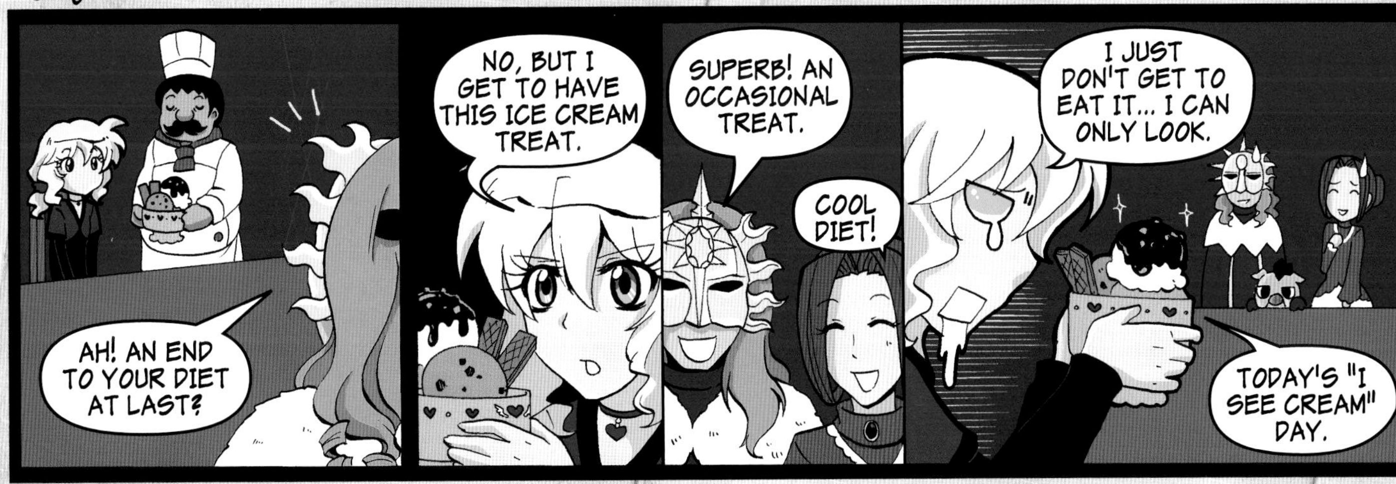
AH! AN END TO YOUR DIET AT LAST?
NO, BUT I GET TO HAVE THIS ICE CREAM TREAT.
SUPERB! AN OCCASIONAL TREAT.
COOL DIET!
I JUST DON'T GET TO EAT IT... I CAN ONLY LOOK.
TODAY'S "I SEE CREAM" DAY.

Chalkolate

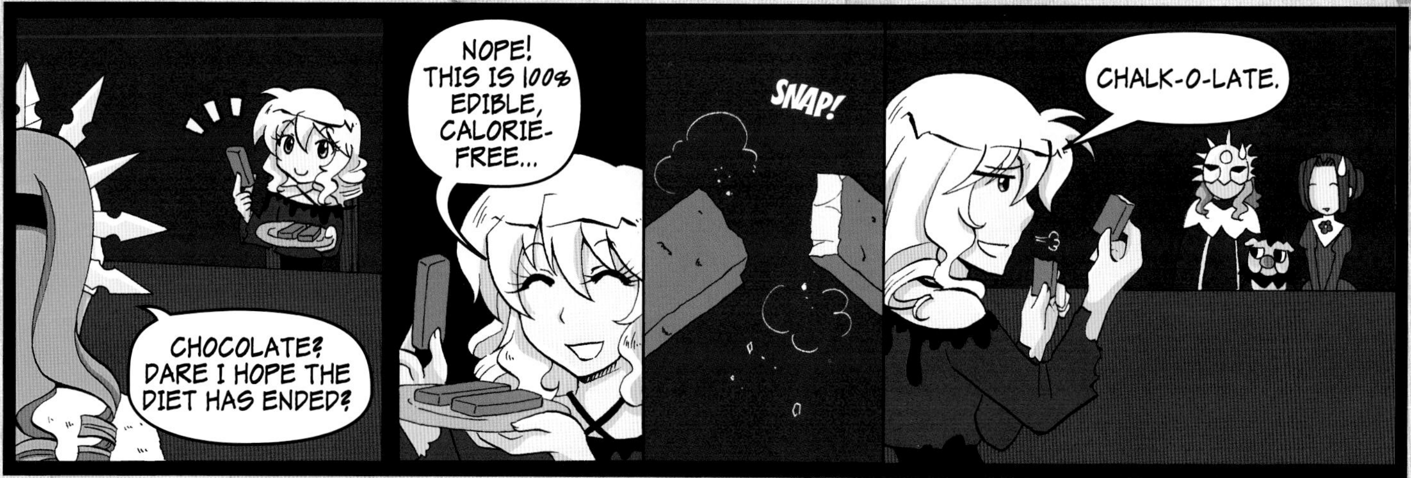
CHOCOLATE? DARE I HOPE THE DIET HAS ENDED?
NOPE! THIS IS 100% EDIBLE, CALORIE-FREE...
SNAP!
CHALK-O-LATE.

Special Soup

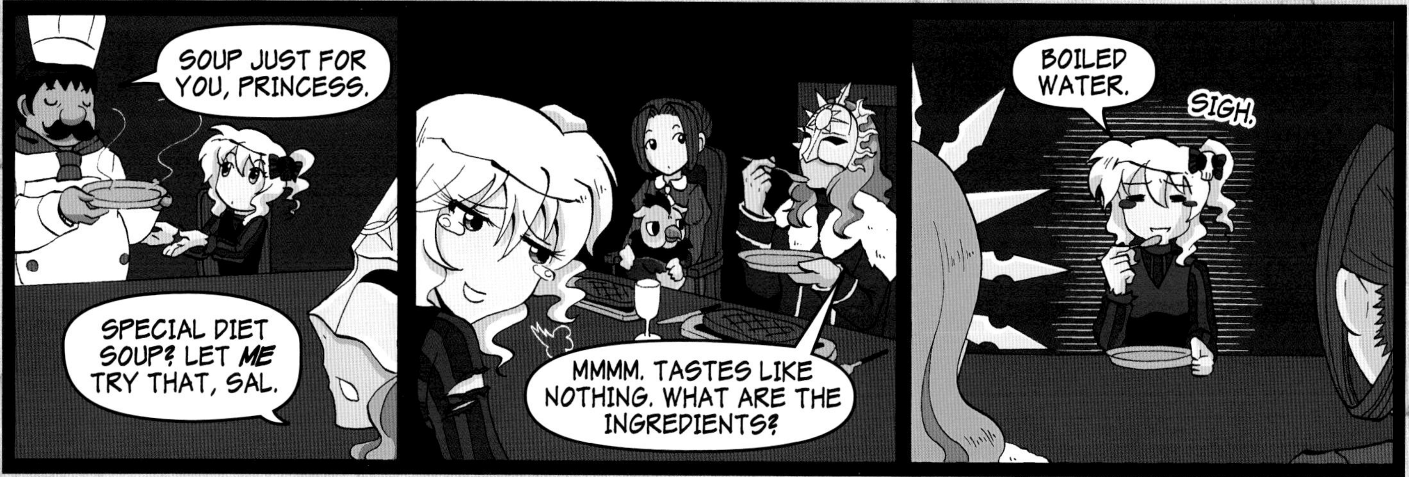
SOUP JUST FOR YOU, PRINCESS.
SPECIAL DIET SOUP? LET *ME* TRY THAT, SAL.
MMMM. TASTES LIKE NOTHING. WHAT ARE THE INGREDIENTS?
BOILED WATER.
SIGH.

dear d**Ai**ry

You know, it really stinks to be on a diet when you love food. When people talk about self-discipline, I think they really mean self-infliction--The pain! The pain! So why am I doing this to myself? I guess this means that I'm self-conscious and insecure. Lissa says I'm already skinny enough, but I only wanted to lose 10 extra pounds. Then would I be happy? I'm not so sure anymore. Maybe I just shouldn't worry about it and just try to be comfortable with who I am...

love forever

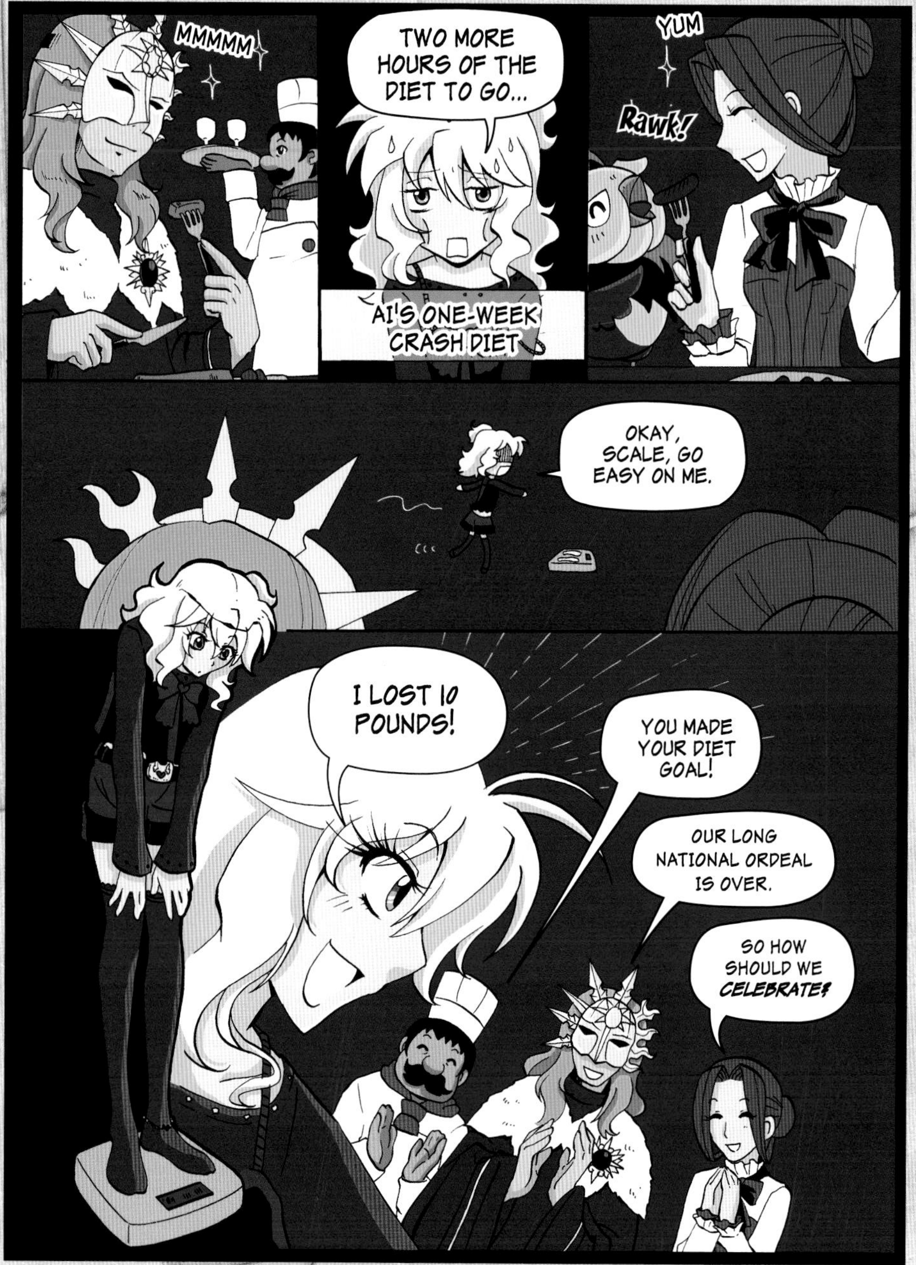
MMMMM
TWO MORE HOURS OF THE DIET TO GO...
AI'S ONE-WEEK CRASH DIET
YUM
Rawk!
OKAY, SCALE, GO EASY ON ME.
I LOST 10 POUNDS!
YOU MADE YOUR DIET GOAL!
OUR LONG NATIONAL ORDEAL IS OVER.
SO HOW SHOULD WE CELEBRATE?

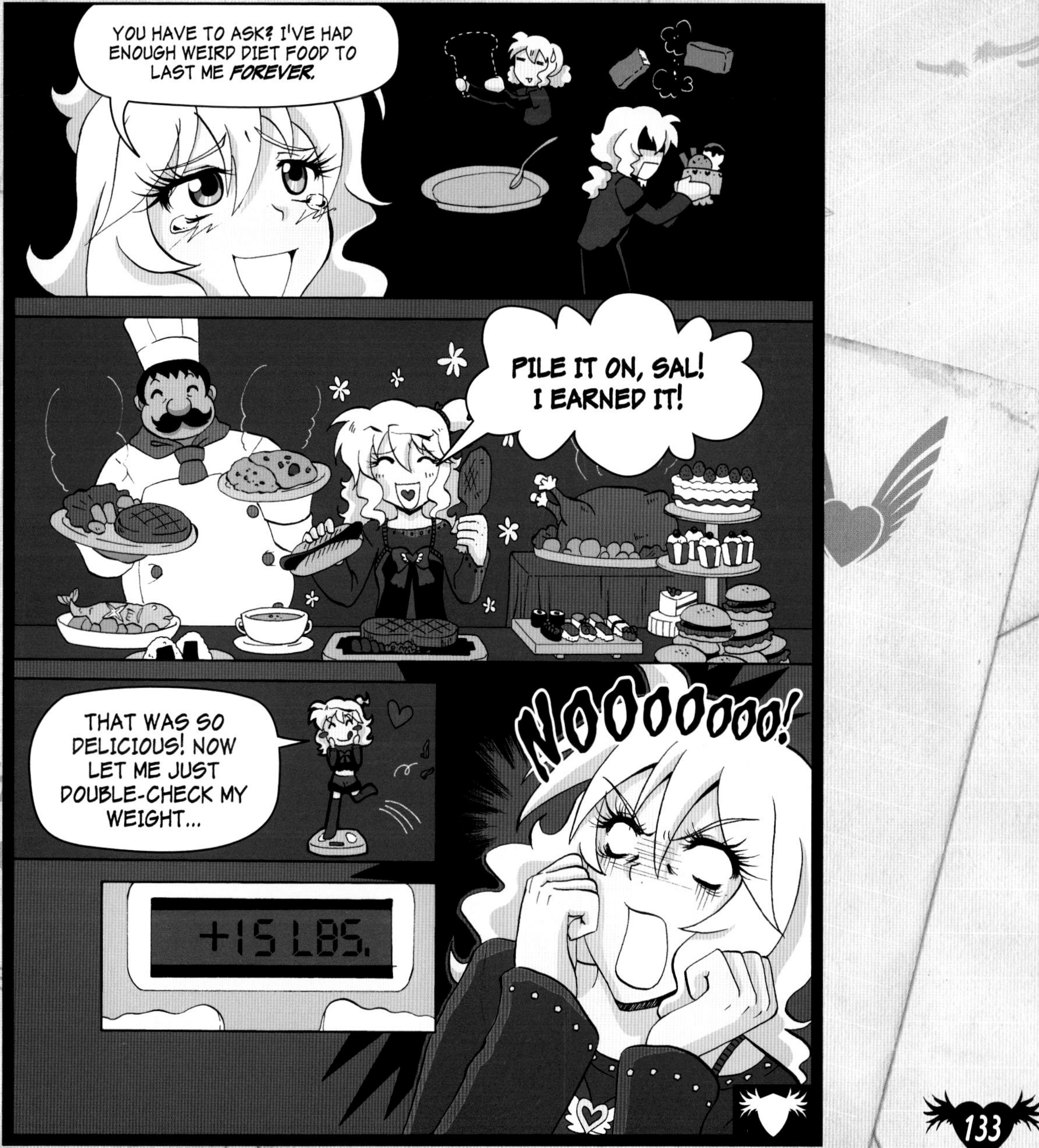
YOU HAVE TO ASK? I'VE HAD ENOUGH WEIRD DIET FOOD TO LAST ME *FOREVER.*
PILE IT ON, SAL! I EARNED IT!
THAT WAS SO DELICIOUS! NOW LET ME JUST DOUBLE-CHECK MY WEIGHT...
+15 LBS.
NOOOOOOO!

Firewood

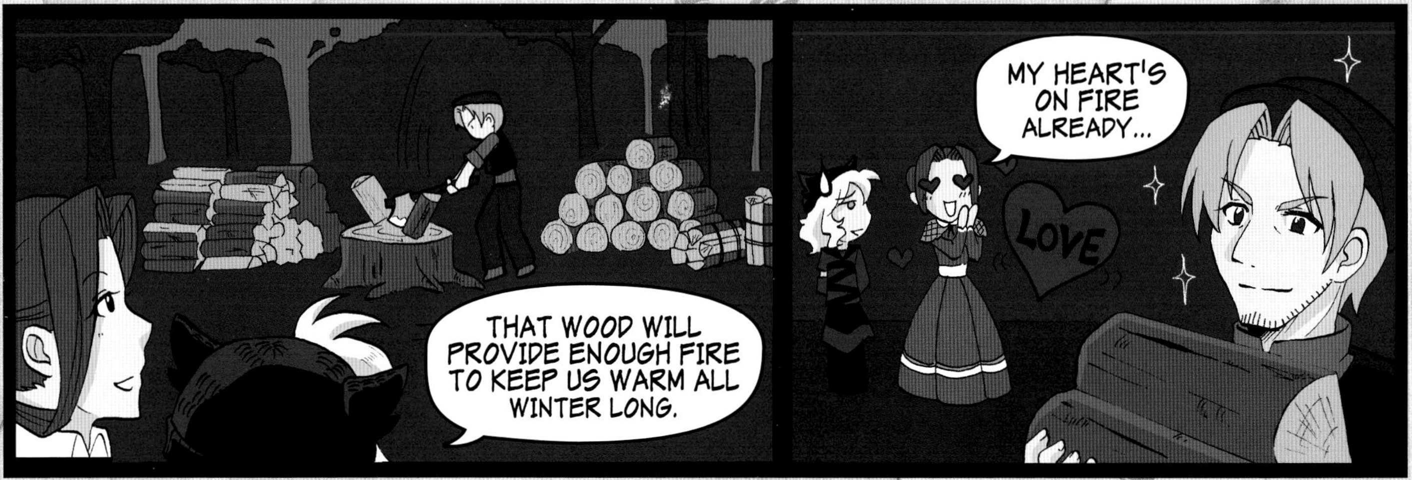
THAT WOOD WILL PROVIDE ENOUGH FIRE TO KEEP US WARM ALL WINTER LONG.
MY HEART'S ON FIRE ALREADY...
LOVE

Jacques

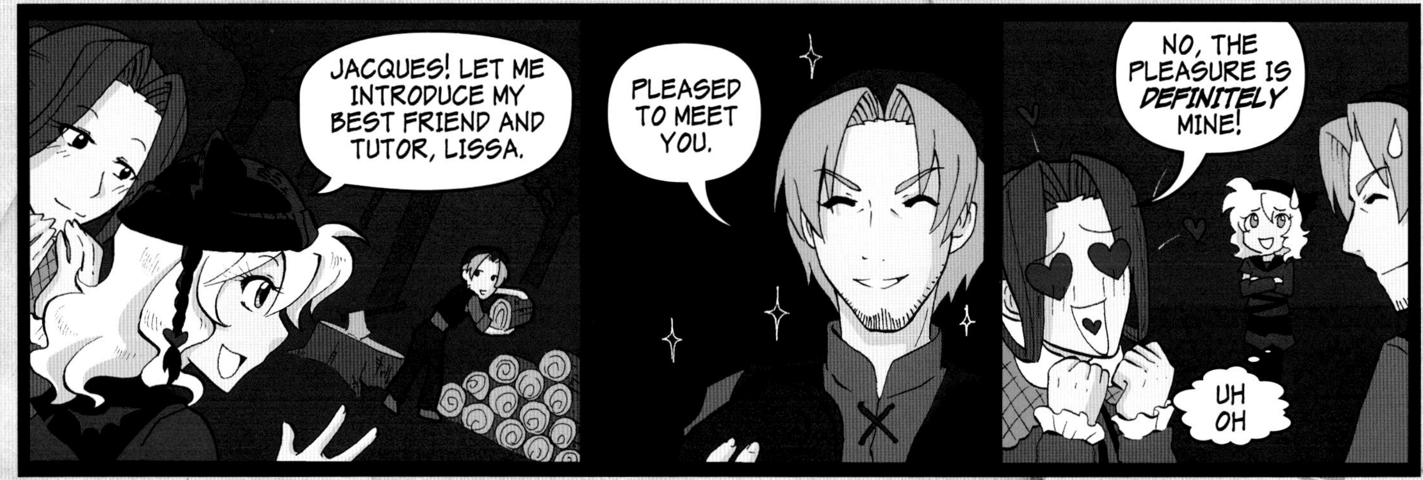
JACQUES! LET ME INTRODUCE MY BEST FRIEND AND TUTOR, LISSA.
PLEASED TO MEET YOU.
NO, THE PLEASURE IS *DEFINITELY* MINE!
UH OH

Wood Chopping

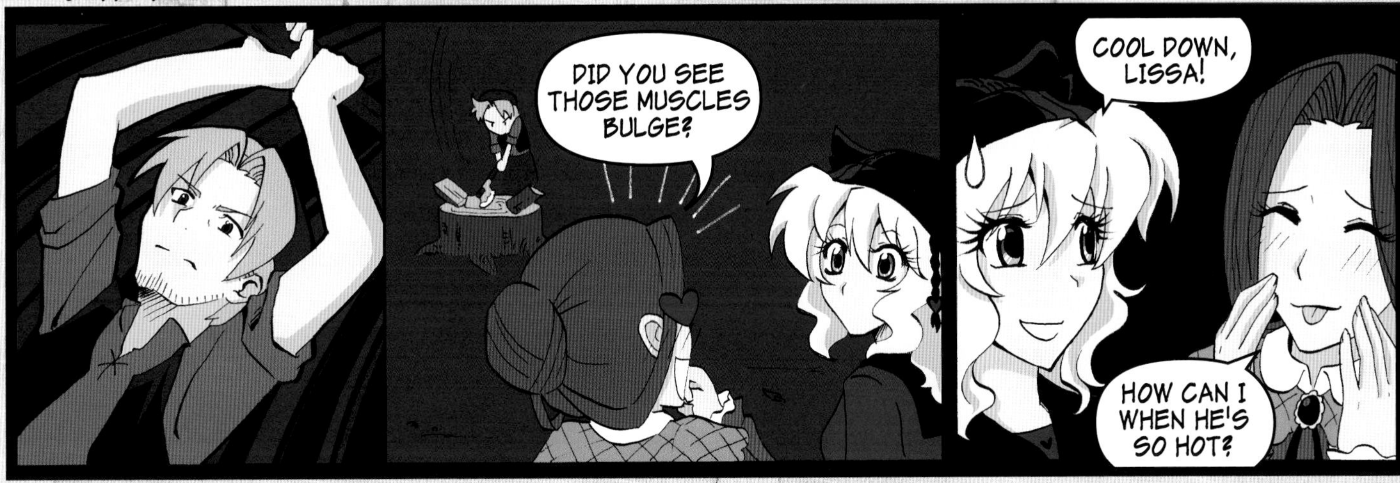
DID YOU SEE THOSE MUSCLES BULGE?
COOL DOWN, LISSA!
HOW CAN I WHEN HE'S SO HOT?

Wood Carrying

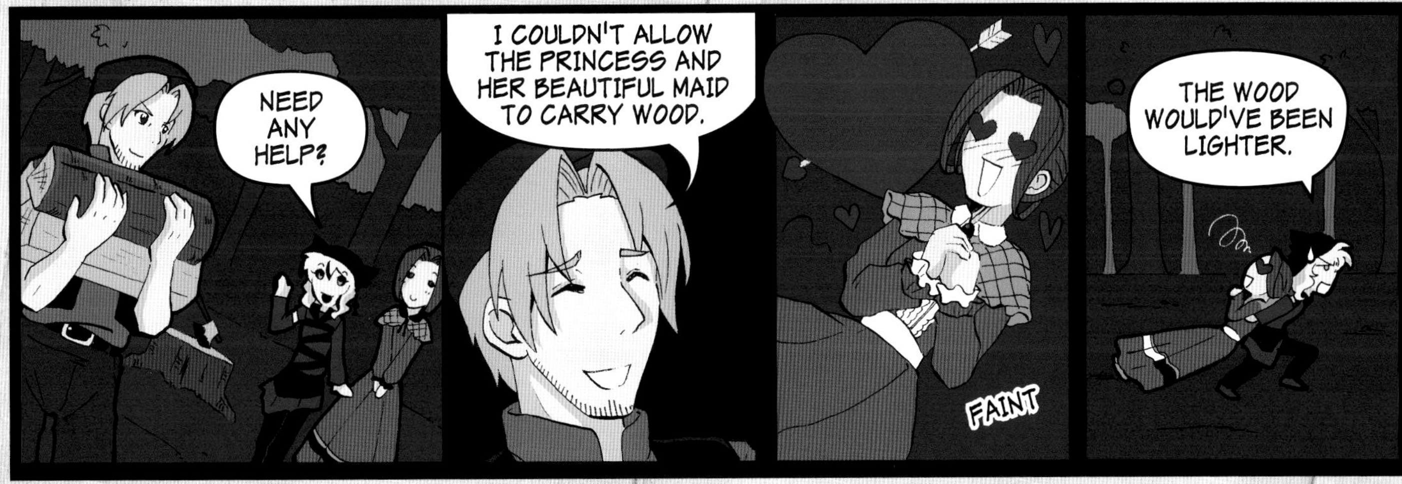
NEED ANY HELP?
I COULDN'T ALLOW THE PRINCESS AND HER BEAUTIFUL MAID TO CARRY WOOD.
FAINT
THE WOOD WOULD'VE BEEN LIGHTER.

Move Out of the Way

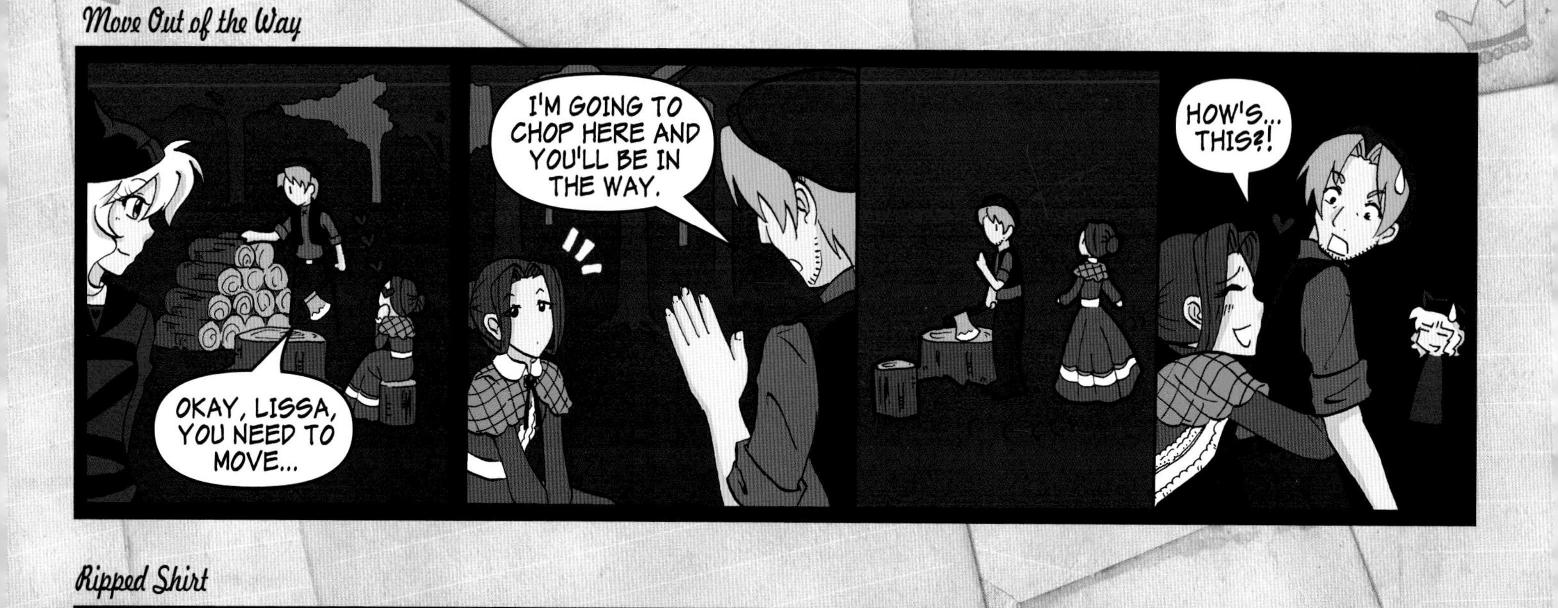
OKAY, LISSA, YOU NEED TO MOVE...
I'M GOING TO CHOP HERE AND YOU'LL BE IN THE WAY.
HOW'S... THIS?!

Ripped Shirt

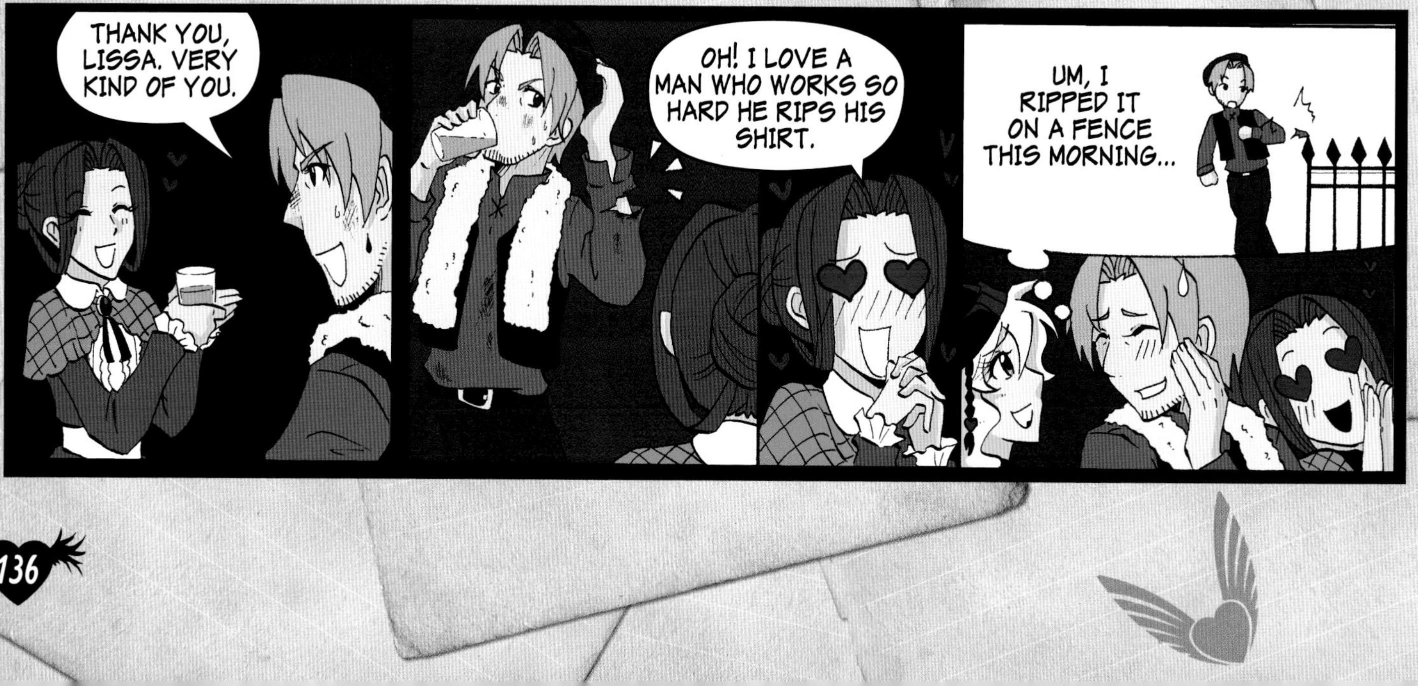
THANK YOU, LISSA. VERY KIND OF YOU.
OH! I LOVE A MAN WHO WORKS SO HARD HE RIPS HIS SHIRT.
UM, I RIPPED IT ON A FENCE THIS MORNING...

dear dry

The Dougen...they're such a mystery. Who were they? It seems that everyone I know has a different opinion. After all, they're practically extinct. Besides Rawk and Daddy's unicorns, I've never even seen them. Some people say they looked like terrible beasts; others say they were angels. Then there was the war. They tried to destroy us--but Daddy drove them off. Will I ever find out their secrets?

love forever

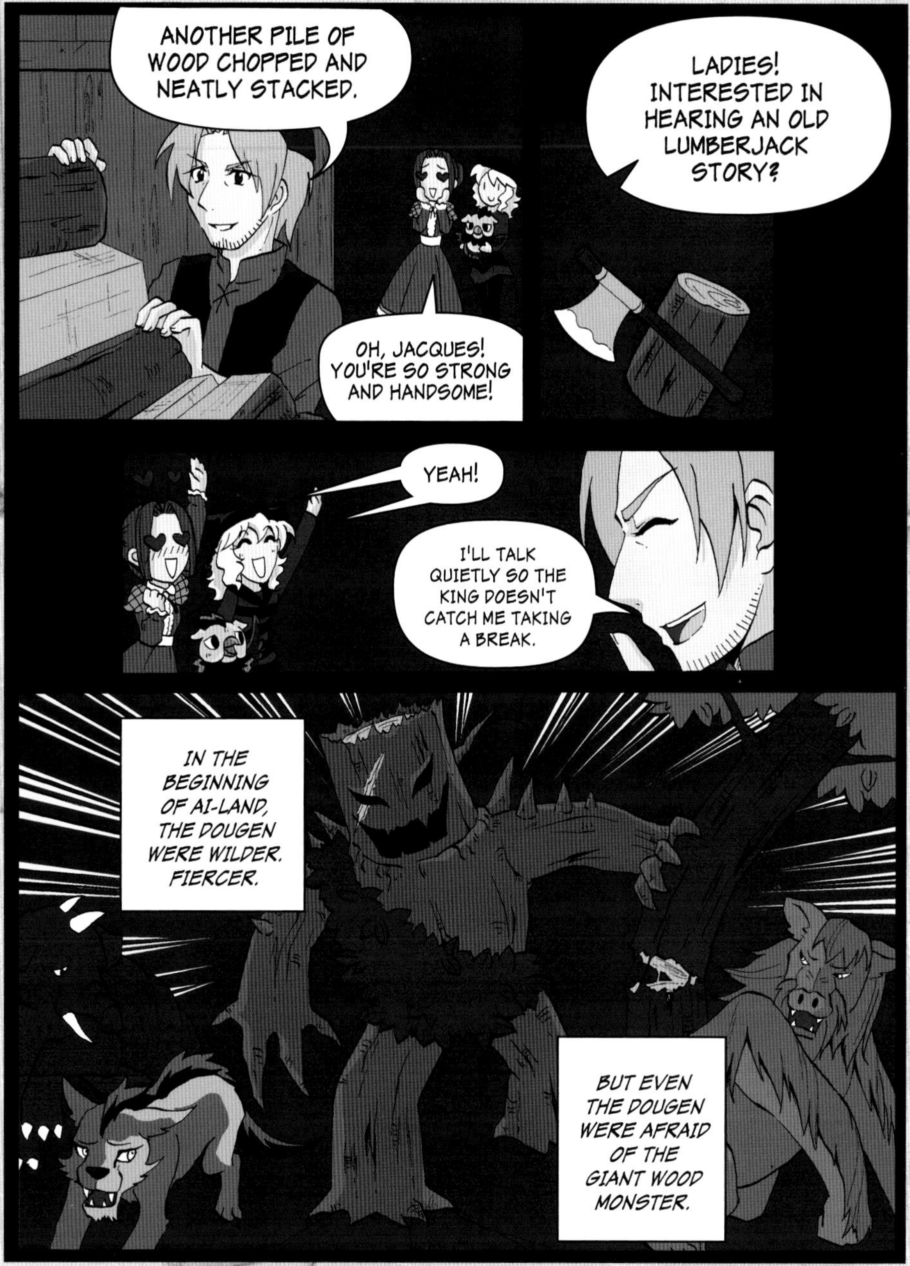
ANOTHER PILE OF WOOD CHOPPED AND NEATLY STACKED.
OH, JACQUES! YOU'RE SO STRONG AND HANDSOME!
LADIES! INTERESTED IN HEARING AN OLD LUMBERJACK STORY?
YEAH!
I'LL TALK QUIETLY SO THE KING DOESN'T CATCH ME TAKING A BREAK.
IN THE BEGINNING OF AI-LAND, THE DOUGEN WERE WILDER. FIERCER.
BUT EVEN THE DOUGEN WERE AFRAID OF THE GIANT WOOD MONSTER.

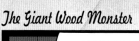

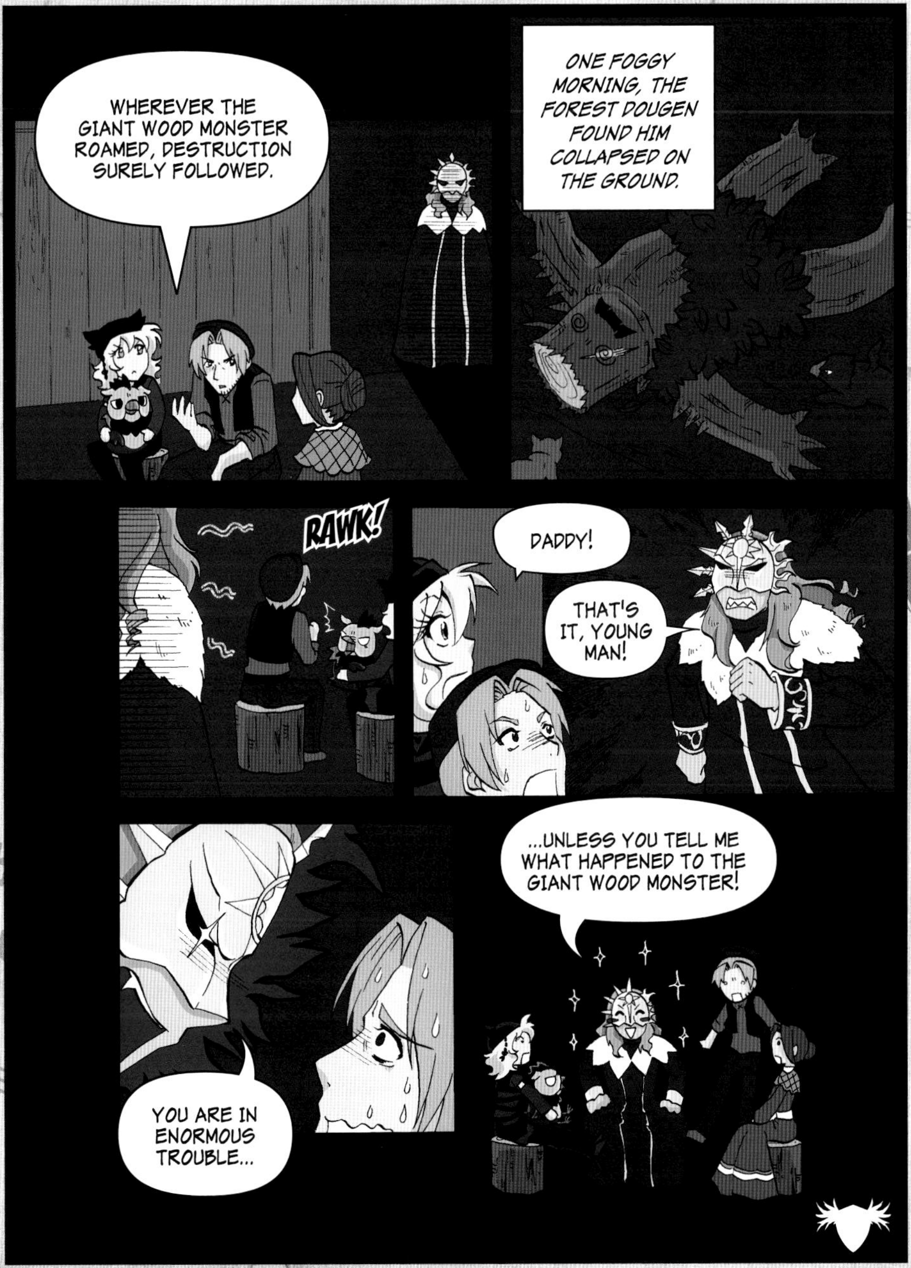
WHEREVER THE GIANT WOOD MONSTER ROAMED, DESTRUCTION SURELY FOLLOWED.
ONE FOGGY MORNING, THE FOREST DOUGEN FOUND HIM COLLAPSED ON THE GROUND.
RAWK!
DADDY!
THAT'S IT, YOUNG MAN!
YOU ARE IN ENORMOUS TROUBLE...
...UNLESS YOU TELL ME WHAT HAPPENED TO THE GIANT WOOD MONSTER!

Tired

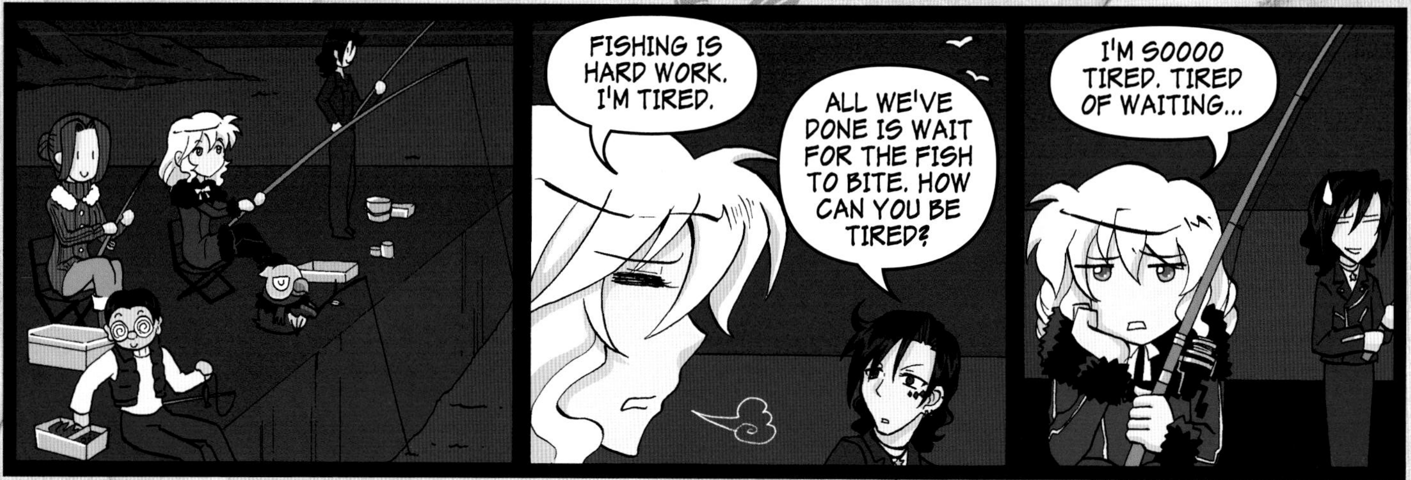
FISHING IS HARD WORK. I'M TIRED.
ALL WE'VE DONE IS WAIT FOR THE FISH TO BITE. HOW CAN YOU BE TIRED?
I'M SOOOO TIRED. TIRED OF WAITING...

Got One

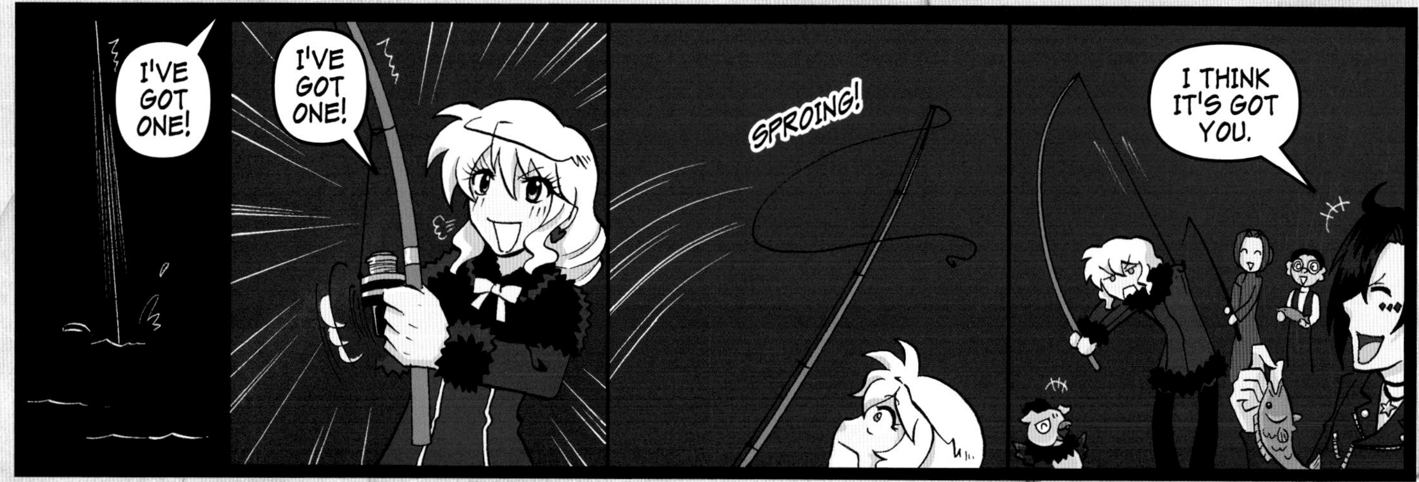
I'VE GOT ONE!
I'VE GOT ONE!
SPROING!
I THINK IT'S GOT YOU.

Big One

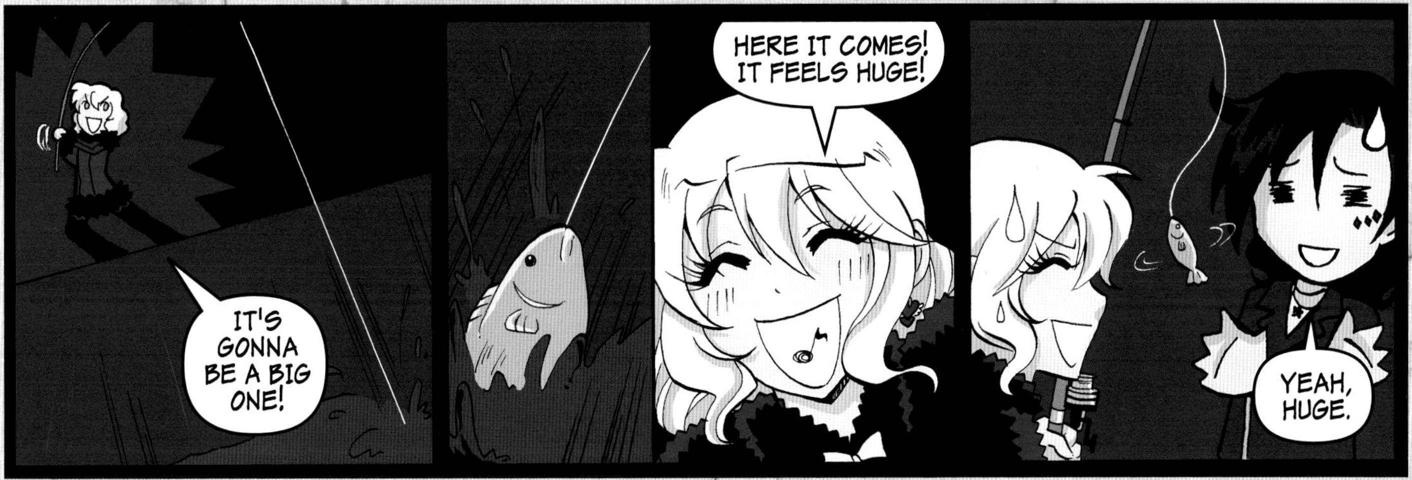
IT'S GONNA BE A BIG ONE!
HERE IT COMES! IT FEELS HUGE!
YEAH, HUGE.

Bait

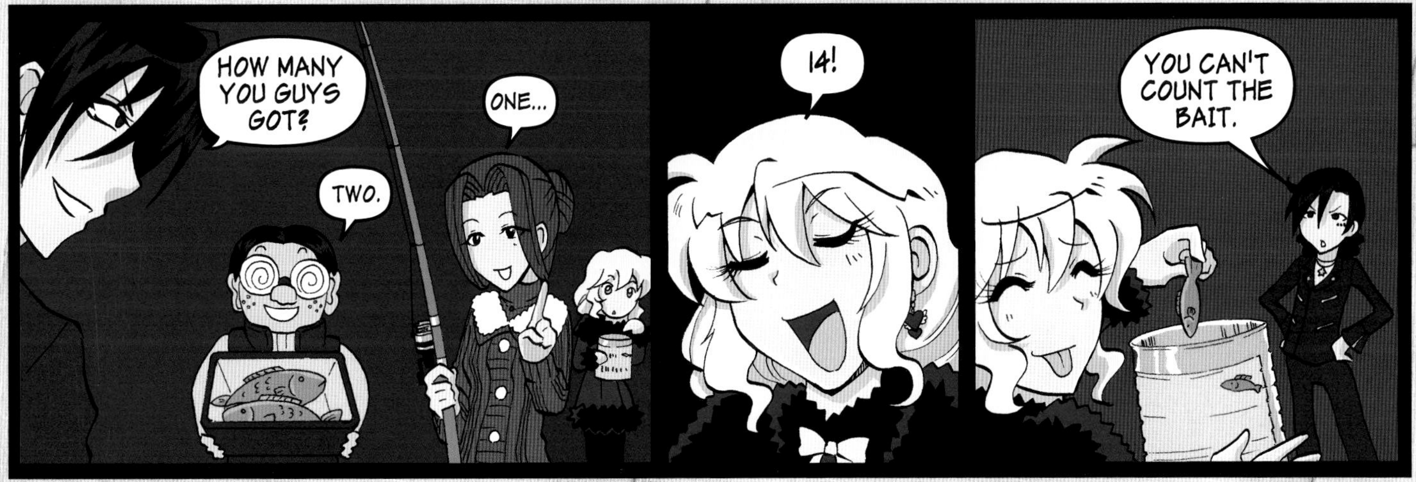
HOW MANY YOU GUYS GOT?
ONE...
TWO.
14!
YOU CAN'T COUNT THE BAIT.

Rawk Lobster

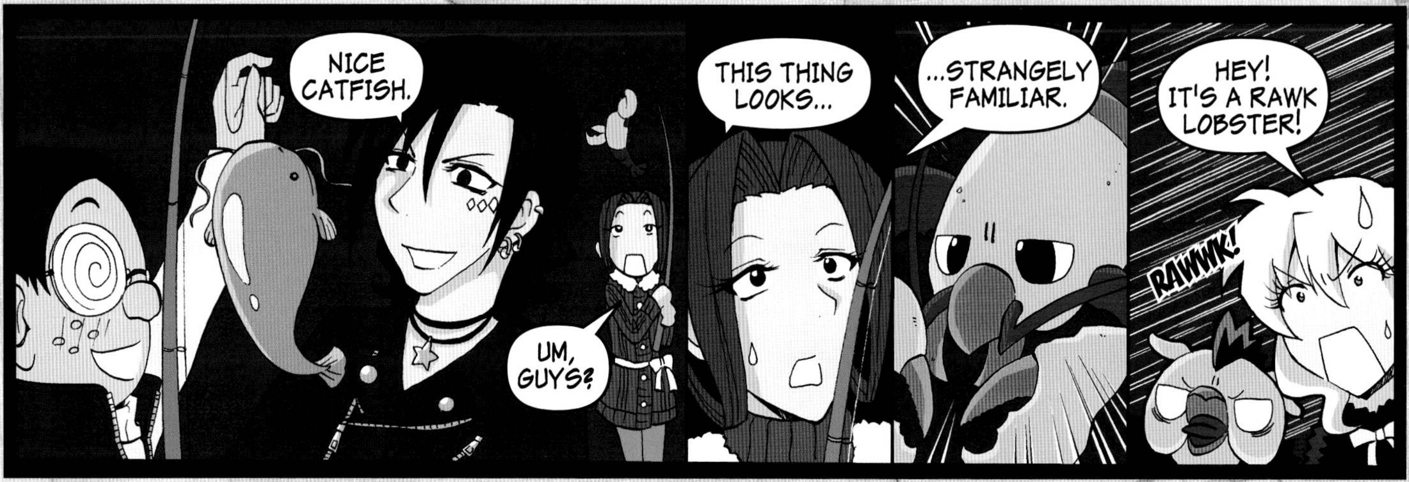
NICE CATFISH.
UM, GUYS?
THIS THING LOOKS...
...STRANGELY FAMILIAR.
HEY! IT'S A RAWK LOBSTER!
RAWWK!

Gum not Fish

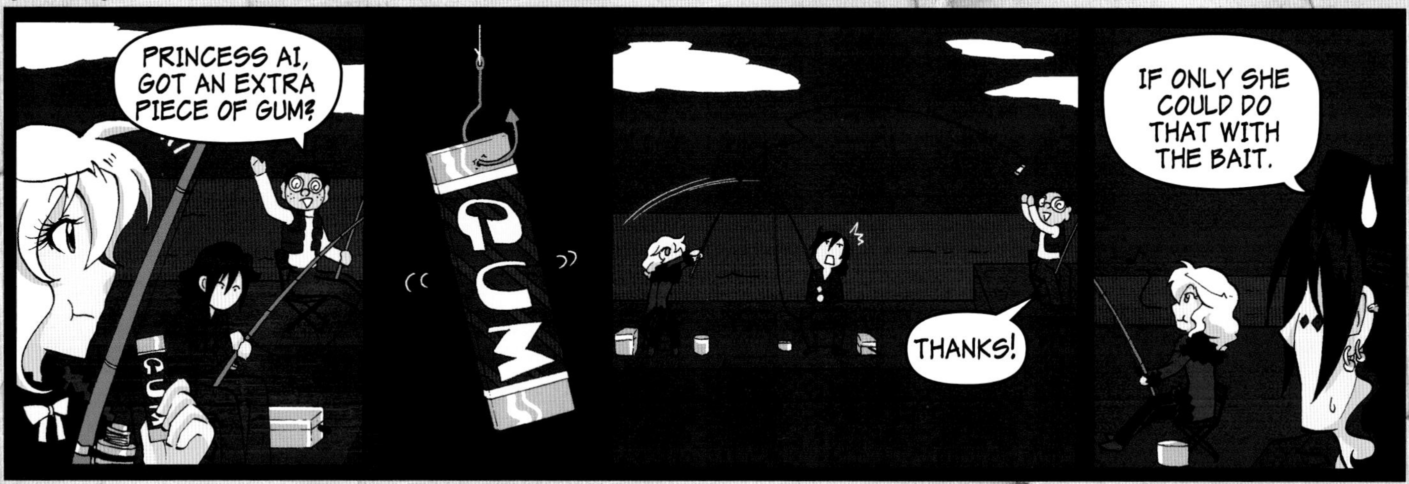
PRINCESS AI, GOT AN EXTRA PIECE OF GUM?
GUM
GUM
THANKS!
IF ONLY SHE COULD DO THAT WITH THE BAIT.

dear d*Ai*ry

Lissa calls my singing magical. I'm not so sure about that, but I definitely feel some sort of magic inside with music. It's almost like my entire body wants to float through the air like musical notes. I don't know why, but it seems like music is its own language, and I'm still learning how to speak it. Maybe no one can quite understand--even I don't get it entirely. I just know that music is something I couldn't live without.

love forever

 Ai

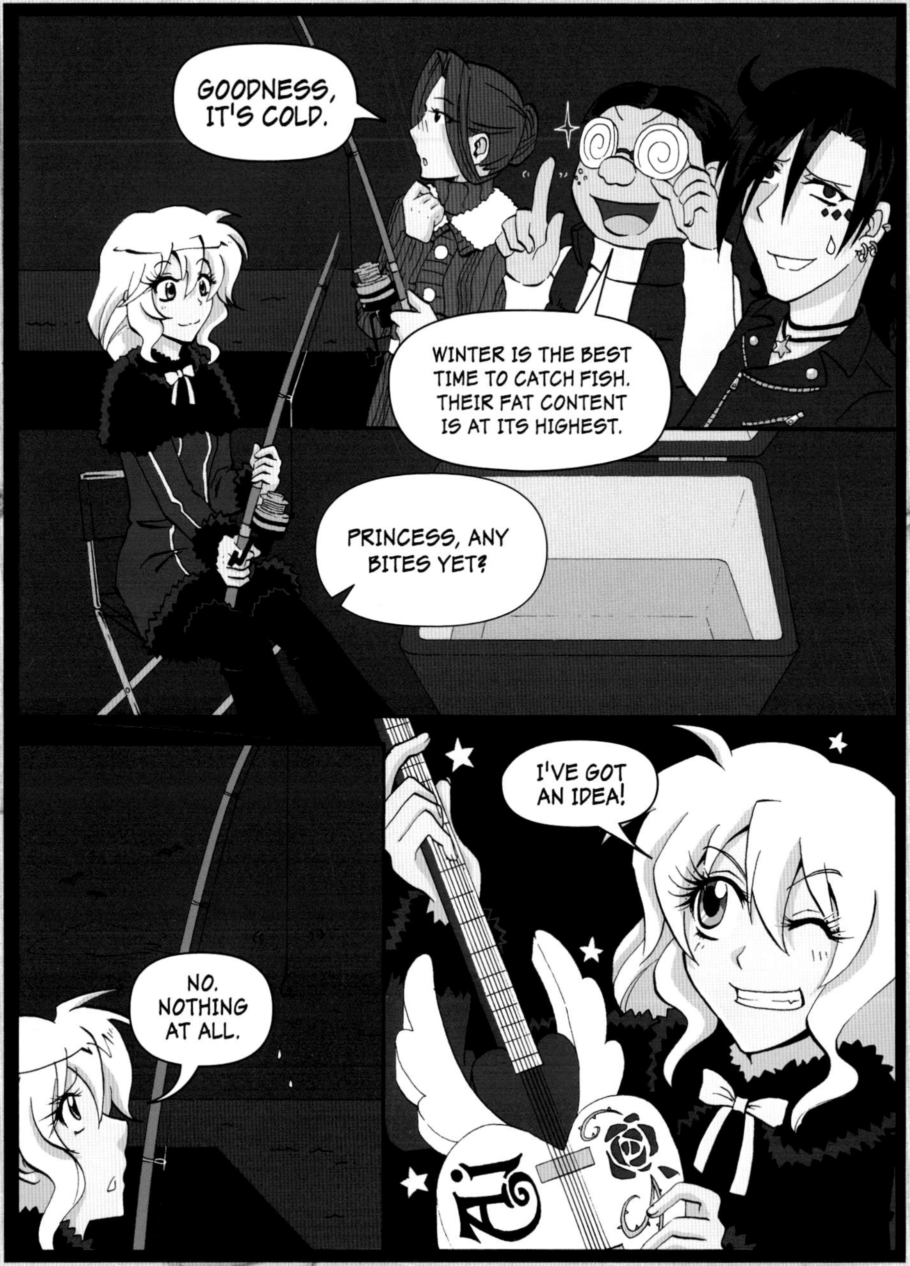
GOODNESS, IT'S COLD.
WINTER IS THE BEST TIME TO CATCH FISH. THEIR FAT CONTENT IS AT ITS HIGHEST.
PRINCESS, ANY BITES YET?
NO. NOTHING AT ALL.
I'VE GOT AN IDEA!

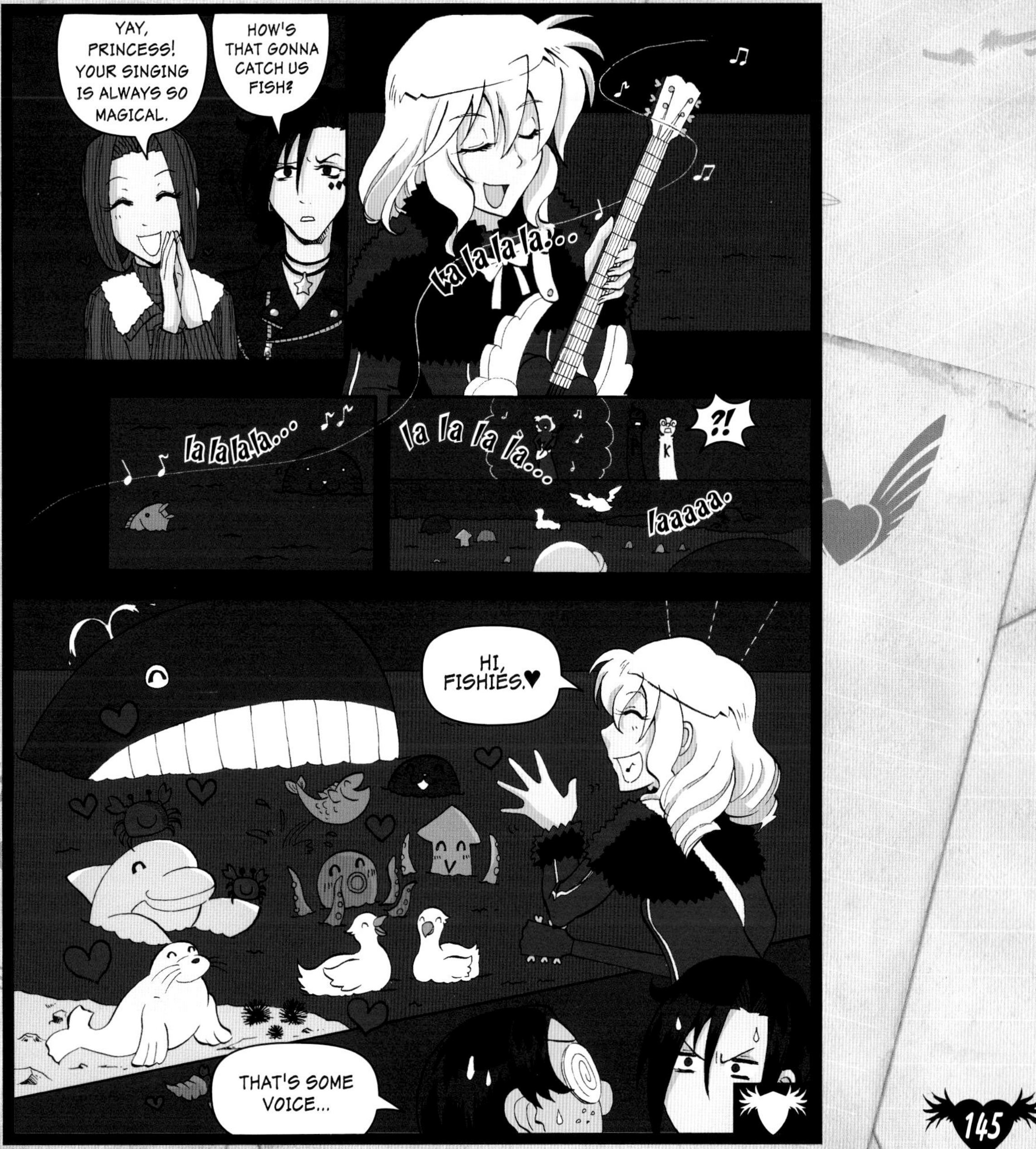
YAY, PRINCESS! YOUR SINGING IS ALWAYS SO MAGICAL.
HOW'S THAT GONNA CATCH US FISH?
la la la la...
la la la la...
la la la la...
?!
laaaaa.
HI, FISHIES.♥
THAT'S SOME VOICE...

Arbor Day

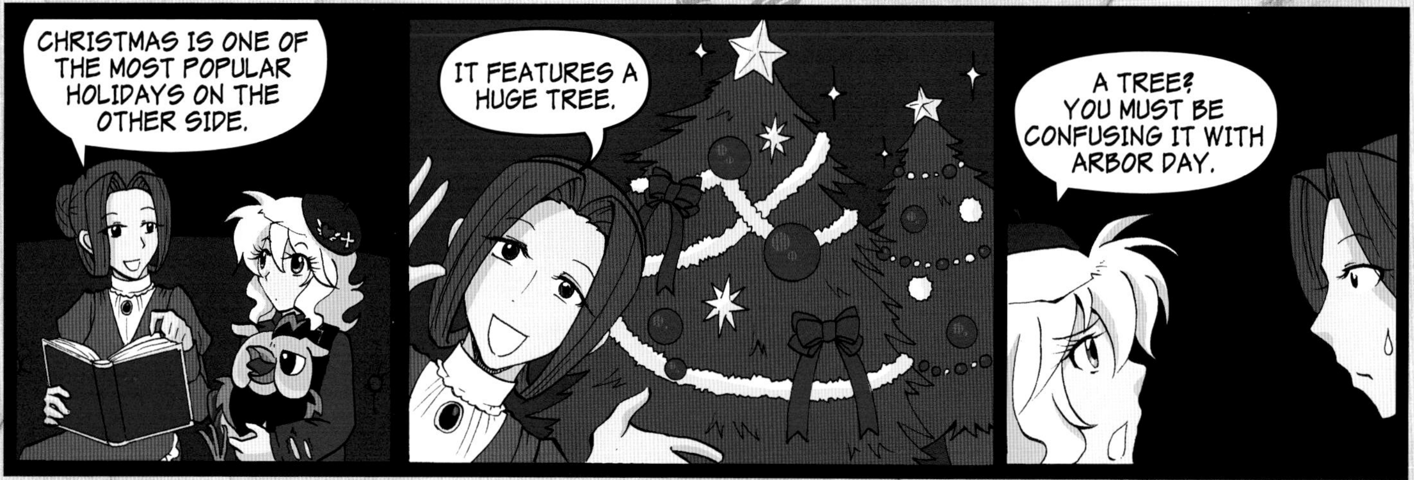
CHRISTMAS IS ONE OF THE MOST POPULAR HOLIDAYS ON THE OTHER SIDE.
IT FEATURES A HUGE TREE.
A TREE? YOU MUST BE CONFUSING IT WITH ARBOR DAY.

White Christmas

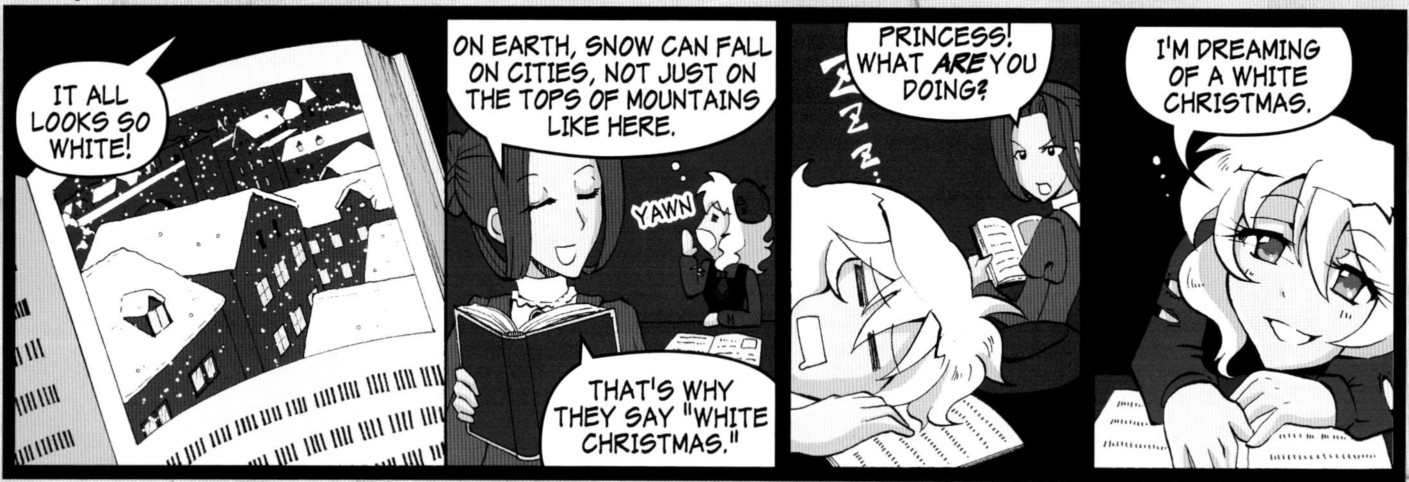
IT ALL LOOKS SO WHITE!
ON EARTH, SNOW CAN FALL ON CITIES, NOT JUST ON THE TOPS OF MOUNTAINS LIKE HERE.
YAWN
THAT'S WHY THEY SAY "WHITE CHRISTMAS."
PRINCESS! WHAT ***ARE*** YOU DOING?
ZZZ...
I'M DREAMING OF A WHITE CHRISTMAS.

Stockings

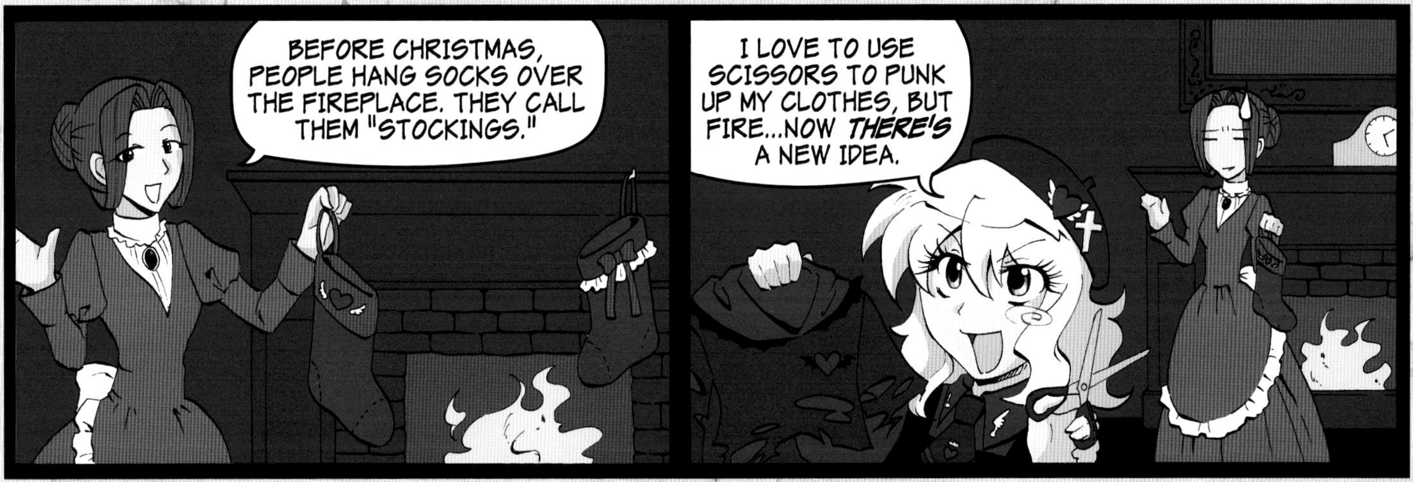

BEFORE CHRISTMAS, PEOPLE HANG SOCKS OVER THE FIREPLACE. THEY CALL THEM "STOCKINGS."
I LOVE TO USE SCISSORS TO PUNK UP MY CLOTHES, BUT FIRE...NOW *THERE'S* A NEW IDEA.

Reindeer

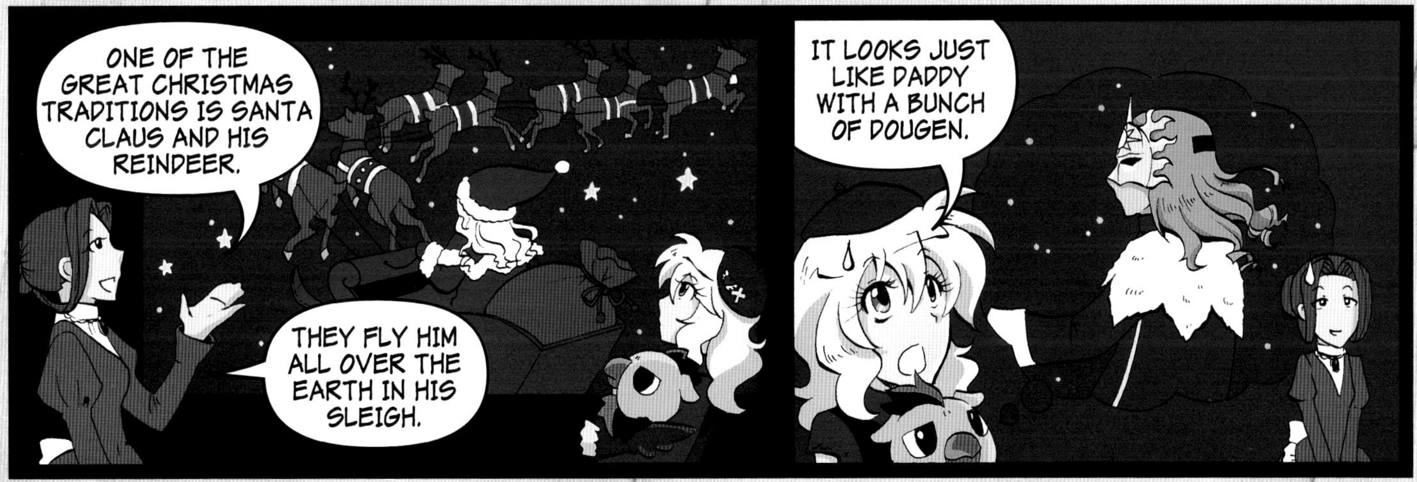

ONE OF THE GREAT CHRISTMAS TRADITIONS IS SANTA CLAUS AND HIS REINDEER.
THEY FLY HIM ALL OVER THE EARTH IN HIS SLEIGH.
IT LOOKS JUST LIKE DADDY WITH A BUNCH OF DOUGEN.

Presents

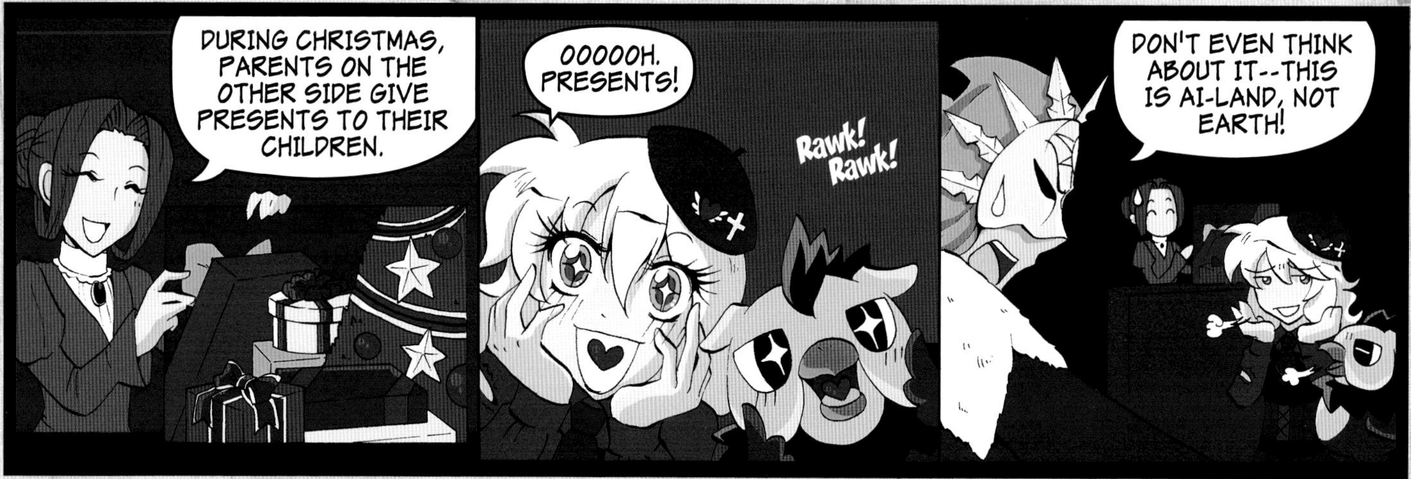
DURING CHRISTMAS, PARENTS ON THE OTHER SIDE GIVE PRESENTS TO THEIR CHILDREN.
OOOOOH. PRESENTS!
Rawk! Rawk!
DON'T EVEN THINK ABOUT IT--THIS IS AI-LAND, NOT EARTH!

X-mas Carols

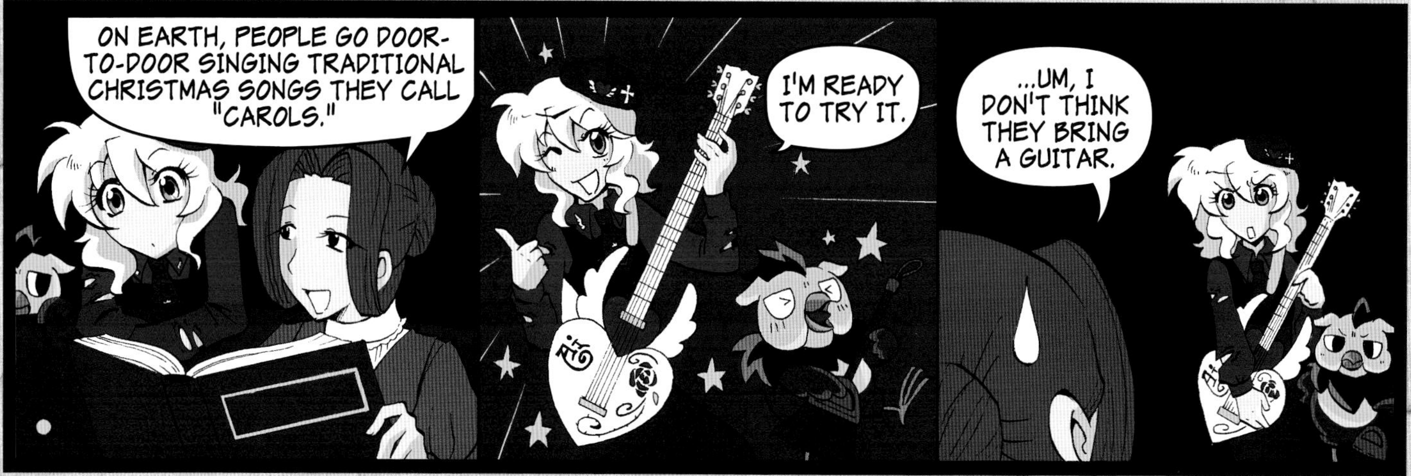
ON EARTH, PEOPLE GO DOOR-TO-DOOR SINGING TRADITIONAL CHRISTMAS SONGS THEY CALL "CAROLS."
I'M READY TO TRY IT.
...UM, I DON'T THINK THEY BRING A GUITAR.

dear dAiry

Ai-Land is sooo boring! Of all the fascinating things I've learned about the Other Side, the most incredible one has got to be the people. What is it about the humans on Earth that makes them so different from us? Maybe it's how, just when it seems they hate each other and are determined to destroy everything around them, they turn around and surprise me with unlimited amounts of love. Not that I would really know, but at least that's what it seems like. How bizarre! One day, my dream is to actually get there, somehow, and meet them in person.

love forever

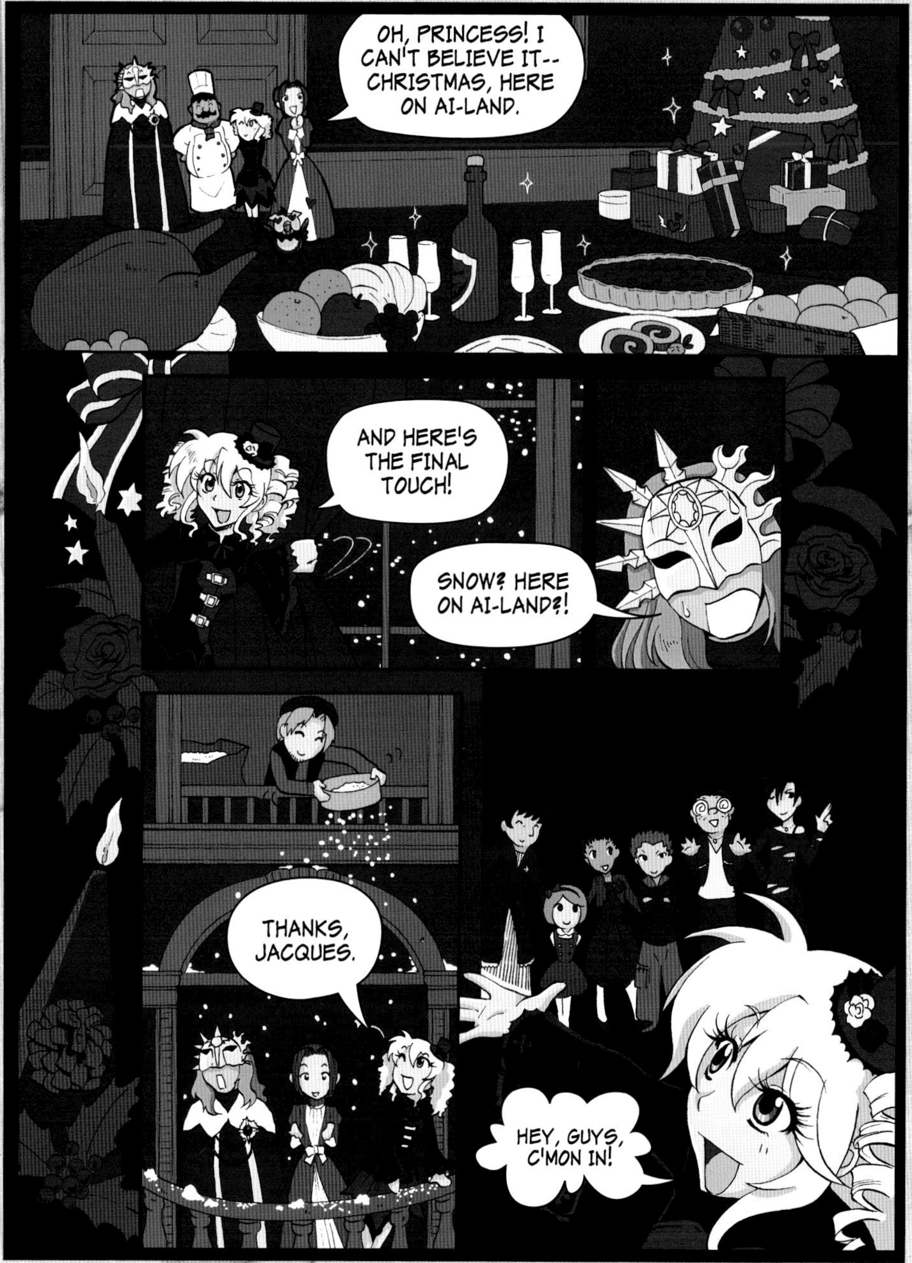
OH, PRINCESS! I CAN'T BELIEVE IT--CHRISTMAS, HERE ON AI-LAND.
AND HERE'S THE FINAL TOUCH!
SNOW? HERE ON AI-LAND?!
THANKS, JACQUES.
HEY, GUYS, C'MON IN!

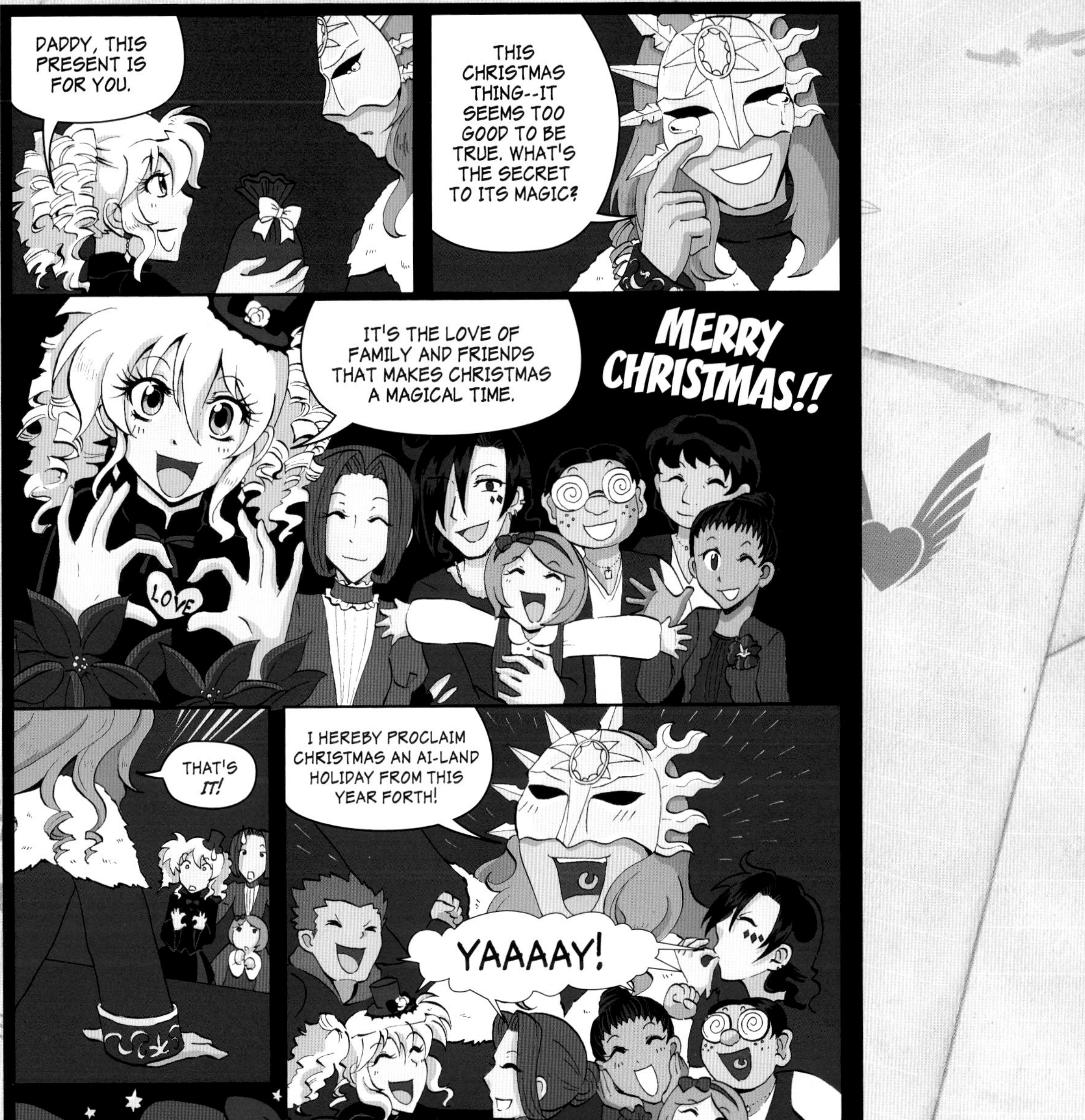
DADDY, THIS PRESENT IS FOR YOU.
THIS CHRISTMAS THING--IT SEEMS TOO GOOD TO BE TRUE. WHAT'S THE SECRET TO ITS MAGIC?
IT'S THE LOVE OF FAMILY AND FRIENDS THAT MAKES CHRISTMAS A MAGICAL TIME.
MERRY CHRISTMAS!!
LOVE
THAT'S *IT!*
I HEREBY PROCLAIM CHRISTMAS AN AI-LAND HOLIDAY FROM THIS YEAR FORTH!
YAAAAY!

Resolution # 1: No Diet

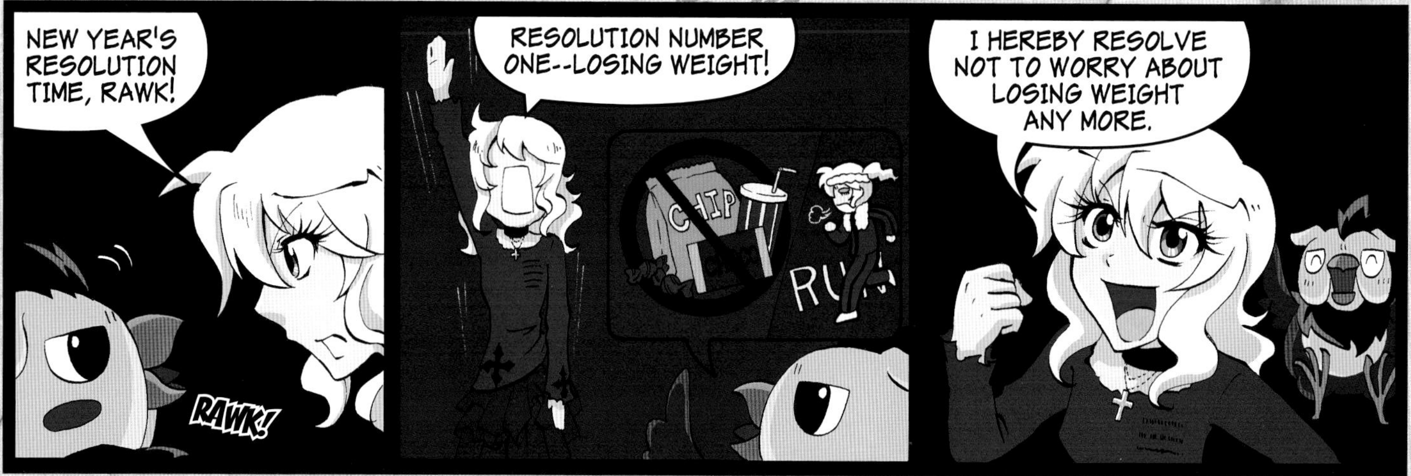
NEW YEAR'S RESOLUTION TIME, RAWK!
RAWK!
RESOLUTION NUMBER ONE--LOSING WEIGHT!
CHIP
I HEREBY RESOLVE NOT TO WORRY ABOUT LOSING WEIGHT ANY MORE.

Resolution # 2: Shop 'Til You Drop

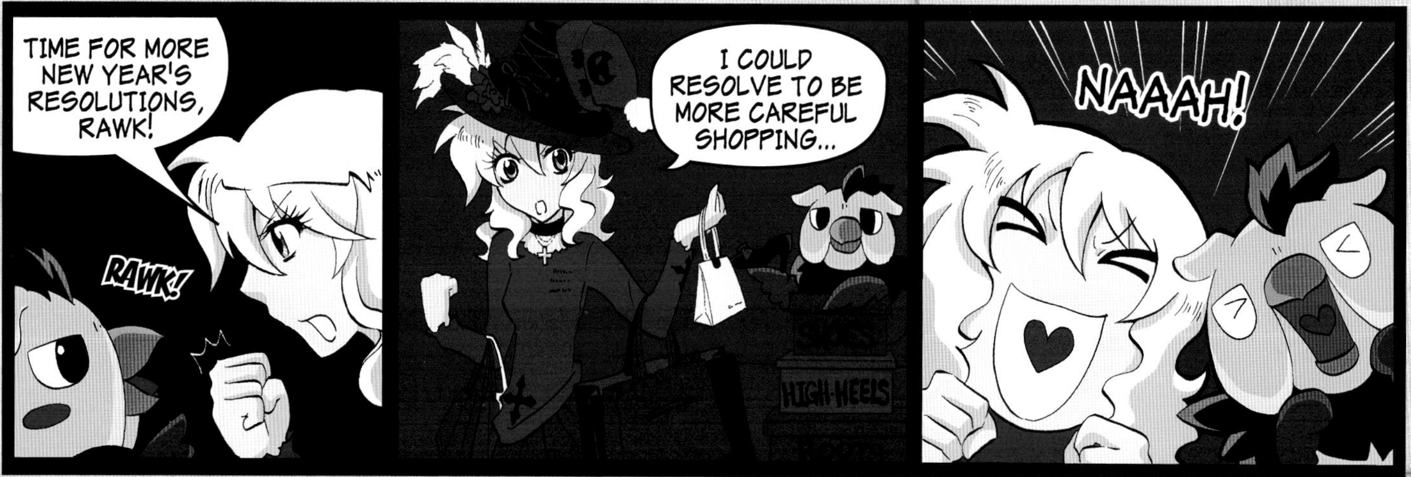
TIME FOR MORE NEW YEAR'S RESOLUTIONS, RAWK!
RAWK!
I COULD RESOLVE TO BE MORE CAREFUL SHOPPING...
HIGH-HEELS
NAAAH!

Resolution # 3: Blisters on Fingers

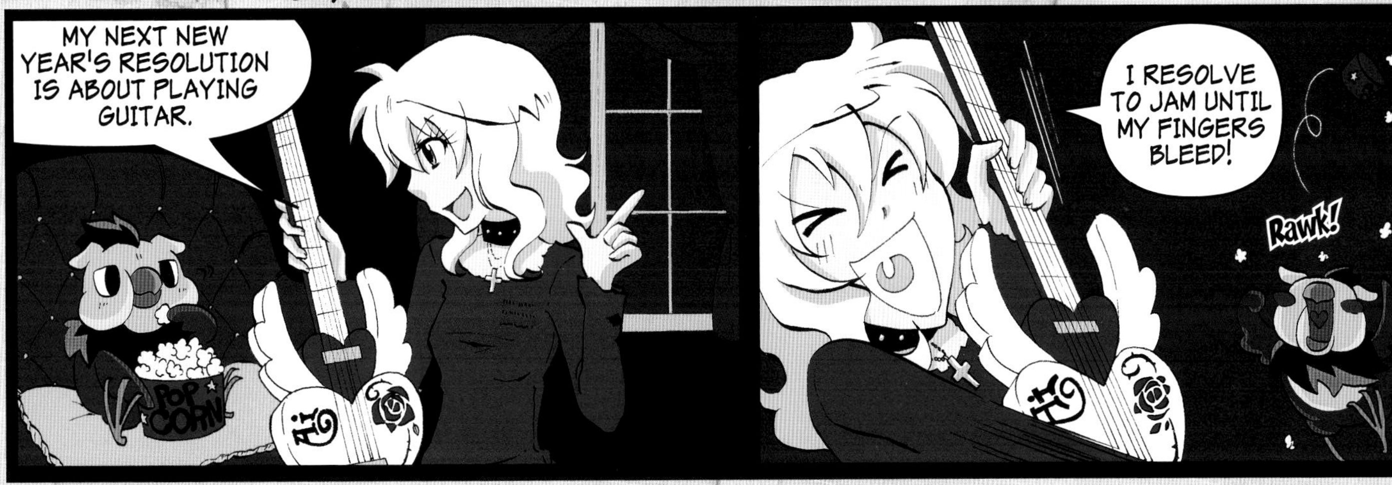
MY NEXT NEW YEAR'S RESOLUTION IS ABOUT PLAYING GUITAR.
POP CORN
I RESOLVE TO JAM UNTIL MY FINGERS BLEED!
RAWK!

Resolution # 4: Find Lissa a Boyfriend

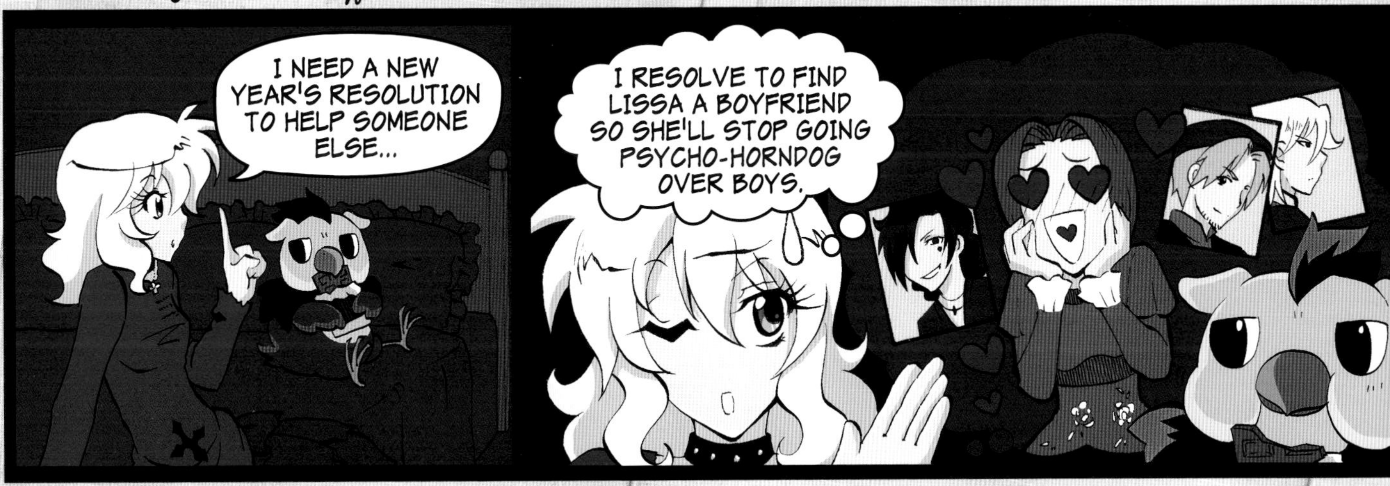
I NEED A NEW YEAR'S RESOLUTION TO HELP SOMEONE ELSE...
I RESOLVE TO FIND LISSA A BOYFRIEND SO SHE'LL STOP GOING PSYCHO-HORNDOG OVER BOYS.

Resolution # 5: Activist

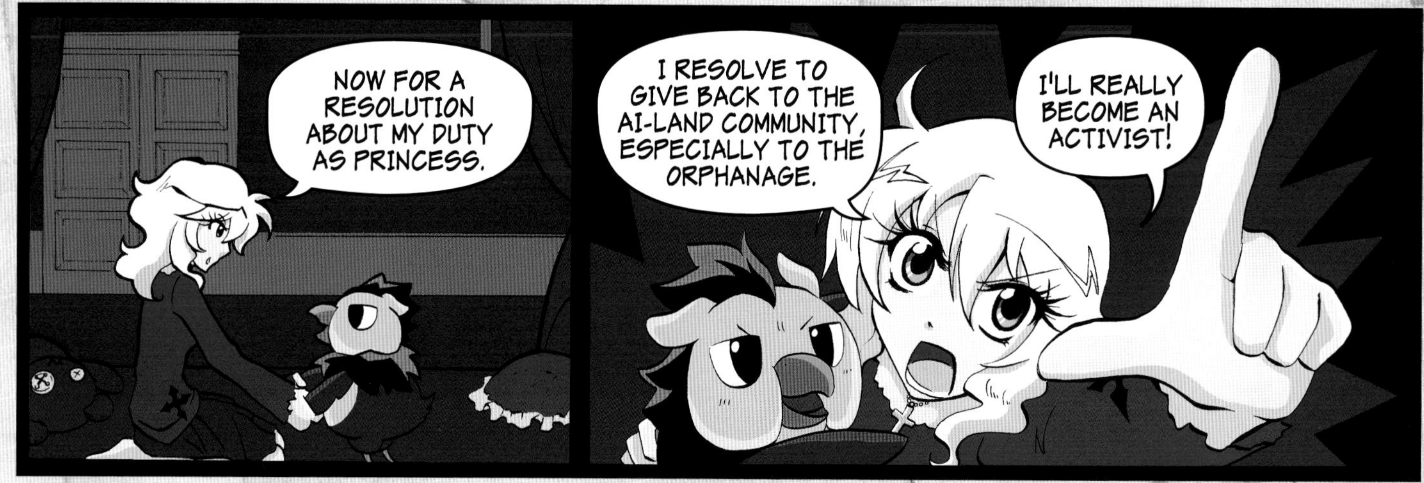
NOW FOR A RESOLUTION ABOUT MY DUTY AS PRINCESS.
I RESOLVE TO GIVE BACK TO THE AI-LAND COMMUNITY, ESPECIALLY TO THE ORPHANAGE.
I'LL REALLY BECOME AN ACTIVIST!

Resolution # 6: Dreadful Wings

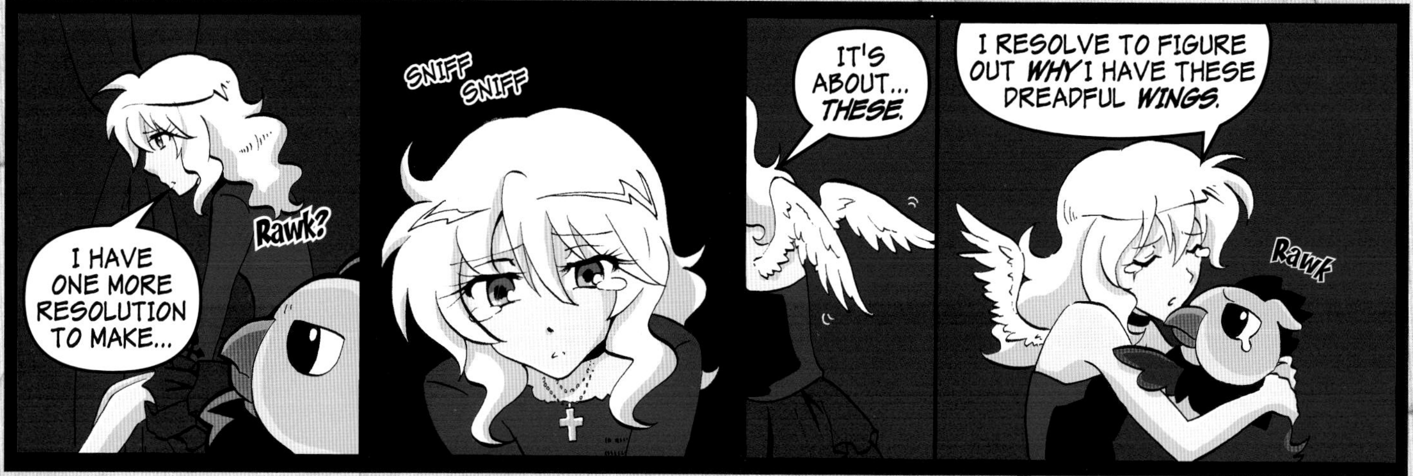
I HAVE ONE MORE RESOLUTION TO MAKE...
Rawk?
SNIFF SNIFF
IT'S ABOUT... THESE.
I RESOLVE TO FIGURE OUT WHY I HAVE THESE DREADFUL WINGS.
Rawk

dear dry

It's New Year's Eve here on Ai-Land, just like it is on the Other Side--Earth. Everyone's making resolutions to change. That's so weird. Every time I try to change, things never turn out like I planned. Like when I try to lose weight. But sometimes, I wake up, and I've just-- changed. I guess that's what growing up is all about. It doesn't always make sense, especially to Daddy. But that's the way it is for me, here on Ai-Land.

love forever

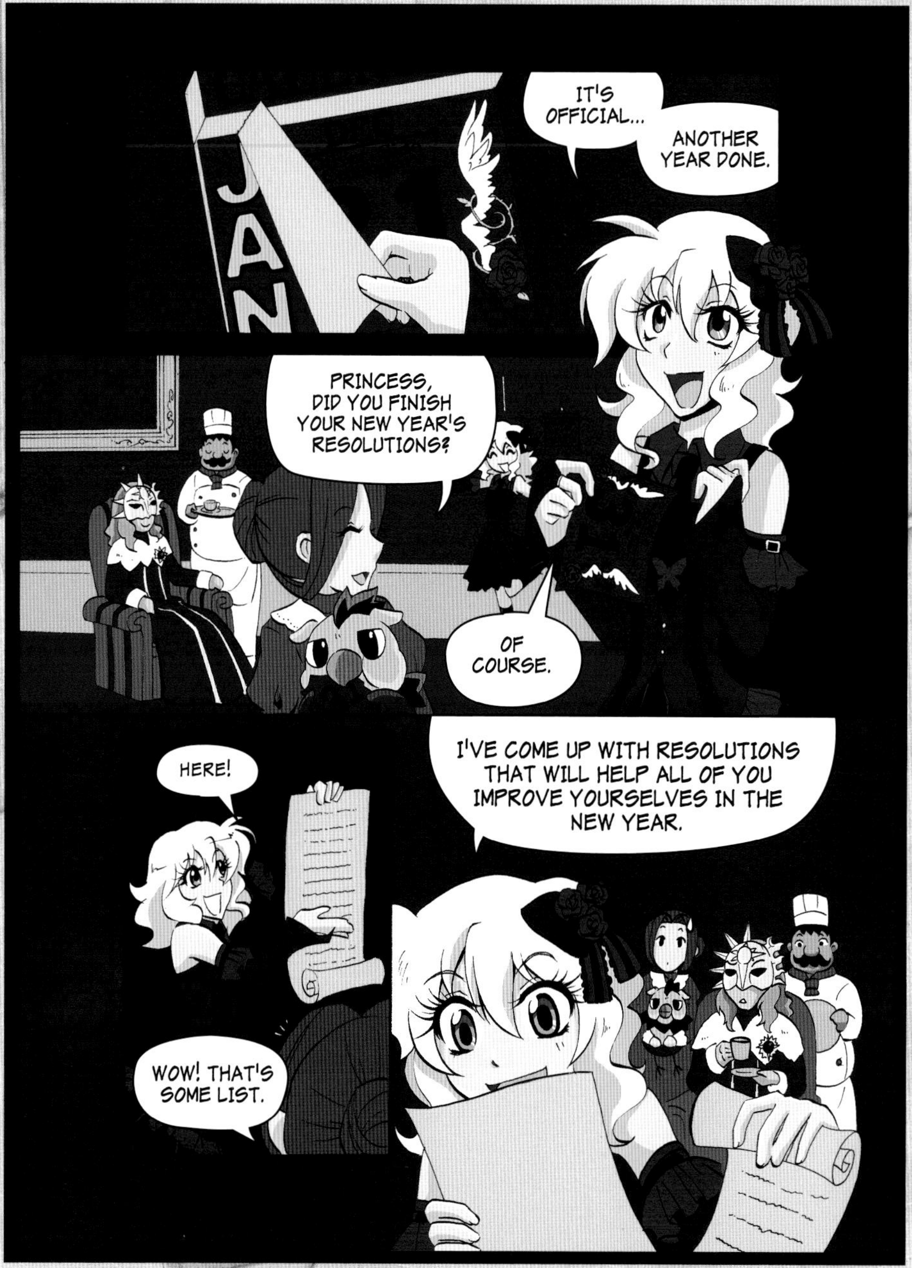
IT'S OFFICIAL...
ANOTHER YEAR DONE.
PRINCESS, DID YOU FINISH YOUR NEW YEAR'S RESOLUTIONS?
OF COURSE.
HERE!
WOW! THAT'S SOME LIST.
I'VE COME UP WITH RESOLUTIONS THAT WILL HELP ALL OF YOU IMPROVE YOURSELVES IN THE NEW YEAR.

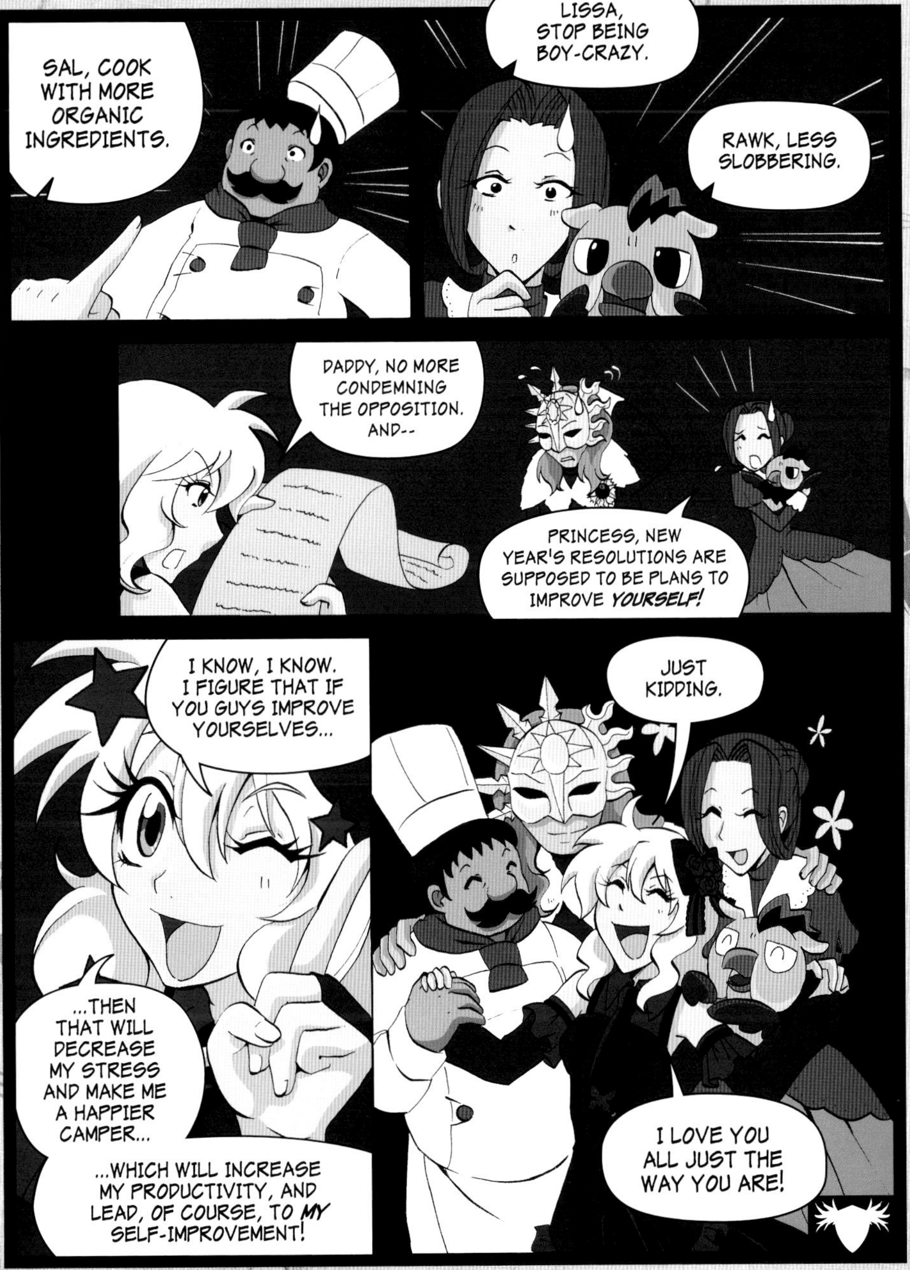
SAL, COOK WITH MORE ORGANIC INGREDIENTS.
LISSA, STOP BEING BOY-CRAZY.
RAWK, LESS SLOBBERING.
DADDY, NO MORE CONDEMNING THE OPPOSITION. AND--
PRINCESS, NEW YEAR'S RESOLUTIONS ARE SUPPOSED TO BE PLANS TO IMPROVE *YOURSELF!*
I KNOW, I KNOW. I FIGURE THAT IF YOU GUYS IMPROVE YOURSELVES...
...THEN THAT WILL DECREASE MY STRESS AND MAKE ME A HAPPIER CAMPER...
...WHICH WILL INCREASE MY PRODUCTIVITY, AND LEAD, OF COURSE, TO *MY* SELF-IMPROVEMENT!
JUST KIDDING.
I LOVE YOU ALL JUST THE WAY YOU ARE!

AVAILABLE NOW

PRINCESS AI: THE MANGA TRILOGY

Princess Ai tries to piece together clues about how she ended up on Earth, as the forces of love and chaos close in around her...

PRINCESS AI: THE ULTIMATE EDITION

All volumes in the manga trilogy are collected here, with never-before-seen bonus material.

PRINCESS AI: RUMORS FROM THE OTHER SIDE

Who would dare print rumors, innuendo and bald-faced lies about everyone's favorite international rock diva Princess Ai?

PRINCESS AI: ROSES & TATTOOS

This limited edition full-color book features new art and poetry by the Princess Ai creators.

EXPLORE
THE WORLD OF

The manga was just the beginning! There's so much going on in the world of Princess Ai—and so much more to come. Here's a peek at the past, present, and future of Ai Land.

AVAILABLE WHEREVER BOOKS ARE SOLD, OR VISIT WWW.TOKYOPOP.COM/SHOP KEYWORD: "PRINCESS AI"

COMING SOON

Stay tuned to www.TOKYOPOP.com for more information!

PRINCESS AI HITS THE BIG SCREEN

This groundbreaking feature film is a Gothic Rock Opera! The Japan-U.S. co-production is a stunning blend of live action and anime.

PRINCESS AI: AI-TUNES

The long-awaited soundtrack to the original manga trilogy.

PRINCESS AI: THE PRISM OF MIDNIGHT DAWN

The stunning new manga sequel! In this new trilogy, Princess Ai ventures to the Other Side to retrieve the stolen Prism of Midnight Dawn...

PRINCESS AI BROKEN LEASH

The sizzling music video for "Broken Leash"—from the collection of music videos being produced by the creative team behind the upcoming feature film.

PRINCESS AI: ENCOUNTERS

A collection of stories following Ai as she journeys across the TOKYOPOP Universe—and into bestselling manga series.

TOKYOPOP

Princess Ai of Ai-Land: The Comic Strip Collection
Written by Stu "Milky" Levy
Illustrated by Pauro Izaki
Princess Ai Created by Courtney Love and Stu "Milky" Levy

Lettering - Jennifer Carbajal, Chelsea Windlinger, and Fawn Lau
Cover Design - Jennifer Carbajal
Cover Art - Pauro Izaki
Color and Tones - Mara Aum

Editors - Rie Shiramizu and Jeremy Ross
Digital Imaging Manager - Chris Buford
Pre-Production Supervisor - Lucas Rivera
Production Manager - Elisabeth Brizzi
Managing Editor - Vy Nguyen
Creative Director - Anne Marie Horne
Editor-in-Chief - Rob Tokar
Publisher - Mike Kiley
President and C.O.O. - John Parker
C.E.O. and Chief Creative Officer - Stu Levy

A  TOKYOPOP® Manga

TOKYOPOP and are trademarks or registered trademarks of TOKYOPOP Inc.

TOKYOPOP Inc.
5900 Wilshire Blvd. Suite 2000
Los Angeles, CA 90036

E-mail: info@TOKYOPOP.com
Come visit us online at www.TOKYOPOP.com

The author and editors would like to give their appreciation for the wonderful people at Andrews McMeel Universal who syndicated *Princess Ai of Ai-Land* in newspapers. Special thanks to John Glynn, Cathy Kirkland, Lucas Wetzel, Patty Adams, Chris Craver, Robert Hightower and the rest of the AMU team.

ISBN: 978-1-4278-1163-9

First TOKYOPOP printing: July 2008
10 9 8 7 6 5 4 3 2 1
Printed in China